W9-BYR-478

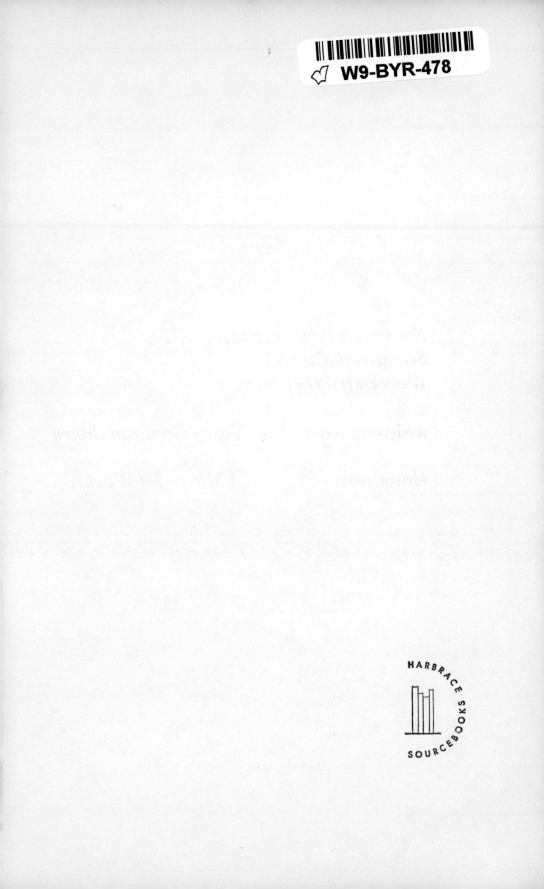

HARBRACE SOURCEBOOKS

Documents Pertaining to the
Seventeenth-Century
Witchcraft Trials

NATHANIEL HAWTHORNE   *Young Goodman Brown*

ESTHER FORBES   *A Mirror for Witches*

WHAT HAPPENED IN SALEM? *Second Edition*

David Levin
STANFORD UNIVERSITY

Harcourt, Brace & World, Inc.

NEW YORK   CHICAGO   SAN FRANCISCO   ATLANTA

A Note on the Cover

The drawings are reproduced from the frontispiece to Part II of Joseph Glanvill's *Saducismus Triumphatus: Or, a Full and plain Evidence, Concerning Witches and Apparitions,* London, 1681. To Glanvill's age Part II proved "(Partly by Holy Scripture, partly by a choice Collection of modern Relations) the real Existence of APPARITIONS, SPIRITS, and WITCHES."

Acknowledgments

Parts I, II, and III (exclusive of "Resolve of Massachusetts General Court, August 28, 1957") of this book are reprinted from *Handbook for English A,* sixth edition, 1950, by permission of the President and Fellows of Harvard College.

A Mirror for Witches by Esther Forbes, Houghton Mifflin Company, Boston. Copyright 1928, © 1956 by Esther Forbes Hoskins. Reprinted by permission of the publisher.

© 1960 by Harcourt, Brace & World, Inc.

All rights reserved. No part of this publication may be reproduced or transmitted in any form or by any means, electronic or mechanical, including photocopy, recording, or any information storage and retrieval system, without permission in writing from the publisher.

Library of Congress Catalog Card Number 60-8494

Printed in the United States of America

To Theodore Morrison

PREFACE

The Introduction and Parts I and II of this book were first published at Harvard in the sixth edition, 1950, of the *Handbook for English A,* under the supervision of Theodore Morrison. With the permission of the President and Fellows of Harvard University, who have also consented to this second edition, the materials were reprinted under the present title by Twayne Publishers, Inc., in 1952. I have always recommended that students be advised to consider a few works of historical fiction and drama that might be successfully studied in conjunction with the historical documents. This new edition makes two of the best of those works—Nathaniel Hawthorne's short story "Young Goodman Brown" and Esther Forbes's novel *A Mirror for Witches*—more accessible. Students should also note that Arthur Miller's play *The Crucible* is now available in an inexpensive reprint.

In editing the seventeenth-century texts, I have modernized all spelling but have left unchanged the original punctuation and such other peculiarities of the time as inconsistent capitalization.

Footnote Form

A book of this kind requires some special arrangement for the citation of sources, in order to afford students practice in acknowledging the various kinds of documents represented here. The editors of some comparable books have therefore interpolated the page numbers of the original sources in brackets throughout the text, and they have asked students to cite the original page numbers. Their purpose, of course, is to avoid endless repetition of *"What Happened in Salem?* p. 25," and *"Ibid.,* p. 38."

For the witchcraft materials another solution seems to me far less complicated. Since the original trial documents, a large portion of which I have checked against Woodward's transcription, have no page numbers, reprinting Woodward's page numbers would only have offered the following dilemma: repeated citations of Woodward or repeated citations of Levin. Even with the other materials, moreover, inclusion of the original page numbers cannot change the fact that the student pretends to be using another edition of Mather or Hawthorne than the one he has actually read. I believe that he can pretend less confusingly if he has only one set of page numbers.

I therefore recommend the following procedure: (1) that every note acknowledging materials in *What Happened in Salem?* follow the form appropriate to the relevant document *without mentioning the title of this book;* (2) that each of these notes cite the appropriate page number in *What Happened in Salem?* A note citing Cotton Mather, for example, would thus read:

[1] Cotton Mather, *The Wonders of the Invisible World* (London, 1862), p. 112.

Although all of the seventeenth-century materials in this book had been published before, most of them were available only in extremely rare editions. For access to them I am indebted to the Harvard College Library, the Houghton Library, and the Massachusetts Historical Society.

D. L.

Stanford University
Stanford, California
November 5, 1959

CONTENTS

INTRODUCTION

I

Between June 10 and September 22, 1692, nineteen Massachusetts men and women and two dogs were hanged for witchcraft, and one man was pressed to death for refusing to plead to the indictment. When the executions came to an end, fifty-five people had confessed that they were witches, and a hundred and fifty were in jail either waiting to be tried or enduring, as several convicted women did, reprieves granted them so that infants they had already conceived would not be executed with them. It would be easy to dismiss this episode merely as a horrible example of "superstition," as a curious delusion of a curiously demented people; but no one can reach a reasonable judgment without taking history into account, and that means trying to understand the ideas and beliefs which to people of the time seemed to justify the Salem executions.

Toward the end of the seventeenth century, belief in the reality of witchcraft was virtually universal. In European countries both Catholic and Protestant, thousands of "witches" had been executed. Despite important advances toward modern science, few people had thought of criticizing current theology in the light of the newest scientific discoveries. No one used Newton's law of gravitation [1] to challenge Cotton Mather's remarks about the aerial activities of "legions of devils." The "invisible world" was still, for most people, a real one. Even the few articulate critics of the Salem trials did not deny the existence of witchcraft; they attacked the methods used by the Salem judges. The intellectual leaders and, so far as we know, the mass of the people read their Bibles literally, accepting without question the Mosaic pronouncement (Exodus 22. 18): "Thou shalt not suffer a witch to live."

The crime of witchcraft consisted in entering into a contract or "covenant" with the Devil. Belief in a real and energetic Devil was therefore the major premise on which seventeenth-century thinkers based their measures against witchcraft. The Devil was an angel who had rebelled against God and fallen from grace; he worked "in continual opposition to the designs of God." This protracted campaign was doomed to failure, for God was omnipotent, but for reasons of His own God allowed the Devil certain powers over men until the millennium, the beginning on earth of the Kingdom of God. Among other powers, the Devil and his legions were allowed to afflict individuals or communities with special trials or adversities from time to

[1] Set forth in the *Principia*, 1687.

time. At all times the Devil tempted men and women to sin, to transgress against the will of God. Not only could he tempt men to isolated acts of sin; he could go farther and invite them to join a covenant binding all the covenantors to work together against "the children of God." In most of his actions the Devil was, of course, invisible; only the results of his work could be seen. It was the Devil and his invisible hellhounds who entered and controlled the body of a "possessed"—an insane—person. But the Devil and his evil spirits were not always invisible; once a witch had entered the fatal covenant, the Devil or one of his agents could assume the witch's shape when tormenting some other human being.

Although belief in witchcraft and the Devil's evil power was not, in the seventeenth century, restricted to any single branch of Christianity, certain tenets made the Puritan in England and America especially sensitive to Devils and witches, and frontier conditions in New England aggravated this sensitivity. The Puritans believed in the doctrine of original sin, which informed them that they were worms, dogs, potential colleagues of the Devil until the grace of God was, by God's free gift, poured into them. Cotton Mather was not preaching unusual doctrine when he reminded his congregation that "we should every one of us be a *dog* and a *witch* too, if God should leave us to ourselves. It is the mere *grace* of God, the *chains* of which refrain us from bringing the *chains of darkness* upon our souls." Knowing that for all practical purposes he belonged to the Devil anyway, the sincere Puritan who had not yet experienced the gift of God's grace was engaged in a constant struggle to find the weak spots in the "chains of darkness" which held him temporarily and threatened to bind him forever. He wanted no more connection with the Devil than he was born with; conscious of his sinfulness, he wanted to repent, to exorcise the Devil, to be prepared for the gift of grace if and when it came.

The Puritans' struggle against the Devil was external as well as internal. Those who had already experienced the influx of grace knew that their mission was to advance the Bible Commonwealth and also to strike down the Devil wherever he appeared too boldly among their unregenerate brethren. The New England Puritans and some other Englishmen believed, moreover, that the Devil's last and most powerful stronghold was in the wilds of North America. This conviction was supported by the presence of "barbarous savages," the antics of whose medicine men savored of witchcraft; and some Puritans reasoned that Satan and his legions would carefully patrol the heathen and Catholic frontier to defend it against any expansion of the Bible Commonwealth. "If any are scandalized," one English minister wrote, "that *New England,* a place of as serious piety, as any I can hear of under Heaven, should be troubled so much with witches; I think, 'tis no wonder: where will the Devil show most malice, but where he is hated, and hateth most . . . ?" At the same time, the Puritans, schooled in Old Testament history, believed that God visits terrible judgments upon His wayward people. As one means of inflicting this punishment, God permitted the Devil and his witches to torment not only the guilty but their neighbors and countrymen; the Puritans knew that God sometimes chastised a whole nation for the sins of its most wicked citizens.

The Puritans knew, too, that the Devil had little time left before the millennium; one minister estimated that Antichrist had only about twenty years more in which to win converts and torture mankind. The experience of those who had lived through the years from 1684 to 1692 seemed to justify the text Cotton Mather chose for a sermon in the summer of 1692: "Woe to the Inhabitants of the Earth, and of the Sea; for the Devil is come down unto you, having great Wrath; because he knoweth, that he hath but a short time." In 1684, James II had revoked the old charter of Massachusetts Bay, by which the colony had been largely self-governing. In 1688, the French and Indians had made new attacks on the frontier settlements, thus starting a costly war that lasted for years; the colonists suspected Andros, the hated royal governor, of conniving with the Indians; the shops were closed on the "pagan" Christmas Day; an old woman in Boston confessed to witchcraft and was hanged. During the next four years the Indian wars continued; even after the Glorious Revolution in England had turned out King James II in favor of William of Orange, the colony failed to win back its old charter and had to accept a compromise providing for a royally appointed governor. In 1692, the magistrates discovered a witchcraft conspiracy in Salem Village, and while the scope of the plot seemed to be growing the people learned that a devilish earthquake had killed seventeen hundred in Jamaica. The Devil seemed to be striking on several fronts at once.

2

When in February, 1692, Elizabeth Parris, eleven-year-old daughter of the minister at Salem Village, and her cousin Abigail Williams began having violent fits, they behaved as had afflicted children in Sweden in 1669, and the Goodwin children who were bewitched in Boston in 1688. These Goodwin children, whose woes Cotton Mather described in a book about their bewitchment, had been

> handled with . . . many sorts of ails. . . . Sometimes they would be deaf, sometimes dumb, and sometimes blind, and often, all this at once. One while their tongues would be drawn down their throats; another while they would be pulled out upon their chins, to a prodigious length. They would have their mouths opened to such a wideness, that their jaws went out of joint; and anon they would clap together with a force like that of a spring-lock.

Samuel Parris and the doctors he consulted could compare the symptoms of his daughter and niece with accounts of the earlier bewitchments. When they learned, too, that the girls had been taking lessons in palmistry from Tituba, a West Indian slave in the Parris family, they were sure that the Devil had made some converts in Salem Village. Moving cautiously, Parris called in some fellow ministers and asked their advice. They suggested fasting and prayer, the method Cotton Mather had used in curing the Goodwin children four years earlier. They planned on meeting at the Parris house for a fast day, and suggested that he keep the matter quiet.

Parris evidently tried to follow the ministers' advice about comparative secrecy, but one of his parishioners advised Tituba's husband that a witch-cake—made with the urine of the afflicted—would cure the girls. This cake, Parris believed, was the people's real invitation to the Devil, for the good Puritan was forbidden to use the Devil's means, even in fighting against him. Actually, there were more worldly reasons why the affliction spread. On several earlier occasions the Salem Village doctor had diagnosed bewitchment, and there had been no excitement. But this time the victims were girls who were known to have toyed with the dangerous "preternatural"; their tormentors were more persistent; and above all, there was reason to believe that the Devil was making an all-out attack on New England in general and Salem Village in particular.

Besides the general tribulations of New England, Salem Village had its own special problems: boundary disputes with neighboring Topsfield, a reprimand from the General Court of Massachusetts Bay (for an uncharitable attitude toward the minister), a bitter quarrel with the minister over who should supply his firewood, and personal wrangles over true title to certain lands. (One of the first few people accused of witchcraft was Rebecca Nurse, a deaf old woman whose family had for years been contending with the Putnams in a fight for land title.) Then, when the first accused woman confessed in open court, she named her "confederates"; other confessors soon told a weird story of witches' sabbaths held in Salem Village, and implied that they were partners in a well-planned diabolical conspiracy, using Salem Village as a central operations base.

Tituba's public confession set the fatal pattern to which the accusations and trials conformed during the hectic months that followed. The afflicted girls, whose number came to include all those who had watched Tituba's exhibitions of palmistry, continued to enjoy notoriety and public solicitude. Although Cotton Mather offered to take them into his home and try to cure them by prayer, as he had cured the Goodwin children, they remained in Salem Village, where they appeared in court to testify against the people they "cried out upon." When anyone questioned the validity of their accusations, the judges could always point to a penitent witch or two who had confirmed the girls' charges.

The sheriff served the first warrants on February 29, 1692, and Tituba appeared before the magistrates, John Hawthorne and Jonathan Corwin, on the first of March. The three women first accused were likely candidates for the role of witches: Tituba was, of course, a West Indian and a conjurer; Sarah Good was a destitute, wizened, pipe-smoking hag; Sarah Osborne had been suspected of immorality and had not been attending church, though attendance was compulsory. As the number of accusations increased after Tituba's confession, the afflicted accused not only old women, but also some men whom the people might find reason to suspect, and at least six children.

By the time the new governor, Sir William Phips, arrived from London on May 14, the jails were crowded, the Salem court clerk had recorded hundreds of pages of frightening testimony, and the friends of both accused and afflicted were clamoring for trials. Governor Phips had to act fast. He had the attacking Indians to contend with, and the witchcraft accusations were increasing so rapidly that he could not wait for the General Court to convene and pass a law providing for judges to try the cases. The growing number of confessions was also alarming; some official government action, some executions, might show the Devil that his enemies were in no way submissive; and state action might discourage the weak-willed from signing the Devil's book. On May 29, Governor Phips appointed a Special Court of Oyer and Terminer, a court empowered to "hear and determine" cases, with Lieutenant-Governor William Stoughton as chief justice.[2]

The court scheduled the first trial for June 2—three months after the first arrest—and on that day convicted Bridget Bishop, whom Stoughton sentenced to hang. This trial must have caused some dissension among the judges, for Nathaniel Saltonstall resigned his seat, and the court adjourned until June 29. It seems that the judges wanted moral backing; presumably for their guidance, Governor Phips sent the colony's ministers a request for procedural advice. Before the ministers had delivered this "Return," Governor Phips left Boston for a summer campaign against the Indians, and on June 8, Stoughton, as acting governor, ordered the execution of the woman he himself had sentenced six days before. For the rest of the summer Stoughton served both as acting governor and chief justice. A learned man, thoroughly orthodox in his theology, he believed in vigorously prosecuting the witches. When he and his court received the ministers' rather equivocal advice on June 15, they proceeded as before, admitting all kinds of testimony, but professing not to rely wholly on what was called spectral evidence: testimony that a specter in the shape of the accused had tormented the accuser or demanded that he sign the Devil's book.

After the court reassembled on June 29, the trials moved rapidly, for they consisted mostly in the reading of depositions taken earlier from witnesses at "examinations" conducted by the magistrates. Five witches were hanged on July 19; five more on August 19; and eight on September 22. On September 19, Giles Cory, an old man who did not want his heirs to be deprived of his property by a bill of attainder, had to pay for his foresightedness; refusing to plead either guilty or not guilty, he avoided conviction but had to endure being pressed to death under increasing weights of stone as the sheriff, in accordance with British common law, tried to force him to answer the indictment.

During August and September more and more people of all ranks came to suspect that there had been "a going too far" in the witch hunt and trials. Many of those who watched the hangings on August 19 shouted objections against the execution of George Burroughs and John Proctor. In court, several courageous witnesses testified that someone had prompted one of the afflicted girls to cry out the right name in making an accusation; others, that

[2] The other judges were Samuel Sewall, Bartholomew Gedney, Wait Winthrop, Nathaniel Saltonstall, John Richards, William Sergeant, and—after Saltonstall resigned—Jonathan Corwin.

one afflicted girl said she made her accusations "for sport." Some embarrassingly logical critics began to ask why it was that the government had not executed any of the witches who confessed, and rumors said that the sheriff had won some confessions by using force. The common people began to lose confidence in the judges after discovering that some "respectable" people who had been accused were not prosecuted, and that others who had been arrested had managed to escape. Mrs. Thatcher, the mother-in-law of Judge Jonathan Corwin, was repeatedly accused, but no one arrested her; Nathaniel Saltonstall, the judge who had resigned, remained at liberty even though someone had cried out upon him; and many believed the rumor that Lady Phips herself had been accused. At the same time, some of the colony's leading thinkers and most of the socially prominent people were amazed and frightened that such men and women as Saltonstall, Lady Phips, and Mrs. Thatcher—persons "of good conversation"—had been accused at all.

At the end of the summer, when Sir William Phips made his second grand entrance as governor of the colony, he found that witchcraft had again forced him to face an explosive situation. During the summer the affliction had spread to Andover, and officials had captured at least one witch in Maine. Cotton Mather was now convinced that the Devil's strategy was subtly to divide God's people—by *"devices,* of perhaps a finer thread than was ever yet practiced among the world," to force them so far "into a *blind man's buffet"* that they were "even ready to be *sinfully,* yea hotly and madly, mauling one another in the *dark."* By this time it was clear that there was open disagreement between some of the judges on the one hand, and the ministers and several laymen on the other. Governor Phips was alarmed by the dissension and the accusations of "unblamable" persons. He consulted Increase Mather, his most trusted adviser, and learned that the burning issue was the court's admission of spectral evidence. Before the twelfth of October, a week after Increase Mather read the ministers an essay demonstrating the unreliability of spectral evidence, Governor Phips prohibited the arrest "without unavoidable necessity" of any more accused persons; he forbade further executions, pending orders from the King; and he tried to persuade William Stoughton to change the court's methods, to stop relying on the testimony of the bewitched. Stoughton apparently refused, for Phips dismissed the court before the end of the month.

With the fall of the Court of Oyer and Terminer the "witchcraft delusion," at least in its most harmful form, came to an end. There were no more executions, and Phips ordered the jailers to release some prisoners on bail. In November the General Court passed a law creating a Superior Court to judge the remaining cases. With new instructions charging them to give very little weight to spectral evidence, the jurors convicted only three of fifty-two persons tried in January. Stoughton condemned these three and signed the death warrants of five others, four of them confessing witches, who had been granted reprieves; but Phips stayed all the executions. The Court sat again in April, but there were no more convictions, and in May Phips signed a general pardon. The period of penitence began soon afterward, though not before some of the sufferers had their revenge on Samuel Parris, whom they banished from the Salem Village pulpit. In 1697, the General Court proclaimed a fast day, and Samuel Sewall stood in church to hear his own confession of error read to the congregation; several of the jurors who had convicted witches asked public pardon on the same day. During the next ten years there were other personal apologies, and in 1711 a resolution of the General Court reversed the bills of attainder against all the executed witches whose families had sought to have the bills revoked.

3

The sudden reversal of public opinion and official action on Salem witchcraft did not mean that most people renounced their belief in the existence of witches. The central issue in 1692 was not whether witches existed, or whether to execute them, but how to discover them. Once Increase Mather and fourteen other ministers had demonstrated that not only spectral evidence but all the testimony of the afflicted was unreliable, there was no really just basis for convicting a witch except a free confession. At the end of the year, therefore, even those who believed that some of the condemned "witches" had been guilty could offer no consistent formula for distinguishing the guilty from the innocent. Although witchcraft was still a real danger, the crime of spilling innocent blood came to be more frightening than the crime of suffering a witch to live.

Why had the ministers failed to speak out against spectral evidence before October? They had spoken, but in a confused whisper rather than a cry of clear conviction. From the very beginning they cautioned the judges not to rely too heavily on spectral evidence, since the Devil could, they said, assume the shape of an innocent person while tormenting a victim. They saw, too, that by June 15 the list of alleged witches had grown almost too large to be credible. Yet the tales of confessors, which agreed with each other in the few details they gave, multiplied almost as rapidly as the number of accusations. Such confessors as William Barker and Deliverance Hobbs seemed to prove that the Devil and his three hundred-odd witches had to be stopped quickly. What the ministers wanted most of all from an accused witch was a confession; let the sheriff execute the witch while the minister extricated the soul of the victim. If the defendant did not plead guilty, then the court had to proceed according to the best light it had, and pray for guidance. True, witchcraft was a crime of the invisible world, but God had commanded His people in this world to destroy witches. There must be some way for the enlightened in the visible world to discover and punish the other-worldly criminals. Although the Devil could impersonate an innocent person, the ministers believed that he did not often do so. Thus spectral evidence, while not conclusive of the defendant's guilt, seemed to be reasonable grounds for "presumption" or suspicion; along with other, corroborative evidence, it might help convict a witch.

Seeing that the accusations did not cease after months of trials, and that after twenty executions the basic dilemma remained unsolved, such different men as Increase Mather and Thomas Brattle the merchant began to wonder how much reliance on spectral evidence was "too much." The ministers came to see that the Devil was making almost as much headway through confusion and dissension as he could make by trying to convert New Englanders to witchcraft. Endorsing Increase Mather's *Cases of Conscience,* the ministers denounced spectral evidence and turned wholly to exhortation as a means of inducing their congregations to combat the Devil. Yet it would be a mistake to think that by this book Increase Mather and the other ministers intended to repudiate the judges. They still believed in witchcraft; they still believed that New England was the target of a large-scale witchcraft conspiracy. This book was not a condemnation but an admonition to the judges. It announced that the ministers would not support any further convictions based on the testimony of the afflicted, but it did not say that all those already executed had been innocent. Increase Mather was careful to assure the reader that he himself would have convicted George Burroughs after hearing the evidence against him; that "there was more than that which is called *specter evidence* for the conviction of the persons condemned."

The documents of five trials appear in this collection. The trials include all the kinds of evidence offered in court against the Salem witches. In choosing them, I have also tried to present a cross section of the kinds of people who were convicted and executed in 1692. Bridget Bishop, a widow who had remarried, was the proprietress of a little tavern. Gaudy in her dress, she had long been the subject of community gossip. She had been accused of witchcraft in 1680. Sarah Good, the wife of a propertyless farm worker, was unpopular because of her slothfulness, her sullen temper, and her poverty; she had recently taken to begging, an occupation the Puritans detested. Susanna Martin of Amesbury was an outspoken woman who answered with defiance the slander that had centered around her ever since she was accused of witchcraft in 1669. John Proctor, a farmer who was master of one of the afflicted girls, had won the respect of most of his neighbors; but his honestly vehement expression of skepticism did not help him in 1692. George Burroughs was the only minister tried for witchcraft. As minister at Salem Village in the early 1680's, he had suffered the usual bickering between this parish and its pastor; after a sharp quarrel with some of his parishioners over debts they said he owed them, he had left Salem Village for a small parish in Maine.

The controversy over who was to blame for the Salem executions has continued in historical writing ever since Cotton Mather, in the first history of Salem witchcraft, blamed the Devil. But aside from this search for heroes and villains, other questions remain unsolved. How large a part did spectral evidence play in some of the convictions? In a trial involving the invisible world, where did "spectral" evidence end and "concrete," human evidence begin? What was the psychology of the afflicted girls? Of the confessed witches? Were any of the condemned witches really "guilty"? The materials of the Salem witchcraft trials are worth studying today not only for the historical exercise of reconstructing human drama, but also because the problem of dealing with heresy and even conspiratorial opinion seems to be a perennial one, as does the question of assigning to individuals responsibility for collective error.

TRIAL EVIDENCE

The documents concerning the following
five convicted witches are reprinted from
William E. Woodward's *Records of Salem
Witchcraft* . . . , 2 vols., Roxbury, Mass.,
1864. The original documents are in the
Essex County Archives.

SARAH GOOD

Warrant vs. Sarah Good.

Salem February the 29th 1691-92 [1]

Whereas Messrs. Joseph Hutchinson, Thomas Putnam, Edward Putnam, and Thomas Preston, Yeomen of Salem Village in the County of Essex, personally appeared before us and made Complaint on Behalf of their Majesties against Sarah Good the wife of William Good of Salem Village abovesaid for suspicion of Witchcraft by her Committed, and thereby much Injury done by Eliz. Parris, Abigail Williams, Ann Putnam and Elizabeth Hubbard all of Salem Village aforesaid Sundry times within this two months and Lately also done, at Salem Village Contrary to the peace of our Sovereign Lord and Lady William & Mary, King & Queen of England etc.—You are therefore in their Majesties' names hereby required to apprehend & bring before us, the said Sarah Good tomorrow about ten of the clock in the forenoon at the house of Lt Nathaniel Ingersoll in Salem Village or as soon as may be then and there to be Examined Relating to the abovesaid premises and hereof you are not to fail at your peril.

Dated. Salem, february 29th 1691-92

JOHN HAWTHORNE [2]
JONATHAN CORWIN
} Assistants.

To Constable George Locker.

Officer's Return.

I brought the person of Sarah Good the wife of William Good according to the tenor of the within warrant, as is Attest by me

GEORGE LOCKER—Constable

1 March 1691-92

[1] Before 1752, British papers dated between January 1 and March 24 often listed two years (as in 1691-92). Since the British new year did not officially begin until March 25 (the Feast of the Annunciation), the double dates were used to avoid confusion resulting from the unofficial British custom (and the official practice in other countries) of considering January 1 as New Year. Not until 1752 did Parliament finally replace the "Old Style," or Julian Calendar, with the "New Style," or Gregorian.

[2] The name was spelled "Hathorne" until Nathaniel Hawthorne (1804-1864) added the "w."

3

Examination of Sarah Good.

The examination of Sarah Good before the worshipful Assistants John Hawthorne Jonathan Corwin

Q. Sarah Good what evil Spirit have you familiarity with

A. None

Q. Have you made no contract with the devil

Good answered no.

Q. Why do you hurt these children

A. I do not hurt them. I scorn it.

Q. Who do you employ then to do it.

A. I employ nobody

Q. What creature do you employ then.

A. no creature but I am falsely accused.

Q. Why did you go away muttering from Mr Parris his house.

A. I did not mutter but I thanked him for what he gave my child.

Q. have you made no contract with the devil.

A. no.

H[awthorne] desired the children all of them to look upon her and see if this were the person that had hurt them and so they all did look upon her, and said this was one of the persons that did torment them—presently they were all tormented.

Q. Sarah Good do you not see now what you have done, why do you not tell us the truth, why do you thus torment these poor children

A. I do not torment them.

Q. who do you employ then.

A. I employ nobody I scorn it.

Q. how came they thus tormented

A. what do I know you bring others here and now you charge me with it.

Q. why who was it.

A. I do not know but it was some you brought into the meeting house with you.

Q. we brought you into the meeting house.

A. but you brought in two more.

Q. who was it then that tormented the children.

A. it was osborne.

Q. what is it you say when you go muttering away from person's houses

A. if I must tell I will tell.

Q. do tell us then

A. if I must tell, I will tell, it is the commandments. I may say my commandments I hope.

Q. what commandment is it.

A. if I must tell I will tell, it is a psalm.

Q. what psalm.

after a long time she muttered over some part of a psalm.

Q. who do you serve

A. I serve God

Q. what God do you serve.

A. the God that made heaven and earth. though she was not willing to mention the word God. her answers were in a very wicked spiteful manner. reflecting and retorting against the authority with base and abusive words and many lies she was taken in it was here said that her husband had said that he was afraid that she either was a witch or would be one very quickly. the worshipful Mr. Hawthorne asked him his reason why he said so of her, whether he had ever seen anything by her, he answered no, not in this nature, but it was her bad carriage to him, and indeed said he I may say with tears that she is an enemy to all good.

  Salem Village March the 1st 1691-92
    Written by Ezekiel Cheever . . .

                                        Salem Village March the 1st 1691-92
  Sarah Good the wife of William Good of Salem Village Laborer Brought before us by George Locker Constable in Salem to Answer, Joseph Hutchinson Thomas Putnam etc. of Salem Village yeomen (Complainants on behalf of their Majesties) against said Sarah Good for Suspicion of witchcraft by her Committed and thereby much Injury done to the Bodies of Elizabeth Parris Abigail Williams Ann Putnam and Elizabeth Hubbard all of Salem Village aforesaid according to their Complaints as per warrants

  Dated Salem March 29th 1691-92.
  Sarah Good upon Examination denieth the matter of fact (viz) that she ever used any witchcraft or hurt the abovesaid children or any of them.
  The above-named Children being all present positively accused her of hurting of them Sundry times within this two months and also that morning.
  Sarah Good denied that she had been at their houses in said time or near them, or had done them any hurt. all the abovesaid children then present accused her face to face upon which they were all dreadfully tortured and tormented for a short space of time and the affliction and tortures being over they charged said Sarah Good again that she had then so tortured them, and came to them and did it, although she was personally then kept at a Considerable distance from them.
  Sarah Good being Asked if, that she did not then hurt them who did it. And the children being again tortured she looked upon them And said that it was one of them we brought into the house with us. We Asked her who it was, she then Answered and said it was Sarah Osborne, and Sarah Osborne was then under Custody and not in the house; And the children being quickly after recovered out of their fit said that it was Sarah Good and also Sarah Osborne that then did hurt & torment or afflict them—although both of them at the same time at a distance or Remote from them personally—there were also sundry other Questions put to her and Answers given thereunto by her according as is also given in.
  p[er]. us.

                                   JOHN HAWTHORNE }
                                   JONATHAN CORWIN } Assistants.

Examination of Tituba Indian.

The examination of Tituba.

Q. Tituba what evil spirit have you familiarity with.
A. none.
Q. why do you hurt these children.
A. I do not hurt them.
Q. who is it then.
A. the devil for aught I know.
Q. Did you never see the devil.
A. The devil came to me and bid me serve him.
Q. Who have you seen.
A. Four women sometimes hurt the children.
Q. Who were they.
A. Goody [3] Osborne and Sarah Good and I do not know who the other were. Sarah Good and Osborne would have me hurt the children but I would not she further saith there was a tall man of Boston that she did see.
Q. when did you see them.
A. Last night at Boston.
Q. what did they say to you.
A. they said hurt the children
Q. and did you hurt them
A. no there is 4 women and one man they hurt the children and they lay all upon me and they tell me if I will not hurt the children they will hurt me.
Q. but did you not hurt them
A. yes, but I will hurt them no more.
Q. are you not sorry you did hurt them.
A. yes.
Q. and why then do you hurt them.
A. they say hurt children or we will do worse to you.
Q. what have you seen.
A. an man come to me and say serve me.
Q. what service.
A. hurt the children and last night there was an appearance that said kill the children and if I would no[t] go on hurting the children they would do worse to me.
Q. what is this appearance you see.
A. Sometimes it is like a hog and sometimes like a great dog, this appearance she saith she did see 4 times.
Q. what did it say to you
A. it . . . the black dog said serve me but I said I am afraid he said if I did not he would do worse to me.
Q. what did you say to it.
A. I will serve you no longer. then he said he would hurt me and then

[3] "Goody" was not a name, but a familiar expression for "Goodwife." "Goodman" and "Goodwife" were approximate equivalents for our "Mr." and "Mrs."

he looked like a man and threatens to hurt me, she said that this man had a yellow bird that kept with him and he told me he had more pretty things that he would give me if I would serve him.

q. what were these pretty things.

a. he did not show me them.

q. what also have you seen

a. two rats, a red rat and a black rat.

q. what did they say to you.

a. they said serve me.

q. when did you see them.

a. last night and they said serve me, but I said I would not

q. what service.

a. she said hurt the children.

q. did you not pinch Elizabeth Hubbard this morning

a. the man brought her to me and made me pinch her

q. why did you go to Thomas Putnam's last night and hurt his child.

a. they pull and haul me and make me go

q. and what would have you do.

a. Kill her with a knife.

Lieutenant Fuller and others said at this time when the child saw these persons and was tormented by them that she did complain of a knife, that they would have her cut her head off with a knife.

q. how did you go

a. we ride upon sticks and are there presently.

q. do you go through the trees or over them.

a. we see nothing but are there presently.

q. why did you not tell your master.

a. I was afraid they said they would cut off my head if I told.

q. would you not have hurt others if you could.

a. They said they would hurt others but they could not

q. what attendants hath Sarah Good.

a. a yellow bird and she would have given me one

q. what meat did she give it

a. it did suck her between her fingers.

q. did not you hurt Mr Currin's child

a. goody good and goody Osborne told that they did hurt Mr Currin's child and would have had me hurt him too, but I did not.

q. what hath Sarah Osborne.

a. yellow dog, she had a thing with a head like a woman with 2 legs, and wings. Abigail Williams that lives with her Uncle Parris said that she did see the same creature, and it turned into the shape of Goody Osborne.

q. what else have you seen with Osborne.

a. another thing, hairy it goes upright like a man it hath only 2 legs.

q. did you not see Sarah Good upon Elizabeth Hubbard, last Saturday.

a. I did see her set a wolf upon her to afflict her, the persons with this maid did say that she did complain of a wolf.

. . . she further saith that she saw a cat with good at another time.

Q. What clothes doth the man go in
A. he goes in black clothes a tall man with white hair I think
Q. How doth the woman go
A. in a white hood and a black hood with a top knot
Q. do you see who it is that torments these children now.
A. yes it is Goody Good, she hurts them in her own shape
Q. and who is it that hurts them now.
A. I am blind now. I cannot see.

Salem Village   Written by Ezekiel Cheever.
March the 1st 1691-92   Salem Village March 1st 1691-92

Evidence vs. Sarah Good.

Tituba's Confession and Examination against herself and Sarah Good abstracted.

Charges Sarah Good to hurt the Children and would have had her done it. 5 were with her last night and would have had her hurt the Children which she refused and that Good was one of them.

Good with others are very strong and pull her with them to Mr. Putnam's and made her hurt the child. Good Cr[4] rode with her upon a pole behind her taking hold of one another, doth not know how they go for she never sees trees nor path but are presently U****

Good Cr tell he[r] she must kill somebody with a Knife and would have had her killed Tho: Putnam's child last night the child at the same time affirmed she would have had her cut off her own head if not Tituba would do it and complained of a knife cutting her.

Good came to her last night when her Mr was at prayer and would not let her hear, hath one yellow bird and stopped her Ears in prayer time, the yellow bird hath been seen by the children and Tituba saw it suck Good between the forefinger and long finger on the right hand.

Saw Good Cr practice witchcraft.

Saw Good have a Cat besides the bird and a thing all over hairy Cr.

Sarah Good appeared like a wolf to Hubbard going to Proctor's and saw it sent by Good to Hubbard

Good Cr hurt the children again and the children affirm the same Hubbard knew th*** not being blinded by them and was once or twice taken dumb herself

Good caused her to pinch the children all in their own persons.

Saw Good's name in the book, and the devil told her they made the marks C said to her she made the mark C it was the same day she went to prison.

Good Cr came to ride abroad with her C the man showed Good's name in the book

Good Cr pinched her on the legs C being searched found it so after confession.

[4] This abbreviation apparently refers to the defendant, but its exact meaning is questionable.

Note S. G. mumbled when she went away from Mr Parris and the children after hurt.

Dorothy Good's charge against her mother Sarah Good. That she had three birds, one black, one yellow and that these birds hurt the children and afflicted persons.

William Allen John Hughes William Good and Samuel Braybrook vs. Sarah Osborne [and Sarah Good].

March 5th 1691-92

William Allen saith that on the 1st of March at night he heard a strange noise not usually heard, and so continued for many times so that he was affrighted and coming nearer, to it he there saw a strange and unusual beast lying on the Ground so that going up to it, the said Beast vanished away and in the said place start up 2 or 3 women and fled from me not after the manner of other women but swiftly vanished away out of our sight which women we took to be Sarah Good, Sarah Osborne an[d] Tituba the time was about an hour within night and I John Hughes, saith the same being in Company then with said Allen. as witness our hands.

William Allen
john hughes.

William Allen further saith that on the 2d day of March the said Sarah Good visibly appeared to him in his chamber said allen being in bed and brought an unusual light in with her, the said Sarah came and sat upon his foot the said allen went to kick at her upon which she vanished and the light with her.

William Good saith that the night before his said wife was Examined he saw a wart or teat a little below her Right shoulder which he never saw before and asked Goodwife Ingersoll whether she did not see it when she searched her.

John Hughes. further saith that on the 2d day of March that coming from Goodman Sibley's about Eight of the clock in the night he saw a Great white dog whom he came up to but he would not stir but when he was past he the said dog followed him about 4 or 5 pole and so disappeared the same night the said John Hughes being in Bed in a closed Room and the door being fast so that no cat nor dog could come in the said John Saw a Great light appear in the said Chamber and Rising up in his bed he saw a large Gray Cat at his bed's foot.

March the 2d Samuel Braybrook saith that Carrying Sarah Good to ipswich the said Sarah leapt off her horse 3 times which was between 12 and 3 of the clock, of the same day which the daughter of Thomas Putnam declared the same at her father's house, the said Braybrook further Saith that said Sarah Good told him that she would not own herself to be a witch unless she is proved one, she saith that there is but one evidence and that an Indian and therefore she fears not, and so continued Railing against the Magistrates and she Endeavored to kill herself.

Salem March the 7th 1691-92

Sarah Good, Sarah Osborne, and Tituba an Indian Woman all sent to the Jail in Boston according to their mittimusses then sent: to their Majesties' Jail Keeper.

Abigail Hobbs's Examination No. 1.

Abigail Hobbs's Examination 20. April 1692 in Salem Prison.

This Examinant declares that Judah White a Jersey maid that Lived with Joseph Ingersoll at Casco but now lives at Boston with whom this Examinant was very well formerly acquainted came to her yesterday in apparition together with Sarah Good as this Examinant was going to Examination and advised her to fly and not to go to be Examined she told them that She would go. They Charged her if she did go to Examination not to confess anything. She said that She would Confess all that She knew. They told her Also that Goody Osborne was a witch. This Judah White came to her in fine clothes in a Sad colored Silk Mantle with a Top knot and an hood.

She confesseth further that the Devil in the Shape of a man came to her and would have her to afflict Ann Putnam Mercy Lewis And Abigail Williams and brought their Images with him in Wood like them and gave her thorns and bid her prick them into these images which she did accordingly into each of them one and then the Devil told her they were afflicted which accordingly they were and Cried out they were hurt by Abigail Hobbs, She confesseth She was at the great meeting in Mr Parris's Pasture when they administered the Sacrament and did eat of the Red Bread and drink of the Red wine at the same time.

Deliverance Hobbs's Confession.

being at a meeting of the witches in Mr. Parris's field when Mr. Burroughs preached and administered the sacrament to them saw Good amongst the rest and this fully agrees with what the afflicted persons relate 22th Apr. (92)

Indictment vs. Sarah Good, No. 1.[5]

Anno: Regis and Reginee William et Mariae nunc Anglice etc. Quarto Essex ss.

The Jurors for our Sovereign Lord and Lady the King and Queen, present, That Sarah Good the wife of William Good of Salem Village in the County of Essex, Husbandman, the Second Day of May in the fourth year of the Reign of our Sovereign Lord and Lady William and Mary by the Grace of God of England, Scotland France & Ireland King and Queen Defenders of the Faith etc. and Divers other Days and times as well before as after, certain Detestable arts called Witchcraft and Sorceries, Wickedly and Feloniously hath used, Practiced and Exercised, at and within the Township of Salem in the County of Essex aforesaid, in, upon and against one Sarah Vibber wife of John Vibber of Salem aforesaid, Husbandman, by which said

[5] In all, there were three indictments against Sarah Good.

wicked Arts, she the said Sarah Vibber the said Second Day of May in the fourth year above-said and divers other Days and times as well before as after was and is Tortured Afflicted, Pined, Consumed, wasted and Tormented, and also for Sundry other Acts of witchcraft by said Sarah Good committed and done before and since that time against the Peace of our Sovereign Lord & Lady the King & Queen their Crown and Dignity and against the form of the Statute in that case made and Provided.

        Witnesses
    Sarah Vibber Jurat
    Abigail Williams Jurat
    Elizabeth Hubbard"
    Ann Putnam Jurat
    Jno Vibber Sworn

Mittimus vs. Sarah Good.

To the Keeper of their Majesties' Jail in Boston
    You are in their Majesties' names hereby required to take into your care and safe Custody the Bodies of Sarah Good the wife of William Good of Salem Farms husbandman and Tituba an Indian Woman belonging unto Samuel parris of Salem Village minister, who stand Charged on behalf of their Majesties for their feloniously Committing Sundry acts of Witchcraft at Salem Village on the Bodies of Elizabeth Parris Eliz Hubbard Abigail Williams and Ann Putnam of Salem Village, whereby great hurt hath been done to their Body contrary to the peace of our Sovereign Lord & Lady William & Mary of England etc. King & Queen.
    Whom you are well to secure until they shall thence be delivered by due order of Law and hereof you are not to fail.
    Dated Boston May the 25th, 1692.

p us   JOHN HAWTHORNE   } Assistants.
                              JONATHAN CORWIN

Examination of [Sarah Good and] Bridget Bishop & als. No. 1.

1692. Salem June 2d about 10 in Morning.
    We whose names are underwritten being commanded by Capt George Corwin Esq. Sheriff of the County of Essex, this 2d day of June 1692 for to view the bodies of Bridget Bishop alias Oliver.

Rebecca Nurse   Elizabeth Proctor.
Alice Parker   Susanna Martin
Sarah Good

                        The first three, namely: Bishop. Nurse: Proctor by diligent search have discovered a preternatural Excrescence of flesh between the pudendum and Anus much like to teats and not usual in women and much unlike to the other three that hath been searched by us and that they were in all the three women near the same place

J BARTON Surgeon

Alice   pickering
HER MARK

Jane Woolings
HER MARK

Margery   Williams
HER MARK

Anna Stephens
HER MARK

Elizabeth Hill
HER MARK

Eleanor Henderson
HER MARK

Rebecca   Sharpe
HER MARK

Lydia Peckman
HER MARK

Hannah Kezer.

Sworn in Court June 2d 1692

Attest STEPHEN SEWALL Cle.

Summons for Witnesses vs. Mary Good.

William & Mary By the grace of God of England Scotland France & Ireland
    King & Queen defenders of the faith etc.

    To Samuel Abbey & his Wife, Joseph Herrick & his Wife, Goodwife
Vibber, Abigail Williams, Elizabeth Hubbard, Mary Walcott, Ann Putnam,
Mercy Lewis, Samuel Braybrook

    We command you and Every of you all Excuses set apart to appear at
the Special Court of Oyer and Terminer to be held at Salem for the County
of Essex, on the 28th of this Instant Month at nine of the Clock in the morning, there to testify the truth to the best of your knowledge on Several Indictments then and there to be Exhibited against Sarah Good for Sundry acts
of Witchcrafts by her Committed and done. hereof make return fail not.
    Dated in Salem. June 27, 1692.

STEP: SEWALL. Clerk.

To the Constables of Salem or any of them.

Greeting.

Officer's Return.

    Dat. 28 June 1692. I have warned the persons above-named according to
tenor of this Summons by me

JOHN PUTNAM Constable of Salem.

Abigail Hobbs's Confession.

was in company with Sarah Good and knows her to be a witch and afterwards was taken deaf and Mary Walcott . . . saw Good and Osborne run their fingers into this   ears and a little after she spoke and said Good told her she should not speak.

Mary Warren's Confession.

That Sarah Good is a Witch and brought her the book to sign to it.
Elizabeth Hubbard
Mary Walcott
Ann Putnam
Mercy Lewis
Sarah Vibber
Abigail Williams afflicted by Sarah Good and saw her shape
Richard Patch
William Allen that she appeared to him when abed
William Good that she hath a strange Teat or wart.
John Hughes that he saw strange sights.
Sam; Braybrook that she said she would not confess unless proved against her and that there was but one Evidence and that an Indian and therefore did not fear.

Samuel Abbey & Ux vs. Sarah Good.

Samuel Abbey of Salem Village Aged 45 years or thereabouts and Mary Abbey his wife aged 38 years or thereabouts, Deposeth and Saith.

That about this Time Three Years past William Good and his wife Sarah Good being destitute of a house to dwell in, these Deponents out of Charity; they being Poor let them live in theirs some time until that the said Sarah Good was of so Turbulent a Spirit, Spiteful and so Maliciously bent, that these Deponents could not suffer her to Live in their house any Longer and was forced for Quietness' sake to turn she the said Sarah with her husband out of their house ever since, which is about two years 1/2 agone, the said Sarah Good hath carried it very Spitefully and Maliciously, towards them, the winter following after the said Sarah was gone from our house we began to Lose Cattle and Lost several after an unusual manner, in a drooping condition Condition and yet they would Eat: and your Deponents have Lost after that manner 17 head of Cattle within this two years besides Sheep and Hogs, and both do believe they Died by witchcraft, the said William Good on the last of May was twelve months went home to his wife the said Sarah Good and told her, what a sad Accident had fallen out, she asked what, he answered that his neighbor Abbey had lost two Cows, both dying within half an hour of one another, the said Sarah good said she did not care if he the said Abbey had Lost all the Cattle he had as the said Jno Good told us. Just that very Day that the said Sarah Good was taken up, we your Deponents had a Cow that could not rise alone, but since presently after she was taken up, the said Cow was well and could rise so well. as if she had ailed nothing. she the said Sarah good ever since these Deponents turned her out of their house she hath behaved herself very crossly and maliciously to them and their Children calling their Children vile names and hath threatened them often.

Jurat in Curia.

Sarah Gadge vs. Sarah Good.

The deposition of Sarah Gadge the wife of Thomas Gadge aged about 40 years, this deponent testifieth and saith that about two years and an half agone. Sarah Good Came to her house and would have come unto the house, but said Sarah Gadge told her she should not come in for she was afraid she had been with them that had the Small pox and with that she fell to muttering and scolding extremely and so told said Gadge if she would not let her in she should give her something and she answered she would not have anything to do with her and the next morning after to said Deponent's best remembrance one of said Gadge's Cows Died in A Sudden terrible and Strange unusual manner so that some of the neighbors and said Deponent did think it to be done by witchcraft and further saith not.

Thomas Gadge vs. Sarah Good.

And Thomas Gadge husband of said Sarah testifieth that he had a Cow so Died about the time above-mentioned and though he and some neighbors opened the Cow yet they could find no natural Cause of said Cow's Death and further saith not.

Thomas Gadge and Sarah Gadge owned this to be the truth on their oath before us; the Jurors for Inquest, this 28 of June: 92.

Joseph Herrick Sr. and ux vs. Sarah Good.

The Deposition of Joseph Herrick senior who testifieth and saith that on the first day of March 1691-92 being the Constable for Salem, there was delivered to me by warrant from the worshipful Jno Hawthorne and Jonathan Corwin Esqrs. Sarah Good for me to carry to their majesties' Jail at Ipswich and that night I set a guard to watch her at my own house, namely Samuel Braybrook Michael dunell Jonathan Baker and the aforenamed persons, Informed me in the morning that that night Sarah Good was gone for some time from them both barefoot and barelegged, and I was also Informed that that night Elizabeth Hubbard one of the afflicted persons Complained that Sarah Good came and afflicted her being foot and barelegged, and Samuel Sibley that was one that was attending of Eliza Hubbard Struck Sarah Good on the Arm as Elizabeth Hubbard said, and Mary Herrick the wife of the abovesaid Joseph Herrick testifieth that on the 2th March 1691-92 in the morning I took notice of Sarah Good in the morning and one of her

Arms was bloody from a little below the Elbow to the wrist, and I also took notice of her Arms on the night before, and then there was no sign of blood on them.

Joseph Herrick senior and Mary herrick appeared before us the Jury for Inquest, and did on the oath which the[y] had taken on this their evidence to be the truth this 28. of June 1692

Sworn in Court.

Batten and Shaw vs. Sarah Good.

The testimony of William Batten aged 76 years or thereabouts and William Shaw aged about 50 years and Deborah his wife aged about 40 years, these all testify and say that this day was a week ago Susanna Sheldon being at the house of William Shaw she was tied her hands a rope in such a manner we were forced to cut the string before we could get her hand loosed and when she was out of her fit she told us it *was* Goody Dustin that did tie her hands after that manner, and 4 times she hath been tied in this manner in two weeks' time, the 2 first times she saith it was Goody Dustin and the 2 last times it was Sarah Good that did tie her, we further testify that whenever she doth but touch this string she is presently bit.

We further testify that in this time there was a broom carried away out of the house in to us and put in a apple tree two times and a shirt once and a milk tube once was carried out of the house three poles from the house into the woods and she saith that it this persons above-named upon their oath owned this their testimony to be the truth before us Jurors for Inquest, this 28 of June, 1692.

Jurat in Curia.

Joanna Chibbun vs. Sarah Good.

The deposition of Joanna Chibbun testifieth and saith that upon 2d of June 1692 that the apparition of Sarah Good and her least child did appear to her and the child did tell its mother that she did murder it, to which Sarah Good replied that she did it because that she could not attend it, and the Child told its mother that she was a witch and then Sarah Good said she did give it to the devil.

Henry Herrick and Jonathan Batchelor vs Sarah Good.

The deposition of Henry Herrick aged about 21 one years this deponent testifieth and saith that in Last March was two year Sarah Good came to his father's house and desired to lodge there and his father forbid it and she went away Grumbling and my father bid us follow her and see that she went away clear, lest she should lie in the barn: and by smoking of her pipe should fire the barn and said deponent with Jonathan Batchelor seeing her make a stop near the barn, did her be gone or her would set her further off. to which she replied that then it should Cost his father Zachariah Herrick one or two of the best Cows which he had

And Jonathan Batchelor aged 14 year testifieth the same above-written and doth further testify that about a week after two of his grandfather's Master Cattle were removed from their places and other younger Cattle put in rooms and since that several of their Cattle have been set loose in a strange manner

Jurat in Curia

Elizabeth Hubbard vs Sarah Good.

The Deposition of Elizabeth Hubbard aged about 17 years, who testifieth and saith that on the 28 February 1691-92 I saw the Apparition of Sarah Good who did most grievously afflict me by pinching and pinching me, and so she continued hurting of me till the first day of March being the day of her examination, and then she did also most grievously afflict and torture me also during the time of her examination and also several times since she hath afflicted me and urged me to writ[e] in her book. also on the day of her examination I saw the apparition of Sarah Good go and hurt and afflict the bodies of Elizabeth Parris Abigail Williams and Ann Putnam junior and also I have seen the the Apparition of Sarah Good afflicting the body of Sarah Vibber

MARK
Elizabeth   Hubbard

also in the night after Sarah Good's Examination: Sarah Good came to me barefoot and barelegged, and did most grievously torment me by pricking and pinching me and I verily believe that Sarah Good hath bewitched me and also that night Samuel Sibley that was then attending me struck Sarah Good on her Arm.

Susanna Sheldon vs Sarah Good.

The Deposition of Susanna Sheldon aged about 18 years who testifieth and saith that since I have been afflicted I have very often been most grievously tortured by Apparition of Sarah Good who has most dreadfully afflicted me by biting pricking and pinching me and almost choking me to death, but on the 26 June 1692 Sarah Good most violently pulled down my head behind a chest and tied my hands together with a wheel band and almost choked me to death and also several times since the Apparition of Sarah Good has most grievously tortured me by biting pinching and almost Choking me to death, also William Battin and Thomas Buffington Junior, were Forced to cut the wheel band from off my hands for they could not untie it.

And farther said Sheldon upon giving in this testimony to the grand jury was seized with sundry fits which when she came to herself, she told the said jury, being asked, that it was the said Good that afflicted her and a little after Mary Warren falling into a fit said Sheldon affirmed to the Grand jury that she saw said Good upon her and also a saucer being by invisible hands, taken from a Table and carried out of doors, said Sheldon affirmed she saw said Sarah Good carry it away and put it where it was found abroad.

Susanna Sheldon owned this her testimony to be the truth before the Jurors of Inquest on the oath which she had taken this. 28. of June 1692.

Ann Putnam Jr. vs Sarah Good.

The Deposition of Ann putnam Junior who testifieth and saith, that on the 25th of february 1691-92 I saw the Apparition of Sarah Good which did torture me most grievously, but I did not know her name till the 27th of february and then she told me her name was Sarah good and then she did prick me and pinch me most grievously, and also since several times urging me vehemently to writ[e] in her book and also on the first day of March being the day of her Examination Sarah Good did most grievously torture me and also several times since, and also on the first day of March 1692. I saw the Apparition of Sarah Good go and afflict and torture the bodies of Elizabeth parris Abigail Williams and Elizabeth Hubbard also I have seen the Apparition of Sarah Good afflicting the body of Sarah Vibber.

MARK

Ann   putnam

Ann Putnam owned this her testimony to be the truth on her oath; before the Jurors of Inquest this 28: of June 1692.

And further says that she verily believes that Sarah Good doth bewitch and afflict her.

Sworn before the Court

Sarah Vibber vs. Sarah Good.

The Deposition of Sarah Vibber aged about 36 years, who testifieth and saith, that since I have been afflicted I have often seen the Apparition of Sarah Good but she did not hurt me till the 2 day of May 1692 tho[ugh] I saw her Apparition most grievously torture Mercy Lewis and Jno Indian at Salem on the 11th of April 1692, but on the 2: May 1692 the Apparition of Sarah Good did most grievously torment me by pressing my breath almost out of my body and also she did Immediately afflict my child by pinching of it that I could hardly hold it, and my husband seeing of it took hold of the child but it cried out and twisted so dreadfully by reason of the torture that the Apparition of Sarah Good did afflict it with—all [i.e., withal?] that it got out of its father's Arms, to[o.] also severally times since the Apparition of Sarah Good has most grievously tormented me by pinching and beating

me and almost Choking me to death and pricking me with pins after a most
dreadful manner,

Sarah Vibber owned this her testimony to be the truth on the oath she
had taken; before us the Jurors for Inquest this 28: day of June 1692.

Sworn in Court June 29th 1692.

And further Adds that she very believes upon her oath that Sarah Good
had bewitched her.

Sarah Vibber vs. Sarah Good.

The Deposition of Sarah Vibber aged 36 years, testifieth and saith that
the Saturday night before Goody Dustin of Reading was examined I saw
the apparition of Sarah Good standing by my bedside and she ptt [6] pulled
aside the curtain and turned down the sheet and looked upon my child
about 4 years old and presently upon it the child was struck into a great
fit that my husband and I could hardly hold it.

Sarah Vibber on her oath did own this her testimony before the Jurors
for Inquest this 28: of June 1692

Jurat Sarah Vibber

Mary Walcott vs. Sarah Good.

The Deposition of Mary Walcott aged about 17 years who testifieth and
saith that since I have been afflicted I have often seen the apparition of
Sarah Good amongst the witches who has also afflicted me and urged me
to writ[e] in her book

The mark of
Mary Walcott
m w

Mary Walcott owned this her testimony to be the truth on her oath before the Jurors for Inquest this 28: of June 1692

Also Mary Walcott testifieth that I have seen Sarah Good afflicting Mercy
lewis and Elizabeth Hubbard and Abigail Williams and I verily believe she
bewitched me

Abigail Williams v. Sarah Osborne and Sarah Good.

The testimony of Abigail Williams testifieth and saith that several times
last February she hath been much afflicted with pains in her head and other
parts and often pinched by the apparition of Sarah Good, Sarah Osborne,
and Tituba Indian all of Salem Village, and also excessively afflicted by the
said apparition of said Goody Osborne and Tituba at their examination before authority the 1st of March last past 1691-92.

[6] The meaning, if any, of these letters is unclear.

Further the said Abigail Williams testifieth that she saw the apparition of Sarah Good at her examination pinch Eliz. Hubbard and set her into fits and also Eliz. Parris, and Ann Putnam

The Mark of
Abigail A. W.   Williams

*Testified before us by Abigail Williams. Salem May the 23d 1692

JOHN HAWTHORNE

JONATHAN CORWIN

per order of the Governor & Council.

Death Warrants.

Warrant for execution of Sarah Good Rebecca Nurse, Elizabeth How Susanna Martin & Sarah Wildes On Tuesday 19 July 1692.

BRIDGET BISHOP

Indictment v. Bridget Bishop No. 1.[7]

Anno Regni Regis et Reginae William et Mariae nunc Anglice 7th Quarto: Essex. ss.

The Jurors for our Sovereign Lord and Lady the King and Queen presents that Bridget Bishop alias Oliver the wife of Edward Bishop of Salem in the County of Essex. Sawyer the nineteenth day of April in the fourth year of the Reign of our Sovereign Lord and Lady William and Mary by the Grace of God of England Scotland France and Ireland King and Queen Defenders of the faith . . . and Divers other days and times a[s] well before as after certain Detestable arts called witchcrafts and Sorceries, wickedly and feloniously hath used Practiced and Exercised at and within the Township of Salem in the County of Essex aforesaid in upon and against one Mercy Lewis of Salem Village in the County aforesaid singlewoman by which said wicked arts the said Mercy Lewis the said nineteenth day of April in the fourth year abovesaid and divers other Days and times as well before as after, was and is hurt Tortured Afflicted Pined Consumed, wasted and tormented against: the Peace of our said Sovereign Lord and Lady the King and Queen and against the form of the Statute in that case made and provided
Witnesses

Mercy Lewis, Mr Samuel Parris, Mary Walcott, Elizabeth Hubbard, Nathaniel Ingersoll, Thomas Putnam Junior, Ann Putnam Junior, Abigail Williams

Billa vera John Ruck Foreman in the name of the Grand Jury.

Deliverance Hobbs v. Bridget Bishop.

Deliverance Hobbs. Examined May 3. 1692 Salem Prison.[8]

Q. what have you done since whereby there is further trouble in your appearance?

A. nothing at all.

Q. but have you not since been Tempted?

A. yes Sir but I have not done it, nor will not do it

Q. here is a great change since we last spoke to you for now you afflict and torment again: now tell us the truth who tempted you to sign again?

[7] In all, there were five indictments against Bridget Bishop.
[8] See pp. 66-69.

20

A. it was Goody Oliver; she would have me to set my hand to the book: but I would not neither have I. neither did consent to hurt them again.

Q. was that true that Goody Wildes appeared to you and tempted you?

A. yes that was true.

Q. have you been tempted since?

A. yes about friday or Saturday night last.

Q. did that [they] bid you that you should not tell.

A. yes they told me so.

Q. but how far did they draw you or tempt you and how far did you yield to the temptation? but do not you acknowledge that that was true that you told us formerly?

A. Yes.

Q. and you did sign then at the first did you not?

A. Yes I did it is true.

Q. did you promise there to deny at last what you said before?

A. Yes I did and it was Goody Oliver alias Bishop that tempted me to deny all that I had confessed before

Q. do you not know the man with the wen?

A. no I do not know who it is. all that I confessed before is true.

Q. who were those you named formerly?

A. Osborne, Good. Burroughs, Oliver, Wildes, Cory and his wife, Nurse, proctor and his wife.

Q. who were with you in the chamber? (it being informed that some were Talking with her there)

A. Wildes and Bishop or Oliver, Good and Osborne, and they had a Feast both of Roast and Boiled meat and did eat and drink and would have had me to have eat and drink with them, but I would not and they would have had me Signed, but I would not then nor when Goody Oliver came to me.

Q. nor did not you consent to hurt these children in your likeness.

A. I do not know that I did.

Q. What is that you have to tell which you cannot tell yet you say?

Examination of Bridget Bishop [19 April 1692].

The examination of Bridget Bishop before the Worshipful John Hawthorne and Jonathan Corwin esq.

Bridget Bishop being now coming in to be examined relating to her accusation of suspicion of sundry acts of witchcrafts, the afflicted persons are now dreadfully afflicted by her as they do say.

(Mr Hawthorne) Bishop what do you say you here stand charged with sundry acts of witchcraft by you done or committed upon the bodies of Mercy Lewis and Ann Putnam and others.

(Bishop) I am innocent I know nothing of it I have done no witchcraft.

H. Look upon this woman and see if this be the woman that you have seen hurting you. Mercy Lewis and Ann Putnam and others do do now charge her to her face with hurting of them.

H. What do you say now you see they charge you to your face

B. I never did hurt them in my life I did never see these persons before I am as innocent as the child unborn.

H. is not your coat cut.

B. answers no, but her garment being Looked upon they find it cut or torn two ways Jonathan Walcott saith that the sword that he struck at Goody Bishop with was not naked but was within the scabbard so that the rent may very probably be the very same that Mary Walcott did tell that she had in her coat by Jonathan's striking at her appearance [that is, her specter].

The afflicted persons charge her with having hurt them many ways and by tempting them to sign the Devil's book at which charge she seemed to be very angry and shaking her head at them saying it was false they are all greatly tormented (as I conceive) by the shaking of her head.

H. Goody Bishop what contract have you made with the devil.

B. I have made no contract with the devil I never saw him in my life. Ann Putnam saith that she calls the devil her God.

H. what say you to all this that you are charged with can you not find in your heart to tell the truth.

B. I do tell the truth I never hurt these persons in my life I never saw them before.

(Mercy Lewis) Oh goody Bishop did you not come to our house the Last night and did you not tell me that your master made you tell more than you were willing to tell.

H. tell us the truth in this matter how comes these persons to be thus tormented and to charge you with doing

B. I am not come here to say I am a witch to take away my life.

H. who is it that doth it if you do not they say it is your likeness that comes and torments them and tempts them to write in the book, what Book is that you tempted them with.

B. I know nothing of it I am innocent.

H. do you not see how they are tormented you are acting witchcraft before us what do you say to this why have you not an heart to confess the truth.

B. I am innocent I know nothing of it. I am no witch I know not what a witch is.

H. have you not given consent that some evil spirit should do this in your likeness.

B. no I am innocent of being a witch I know no man woman or child here.

(Marshall Herrick) how came you into my bed chamber one morning then and asked me whether I had any curtains to sell. She is by some of the afflicted persons charged with murder.

H. what do you say to these murders you are charged with.

B. I am innocent I know nothing of it.

now she lifts up her eyes and they are greatly tormented

H. what do you say to these things here horrible acts of witchcraft.

B. I know nothing of it I do not know whether be any witches or no

H. no have you not heard that some have confessed

B. no I did not. two men told her to her face that they had told her, here she is taken in a plain lie. now she is going away they are dreadfully afflicted 5 afflicted persons do charge this woman to be the very woman that hurts them

This is a true account of what I have taken down at her examination according to best understanding and observation I have also in her examination taken notice that all her actions have great influence upon the afflicted persons and that have been tortured by her

EZEKIEL CHEEVER.

Examination No. 2.

Salem about 4 afternoon June 2d 1692.

We whose names are subscribed to the within mentioned, upon a second search about 3 or 4 hours' distance, did find the said Bridget Bishop alias Oliver in a clear and free state from any preternatural Excrescence as formerly seen by us as also Rebecca Nurse instead of that Excrescence within mentioned it appears only as a dry skin without sense and as for Elizabeth proctor which Excrescence like a teat red and fresh, not anything appears, but only a proper procedeulia Ani and as for Susanna Martin whose breast in the morning search appeared to us very full: the nibs fresh and starting, now at this searching all lank and pendant which is all at present from the within mentioned subscribers and that that piece of flesh of Goodwife Nurse's formerly seen is gone and only a dry skin nearer to the anus in another place.

J. BARTON Surgeon

[Signed by the same persons who examined Sarah Good and others on the morning of June 2, 1692. See pp. 11-12.]

William Stacey v. Bridget Bishop.

William Stacey of the Town of Salem aged Thirty Six years or thereabouts Deposeth and Saith

That about fourteen years agone this Deponent was visited with the Small Pox, then Bridget Bishop did give him a visit and withal Professed a great Love for this Deponent in his affliction more than ordinary, at which this deponent admired some time after this Deponent was well the said Bishop got him to do some work for her for which she gave him three pence which seemed to [t]his Deponent as if it had been good money, but he had not gone not above 3 or 4 Rods before he Looked in his Pocket where he put it for it, but could not find any. sometime after this deponent met the said Bishop in the Street a-going to mill, She asking this Deponent whether his father would grind her grist: he put it to the said Bishop why she asked: she answered because folks counted her a witch this Deponent made answer, he did not question but that his father would grind it: but being gone about 6 Rod from he[r] the said Bishop, with a small load in his cart suddenly the Off wheel Plumped or Sunk down into a hole upon Plain ground, that this Deponent was forced to get one to help him get the wheel out afterwards this Deponent, went back to look for said hole where his wheel sunk in but could not find any hole, sometime after in the winter about midnight this deponent felt something between his lips Pressing hard against his teeth and withal was very cold insomuch that it did awake him so that he got up and sat upon his bed he at the same time seeing the said Bridget Bishop sitting at the foot of the bed, being to his seeming it was then as light as if it had been day, or one in the said Bishop's shape, she having then a black cap and a black hat and a Red coat with two [p]eaks of two Colors then she the said Bishop or her shape clapped her coat close to her legs and hopped upon the bed and about the Room and then went out. and then it was Dark, again some time after the said Bishop went to this De-ponent and asked him whether that which he had reported was true that he had told to several, he answered that was true, and that it was she and bid her deny it if she dare, the said Bishop did not deny it and went away very angry and said that this Deponent did her more mischief than any other body, he asked why: she answered because folks would believe him before anybody Else: sometime after the Said Bishop threatened this Depo-nent and told him he was the occasion of bringing her out about the brass she stole; some time after this deponent in a Dark night was going to the Barn, who was, suddenly taken or hoisted from the Ground and threw against a Stone wall, after that taken up again a-throwed Down a bank at the end of his house; sometime after this deponent met the said Bishop by Isaac Stone's brick kiln after he had Passed by her this Deponent's horse stood still with a small load going up the hill so that the horse striving to draw all his Years and [the?] tackling flew in pieces and the cart fell down.

Afterward this Deponent went to lift a Bag of Corn of about 2 bushels, but could not budge it with all his might.

This Deponent hath met with several other of her Pranks at several times which would take up a great time to tell of.

This Deponent doth verily believe that the said Bridget Bishop was In-strumental to his daughter Priscilla's death: about two years ago, the child was a likely Thriving child. And suddenly screeched out and and so con-tinued in an unusual manner for about a fortnight and so died in that la-mentable manner.

Sworn Salem May the 30th 1692.
before us.

JOHN HAWTHORNE
JONATHAN CORWIN
   } Assistants.

Jurat in Curia June 2d 1692.

Samuel Gray v. Bridget Bishop.

Samuel Gray of Salem aged about 42 years Testifieth and saith that about fourteen years ago he going to bed one Lord's Day at night, and after he had been asleep some time, he awakened and looking up, saw the house light as if a candle or candles were lighted in it and the door locked and that little

fire there was Raked up he did then see a woman standing between the
cradle in the Room and the bed-side and seemed to look upon him so he
did Rise up in his bed and it vanished or disappeared then he went to the
door and found it locked and unlocking and opening the door he went to
the entry door and looked out and then again did see the same woman he
had a little before seen in the Room and in the same Garb she was in before then he said to her in the name of God, what do you Come for. then
she vanished away so he locked the door again and went to bed and between
sleeping and waking he felt something Come to his mouth or lips cold and
thereupon started and looked up and again did see the same woman with
something between both her hands holding before his mouth upon which
she moved and the Child in the cradle gave a great screech out, as if it was
greatly hurt and she disappeared. and taking the child up could not quiet
it in some hours from which time, the child that before was a very likely
Thriving child did pine away and was never well although it Lived some
months after, yet in a sad condition and so died: some time after within a
week or less he did see the same woman in the same Garb and clothes that
appeared to him as aforesaid, and although he knew not her nor her name
before. Yet both by her Countenance and Garb doth testify that it was the
same woman that they now call Bridget Bishop alias Oliver of Salem

SAMUEL GRAY.

Sworn Salem May 30th 1692.
    before me
        JOHN HAWTHORNE Assistant.

John Hale v. Bridget Bishop.

John Hale of Beverly aged about 56 years testifieth and saith that about
5 or 6 years ago Christiana the wife of John Trask (living in Salem bounds
bordering on the abovesaid Beverly) being in full communion in our church
came to me to desire that Goodwife Bishop her neighbor wife of Edw:
Bishop . . . might not be permitted to receive the Lord's Supper in our church
till she had given her the said Trask satisfaction for some offences that were
against her: viz: because the said Bishop did entertain certain people in her
house at unseasonable hours in the night to keep drinking and playing at
shovelboard whereby discord did arise in other families and young people
were in danger to be corrupted and that the said Trask knew those things
and has once gone into the house and finding some at Shovelboard had taken
the pieces they played with and thrown them into the fire and had reproved
the said Bishop for promoting such disorders But received no satisfaction from
her about it.

I gave said Christiana Trask direction how to proceed farther in this
matter if it were clearly proved And indeed by the information I have had
otherwise I do fear that if a stop had not been put to those disorders Edward Bishop's house would have been a house of great profaneness and iniquity.

But as to Christiana Trask the next news I heard of her was that she was distracted and asking her husband Trask when she was so taken, he told me she was taken distracted that night after she came from my house when she complained against Goody Bishop.

She continuing some time distracted we Sought the Lord by fasting and prayer and the Lord was pleased to restore the said Trask to the use of her reason again I was with her often in her distraction (and took it then to be only distraction yet fearing sometimes somewhat worse) but since I have seen the fits of those bewitched at Salem village I call to mind some of hers to be much like some of theirs.

The said Trask when recovered (as I understood it[)] did manifest strong suspicion that she had been bewitched by the said Bishop's wife and showed so much averseness from having any converse **** her that I was then troubled **** as hoping better of Goody Bishop at that time ******* At length said Christiana Trask *** *was* *** again in a distracted fit on a Sabbath day in the forenoon at the public meeting to a public disturbance and so continued sometimes better sometimes worse unto her death manifesting that she was under temptation to kill herself or somebody else.

I inquired of Margaret Ring who kept at or nigh the house, what she had observed of said Trask before this last distraction she told me, Goody Trask was much given to reading and search the prophecies of scripture.

The day before she made that disturbance in the meeting house she came home and said she had been with Goody Bishop and that they two were now friends or to the effect.

I was off praying with and counseling of Goody Trask before her death and not many days before her end being there she seemed more rational and earnestly desired Edw Bishop might be sent for that she might make friends with him. I asked her if she had wronged Edw Bishop she said not that she knew of unless it were in taking his shovelboard pieces when people were at play with them and throwing them into the fire and if she did evil in it she was very sorry for it and desired he would be friends with her or forgive her. this was the very day before she died or a few days before.

Her distraction (for [or] bewitching) continued about a month and in those intervals wherein she was better she earnestly desired prayers, and the Sabbath before she died I received a note for prayers on her behalf which her husband said was written by herself and I judge was her own hand writing being well acquainted with her hand.

As to the wounds she died of I observed 3 deadly ones; a piece of her wind pipe cut out. and another wound above that through the wind pipe and Gulle[t] to the vein they call jugular,, So that I then judged and still do apprehend it impossible for her with so short a pair of scissors to mangle herself so without some extraordinary work of the devil or witchcraft.

Signed 20. May 1692. by John Hale.

To several parts of this testimony new witnesses Major Gedney Mr Parris Joseph Herrick junr and his wife Thomas Raiment and his wife John Trask Margaret King Hannah wife of Colonel Baker Miles and others.

As also about the said Goody Bishop Capt William Raiment his son

Wm Raiment about creatures strangely dying. James Kettle and the above-said Jos. Herrick and Tho. Raiment about Sundry actions that have the appearance of witchcraft.

Samuel Shattuck v. Bridget Bishop.

Samuel Shattuck aged 41 years testifieth that in the year 1680. Bridget Oliver formerly wife to old Goodman Oliver, now wife to Edward Bishop did come to my house pretending to buy an old hogshead [?] which though I asked very little for and for all her pretended want She went away without it and Sundry other times she came in a Smooth flattering manner in very Slightly Errands: we have thought Since on purpose to work mischief: at or very near this time our Eldest Child who promised as much and understanding, both by countenance and actions as any other children of his years: was taken in a very drooping condition, and as she came oftener to the house he grew worse and worse: as he would be standing at the door would fall out and bruise his face upon a great step stone as if he had been thrust out by an invisible hand oftentimes falling and hitting his face against the sides of the house, bruising his face in a very miserable manner. After this the abovesaid Oliver brought me a pair of sleeves to dye and after that Sundry pieces of lace Some of which were So Short that i could not judge them fit for any use: she paid me 2 pence for dyeing them which 2 pence I gave to Henry Williams which lived with me he told me [hc] put it in a purse among some other money which he locked up in a box and that the purse and money was gone out of the Box he could not tell how: and never found it after. just after the dyeing of these things this child taken in a terrible fit: his mouth and eyes drawn aside and gasped in such a manner as if he was upon the point of death: after this he grew worse in his fits and out of them would be almost always crying that for many months he would be crying till nature's strength was spent and then would fall asleep and then awake and fall to crying and moaning: that his very countenance did bespeak compassion: And at length we perceived his understanding decayed. So that we feared (as it has Since proved) that he would be quite bereft of his wits, for Ever Since he has been Stupefied and void of reason his fits still following of him: after he had been in this kind of Sickness Some time he has gone into the garden and has got upon a board of an inch thick which lay flat upon the ground and we have called him: he would come to the Edge of the board and hold out his hand and make as if he would come but Could not till he was helped off the board: other times when he has got upon a board as aforesaid my wife has said she has offered him a Cake and money to Come to her and he has held out his hand and reached after it but Could not Come till he had been helped off the board: by which i judge some enchantment kept him on, about 17 or 18 months after the first of this Illness there came a Stranger to my house and pitied this Child and said among other words we are all born Some to one thing and Some to another: I asked him and what do you say this child is born to he replied he is born to be bewitched and is bewitched. I told him he did not know: he said he did know and said to me you have a neighbor that lives not far off that is a witch. I told him we had no neighbor but what was honest folk, he replied you have a neighbor that is a witch and she has had a falling out with your wife and said in her heart your wife is a proud woman, and she would bring down her pride in this Child: I paused in myself and did remember that my wife had told me that Goodwife Oliver had been at the house and spoke to her to beat Henry Williams that lived with us and that she went away muttering and she thought threatening: but little before our child was taken ill: I told the aforesaid Stranger that there was such a woman as he spoke of: he asked where she lived for he would go and see her if he knew how: I gave him money and bid him ask her for a pot of Cider away he went and I sent my boy with him, who after a short time, both returned: the boy's face bleeding and i asked what was the matter they told me the man knocked at the door and Goody Oliver came to the door and asked the Stranger what he would have, he told her a pot of cider. she said he should have none and bid him get out and took up a spade and made him go out She followed him and when she came without the porch She saw my boy and ran to him and scratched his face and made it bleed: Saying to him thou rogue what dost thou bring this fellow here to plague me: now this man did say before he went: that he would fetch blood of her. And ever Since this child hath been followed with grievous fits as if he would never recover more: his head and Eyes drawn aside so as if they would never Come to rights more: lying as if he were in a manner dead falling anywhere Either into fire or water, if he be not constantly looked to, and generally in such an uneasy and restless frame almost always running to and fro acting so Strange that I cannot judge otherwise but that he is bewitched and by these circumstances do believe that the aforesaid Bridget Oliver now called Bishop is the cause of it and it has been the judgment of Doctors Such as lived her[e] and ferrugriers [surgeons?] that he is under an Evil hand of witchcraft.

Samuel Shattuck and
Sarah Shattuck.

affirmeth upon the oath they have taken to the truth of what is above written.

> Attest STEPHEN SEWALL. Cler.
> Jurat in Curia June 2d 1692.

John Londer v. Bridget Bishop.

John Londer of Salem aged about Thirty two years Testifieth and saith that about seven or eight years since I then living with Mr John Gedney in Salem and having had some Controversy with Bridget Bishop the wife of Edw Bishop of Salem Sawyer about her fowls that used to Come into our orchard or Garden. Some little time after which, I going well to bed: about the dead of the night felt a great weight upon my Breast and awakening looked and it being bright moon-light did clearly see said Bridget Bishop or her likeness sitting upon my stomach and putting my arms off of the bed to free myself from that great oppression, she presently laid hold of my throat and almost choked me and I had no strength or power in my hands to resist or help myself and in this condition she held me to almost day. some time after this my Mistress Susanna Gedney was in our orchard and I was then with her, and said Bridget Bishop being then in her orchard which was next adjoining to ours, my Mistress told said Bridget that I said or affirmed that she came one night and sat upon my breast as aforesaid which she denied and I Affirmed to her face to be true and that I did plainly see her, upon which discourse with her she threatened me. And some time after that I being not very well stayed at home on a Lord's day and on the Afternoon of said day the doors being shut I did see a black pig in the Room Coming towards me so I went towards it to kick it and it vanished away.

Immediately after I sat down in an narrow Bar And did see a black thing jump into the window and came and stood Just before my face upon the bar the body of it looked like a Monkey only the feet were like a Cock's feet with claws and the face somewhat more like a man's than a monkey and I being greatly affrighted not being able to speak or help myself by reason of fear I suppose, so the thing spoke to me and said I am a Messenger sent to you for I understand you are troubled in mind and of [if] you will be ruled by me you shall want for nothing in this world, upon which I Endeavored to clap my hands upon it, and said you devil I will kill you but could feel no substance and it Jumped out of the window again, And Immediately came in by the porch although the doors were shut and said you had Better take my Counsel, whereupon I struck at it with a stick but struck the Groundsill and broke the stick, but felt no substance and that arm with which I struck was presently discnabled, then it vanished away, and I opened the back door and Went out and going towards the house End I Espied said Bridget Bishop in her orchard going towards her house, and seeing her had no power to set one foot forward but returned in again and going to shut the door. I again did see that or the like creature that I before did see within doors in such a posture as it seemed to be agoing to fly at me, upon which I cried out; the whole armor of God to be between me and you. So it sprang back and flew over the appletree flinging the dust with its feet against my stomach, upon which I was struck dumb and so continued for about three days' time and also shook many of the apples off from the tree which it flew over:

John Londer appeared before us this 2 day of June 1692 and on the oath that he had taken did own this testimony to be the truth before us the Juries of Inquest.

Jurat in Curia.

Bridget Bishop alias Oliver on her Trial denied that she knew this deponent though the orchard of this deponent and the orchard of said Bishop Joined and they often had differences for some years.

Jno Bly Sr. and William Bly v. Bridget Bishop.

June 2d 1692. John Bly Senior aged about 57 years and William Bly aged about 15 years both of Salem Testifieth and saith that being Employed by Bridget Bishop Alias Oliver of Salem to help take down the Cellar wall of The Old house she formerly Lived in we the said Deponents in holes in the said old wall belonging to the said Cellar found several puppets made up of Rags And hog's Bristles with headless pins in Them. with the points outward and this was about Seven years Last past.

John Bly Sr. and Rebecca Bly v. Bridget Bishop.

John Bly senior and Rebecca Bly his wife of Salem, both Testify and say that said Jno Bly Bought a Sow of Edwd Bishop of Salem Sawyer and by agreement with said Bishop was to pay the price agreed upon unto Lt. Jeremiah Neale of Salem. and Bridget the wife of Said Edward Bishop because she could not have the money or value agreed for paid unto her, she came to the house of the deponents in Salem and Quarrelled with them about it, soon after which the sow having pigged, she was taken with strange fits Jumping up and knocking her head against the fence and seemed blind and deaf and would not Eat neither Let her pigs suck but foamed at the mouth which Goody Henderson hearing of said she believed she was overlooked and that they had their cattle ill in such a manner at the eastward when she lived there and used to cure them by giving of them, Red Okra and Milk which we also gave the sow: Quickly after eating of which she grew Better and then for the space of near two hours together she getting into the street did set off Jumping and running between the house of said deponents and said Bishops as if she were stark mad, and after that was well again and we did then apprehend or Judge and do still that said Bishop had bewitched said sow.

Jurat in Curia.

Richard Coman v. Bridget Bishop.

Richard Coman aged about 32 years. Testifieth that Sometime about Eight years since I then being in bed with my wife at Salem, one fifth day of the week at night Either in the Latter end of may the Beginning of June, and a light burning in our Room I being awake, did then see Bridget Bishop of Salem Alias Oliver come into the Room we lay in and two women more with her which two women were strangers to me I knew them not, but said Bishop came in her Red paragon Bodice and the rest of her clothing that she then usually did wear, and I knowing of her well also the garb she did use to go in did clearly and, plainly know her, and testifieth that as he locked the door of the house when he went to bed so he found it afterwards when he did rise, and quickly after they appeared the light was out and the Curtains at the foot of the bed opened where I did see her and presently came And lay upon my Breast or body and so oppressed him that he could not speak nor stir no not so much as to awake his wife although he Endeavored much so to do it: the next night they all appeared Again in like manner and she said Bishop Alias Oliver took hold of him by the throat and almost hauled him out of the bed, the Saturday night following: I having been that day telling of what I had seen and how I suffered the two nights before, my kinsman Wm Coman told me he would stay with me and Lodge with me and see if they would come again and advised me to lay my sword on thurt [athwart] my body, quickly after we went to bed that said night and both, well awake and discoursing together in came all the three women again and said Bishop was the first as she had been the other two nights so I told him. Wm hear they be all come again and he was Immediately struck Speechless and could not move hand or foot and Immediately they got hold of my sword and strived to take it from me but I held so fast as they did not get it away and I had then Liberty of speech and Called Wm. also my wife and Sarah Phillips that lay with my wife. Who all told me afterwards they heard me but had not power to speak or stir afterwards. And the first that spoke was Sarah Phillips and said in the name of God Goodman Coman what is the Matter with you, so they all vanished away.

Sworn Salem June 2d. 1692. Before me

Jurat in Curia   JOHN HAWTHORNE.

Sus Sheldon v. Bridget Bishop.

The Deposition of Susanna Sheldon aged about 18 years who testifieth and saith that on the 2 June 1692 I saw the apparition of Bridget Bishop and Immediately appeared to little children and said that they were Thomas two twins and told Bridget Bishop to her face that she had murdered them in setting them into fits whereof they died.

Sus Sheldon v. Bridget Bishop.

on the fourth day at night came Goody Oliver and Mrs English and Goodman Cory and a black man with a high crowned hat with books in their hands Goody Oliver bade me touch her book i would not i did not know her name she told me her name was Goody Oliver and bid me touch her book now I bid her tell me how long she had been a witch she told me she told m . . .

had been a witch above twenty years then there came a stretched snake creeping over her shoulder and creep into her bosom. Mrs English had a yellow bird in her bosom and Goodman Cory had two turcles [turtles?] hang to his coat and he opened his bosom and put his turcles to his breast and gave them suck then . . . Goody Oliver kneeled down before the black man and went to prayer, and then the blackman told me Goody Oliver had been a witch twenty years and an half then they all set to biting me and so went away, ...

the sixth day at night came Goody Oliver and Mrs English Goodman
Cory and his wife.

Goodwife Cory presented me a book i refused it and asked her where
she lived, she told me she lived in [B]oston prison then she pulled out her
breast and the black man gave her a thing like a black pig it had no hairs
on it and she put it to her breast and gave it suck and when it had sucked
one breast she put it to the other and gave it suck there. then she gave it
to the black man then they went to prayer to the black man, then Goody
Oliver told me she had killed four women two of them were the fosters'
wives and John Trask's wife and did not name the other. . . .

Jno Cook v. Bridget Bishop.

John Cook aged about 18 years testifieth that about five or six years ago
one morning about Sun rising as I was in bed before I rose I saw Goodwife
Bishop Alias Oliver Stand in the chamber by the window and she looked
on me and Grinned on me and presently struck me on the side of the head
which did very much hurt me and then I saw he[r] go out under the End
window at a little Crevice about so big as I could thrust my hand into. I
saw her again the same day which was the Sabbath Day about noon walk
across the Room and having at the time an apple in my hand it flew out
of my hand into my mother's lap who sat six or eight foot distance from
me and then she disappeared and though my mother and several others were
in the same room yet they affirmed they saw her not.

John Cook appeared before us the Jurors of Inquest and did own this
to be his testimony on the oath that he hath taken: this 2: day of June. 92.
                                                          Jurat in Curia.

Elizabeth Balch v. Bridget Bishop.

The deposition of Elizabeth Balch of Beverly Aged About Eight and
thirty years and wife unto Benjamin Balch junior This deponent testifieth
hereby and saith that she being at Salem on the very day that Captain George
Corwin was buried and in the evening of said day coming from said Salem
unto said Beverly on horse back with her sister . . . Riding behind her and
as they were Riding as before and were come so far as Crane River Common So called Edward Bishop and his wife overtook us (on horseback) who
are both in u in prison under Suspicion of witchcraft and had some words
of Difference it seemed unto us. said Bishop riding into the brook, pretty
hastily she finding fault with his so doing and said that he would throw
her into the water or words to that purpose, said Bishop answered her that
it was no matter if he Did or words to that effect: and so we rode along
all together towards Beverly and she blamed her husband for Riding so fast
and that he would do her a mischief or words to that purpose, and he answered her it was no matter what was done unto her or words to that purpose, And then said Bishop directed his speech unto us as we Rode along
and said that she had been a bad wife unto him ever since they were mar-

ried and reckoned up many of her miscarriages towards him, but now of late she was worse than ever she had been unto him before (and that the Devil did come bodily unto her and that she was familiar with the Devil and that she sat up all the night Long with the Devil) or words to that purpose and with such kind of discourse he filled up the time until we came to said Bishop's dwelling house and this Deponent did reprove said Bishop for speaking in such a manner unto his wife said Bishop Answered it was nothing but what was truth and said Bishop's wife made very little reply to all her husband's discourse During all the time we were with them and fur- ther saith not.

The mark E of elizabeth Balch.

her Answer. the mark A of Abigail Walden.

if it be so you had need pray, for me.

Death Warrant v. Bridget Bishop.

To George Corwin Gentleman high Sheriff of the County of Essex.
   Greeting.

Whereas Bridget Bishop alias Oliver the wife of Edward Bishop of Salem in the County of Essex, Sawyer, at a special court of Oyer and Terminer held at Salem the second Day of this instant month of June for the Counties of Essex' Middlesex' and Suffolk before William Stoughton Esq. and his As- sociate Justices of the said Court was Indicted and arraigned upon five sev- eral Indictments for using practicing and exercising on the nineteenth day of April last past and divers other days and time before and after certain acts of Witchcraft in and upon the bodies of Abigail Williams Ann putnam Junior Mercy Lewis Mary Walcott and Elizabeth Hubbard of Salem Vil- lage Singlewomen whereby their bodies were hurt afflicted pined, consumed Wasted and tormented contrary to the form of the Statute in that Case made and provided.

To which Indictments the said Bridget Bishop pleaded not guilty and for trial thereof put herself upon God and her Country whereupon she was found guilty of the Felonies and witchcrafts whereof she stood Indicted and sentence of Death accordingly passed against her as the Law, directs.

Execution whereof yet remains to be done.

These are therefore in the name of their Majesties William and Mary now King and Queen over England etc. to will and Command you That upon Friday next being the Tenth day of this instant month of June be- tween the hours of Eight and twelve in the aforenoon of the same day you safely conduct the said Bridget Bishop alias Oliver from their Majesties' Jail in Salem aforesaid to the place of Execution and there cause her to be hanged by the neck until she be dead. and of your doings herein make return to the Clerk of the said Court and precept.

And hereof you are not to fail at your peril.

And this shall be your sufficient Warrant. Given under my hand and seal at Boston the Eighth day of June in the Fourth year of the Reign of our Sovereign Lord and Lady William and Mary now King and Queen over England etc. Annoq Dom 1692.

WM. STOUGHTON

June 10th = 1692.

According to the within Written precept I have taken the body of the within named Bridget Bishop out of their Majesties' Jail in Salem and Safely Conveyed her to the place provided for her Execution and caused the said Bridget to be hanged by the neck until she was dead all which was according to the time within Required and So I make Return by me

GEORGE CORWIN Sheriff.

SUSANNA MARTIN

Indictment v. Susanna Martin No. 1.[9]

Anno Regis et Reginae William et Mariee nunc Anglice etc. Quarto.
Essex ss.

The Jurors for our Sovereign Lord and Lady the King and Queen presents that Susanna Martin of Amesbury in the County of Essex, widow the Second day of May in the fourth year of the Reign of our Sovereign Lord and Lady William and Mary by the Grace of God of England Scotland France and Ireland King and Queen Defenders of the faith etc and divers other Days and Times as well before as after certain detestable arts called witchcrafts and Sorceries wickedly and Feloniously hath used Practiced and Exercised at and within the Township of Salem in the County of Essex, aforesaid in upon and against one Mary Walcott of Salem Village singlewoman, by which said wicked arts the said Mary walcott the second day of May in the fourth year aforesaid and at Divers other Days and times as well before as after was and is Tortured Afflicted Pined wasted and Tormented as also for Sundry other acts of witchcrafts by said Susanna Martin committed and done before and Since that time against the Peace of our Sovereign Lord and Lady William and Mary King and Queen of England their Crown and Dignity and against the Form of the statute in that case made and Provided.

        Witnesses.
Sarah Vibber Sworn.
Mary Walcott Sworn.
Mr Samuel Parris Sworn
Elizabeth Hubbard
Mercy Lewis. . . .

Sheriff's Report.

according to this warrant I have apprehended Susanna Martin widow of Amesbury and have brought or caused her to be brought to the place appointed for her Examination

                  p me ORLANDO: BAGLEY Constable of Amesbury.
Salem Village this 2th May 1692.

[9] There were two indictments against Susanna Martin.

Examination of Susanna Martin No. 1.

The Examination of Susanna Martin 2. May 1692.
As soon as she came in many had fits.
Do you know this woman
Abig. Williams saith it is Goody Martin she hath hurt me often. Others by fits were hindered from speaking. Eliz Hubbard said she hath not been hurt by her. John Indian said he hath not seen her. Mercy Lewis pointed to her and fell into a little fit. Ann Putnam threw her glove in a fit at her. The examinant laughed.

What, do you laugh at it?
Well I may at such folly
Is this folly? The hurt of these persons?
I never hurt man woman or child
Mercy Lewis cried out she hath hurt me a great many times and pulls me down
Then Martin Laughed again
Mary Walcott saith this woman hath hurt me a great many times Sus Sheldon also accused her of afflicting her.
What do you say to this?
I have no hand in witchcraft.
What did you do? Did not you give your consent?
No never in my life.
What ails this people?
I do not know.
But what do you think?
I do not desire to spend my judgment upon it.
Do not you think they are Bewitched?
No I do not think they are?
Tell me your thoughts about them?
Why my thoughts are my own, when they are in, but when they are out they are another's.
You said their Master—who do you think is their master?
If they be dealing in the black art you may know as well as I.
Well what have you done towards this?
Nothing.
Why it is you or your appearance.
I cannot help it.
That may be your master.
I desire to lead myself according to the word of God.
Is this according to God's word?
If I were such a person I would tell you the truth.
How comes your appearance just now to hurt these?
How do I know?
Are not you willing to tell the truth?
I cannot tell: He that appeared in Sam[uel]: shape a glorified saint can appear in anyone's shape.

Do you believe these do not say true?

They may lie for aught I know.

May not you lie?

I dare not tell a lie if it would save my life.

Then you will speak the Truth.

I have spoke nothing else. I would do them any good

I do not think you have such affections for them whom just now you insinuated had the devil for their Master.

Eliz Hubbard was afflicted and then the Marshall who was by her said she [Martin] pinched her hand.

Several of the afflicted cried out they saw her upon the beam.

Pray God discover you, if you be guilty.

Amen: Amen: A false tongue will never make a guilty person.

You have been a long time coming to the Court today you can come fast enough in the night said Mercy Lewis.

No, sweetheart, said the examinant, and then Mercy Lewis and all or many of the rest were afflicted

John Indian fell into a violent fit and said it was that woman, she bites, she bites, and then she was biting her lips.

Have you not compassion for these afflicted?

No I have none.

Some cried out there was the black man with her and Goody Vibber who had not accused her before confirmed it.

Abig Williams upon trial could not come near her. Nor Goody Vibber. Nor Mary Walcott, John Indian cried he would kill her if he came near her but he was flung down in his approach to her.

What is the reason these cannot come near you?

I cannot tell: It may be the Devil bears me more malice than another.

Do not you see how God evidently discovers you?

No. not a bit for that.

All the congregation think so.

Let them think what they will.

What is the reason these cannot come near you?

I do not know but they can if they will, or else if you please I will come to them.

What is the black man whispering to you?

There was none whispered to me.

Abig Williams v. S. Martin.

The Testimony of Abigail Williams witnesseth and saith that she has several times seen, and been afflicted by the apparition of Susanna Martin of Amesbury widow at and before the 2 may 1692.

Wm. Brown v. S. Martin.

The Deposition of William Brown of Salisbury aged: 70 years or thereabout, who testifying saith. That about one or two and thirty years ago Elizabeth his wife being a very rational woman and Sober and one that feared God as was well known to all that knew her and as prudently Careful in her family which woman going upon a time from her own house towards the mill in Salisbury Did there meet with Susanna Martin the then the wife of George Martin of Amesbury Just as they came together the said Susanna Martin vanished away out of her sight which put the said Elizabeth into a great fright. After which time the said Martin did many times afterward appear to her at her house and did much trouble her in any of her occasions and this continued till about feb: following, and then when she did come it was as birds pecking her Legs or pricking her with the motion of their wings and then it would rise up into her stomach with pricking pain as nails and pins of which she did bitterly complain and cry out like a woman in travail and after that it would rise up to her throat in a bunch Like a pullet's egg and then she would turn back her head and say, witch you shan't choke me, In the time of this extremity the church appointed a day of humitting [humility, i.e., fasting] to seek God on her behalf and thereupon her trouble ceased and she saw Goodwife Martin no more for a considerable time for which the church instead of the day of humiliation gave thanks for her Deliverance and she came to meeting and went about her business as before this continued till April following at which time summonses were sent to the said Elizabeth brown Goodwife Osgood by the Court to give their evidences concerning the said Martin and they did before the Grand Jury gave a full account.

After which time the said Elizabeth told this deponent that as she was milking of her cow the said Susanna Martin came behind her and told her that she would make her the miserablest creature for defaming her name at the Court and wept grievously as she told it to this deponent.

About 2 months after this deponent came home from hampton and his said wife would not own him but said they were divorced and Asked him whether he did not meet with one Mr Bent of Abbey in England by whom he was divorced. And from that time to this very day have been under a strange kind of distemper frenzy incapable of any reasonable action though strong and healthy of body. he further testifieth that when she came into that condition this deponent procured Doctor fuller and Crosby to come to her for her relief but they did both say that her distemper was supernatural and no sickness of body but that some evil person had bewitched her

Sworn the eleventh day of May Anno Dom 1692.
                    before me   ROBT PIKE. Assist.

Wm Brown made oath that the above is a true relation according to his wife's complaint in the day of it.

concerning the truth of what is sworn by William Brown concerning his wife with respect to her being a Rational woman before she was so handled and of her now present condition and her so long continuance all that then knew her and now know her can testify to the truth of it for she yet remains a miserable creature of which myself is one as witness my hand 16.3. [May] 1692.

ROBT PIKE.

John Pressey v. Susanna Martin.

The testimony of John Pressey of Amesbury aged 53 years or thereabouts taken before me at my house at Salisbury the eleventh day of May: Ano: Dom. 1692 is as followeth. That about twenty four years ago, he this deponent was at Amesbury Ferry upon a Saturday in the evening near about the shutting in of the daylight (which was about three mile From his house) and as he was going home a little beyond the field of George Martin at a hill called Goodal's hill this deponent was bewildered and Lost his way and having wandered a while he came back again to the same place which he knew by stooping trees in that place.

which perceiving he set out again and steered by the moon which shone bright. and was again Lost and came back again to the same place.

And then set out the 3d time in like manner and was bewildered and came back but not so far as before but knew where he was and so set himself in his way as before and in Less than half a mile going he saw a Light stand on his Left hand about two rod out of the way it seemed to be about the bigness of a half bushel. but this deponent kept on his way and Left it and in a matter of seven or eight rod going it appeared again at the Like distance from him as before and so it did again the 3d time but the deponent passed on his way and in Less than twenty rod going the same or such another Light Lay in his way and he having a stick in his hand did with the end of it endeavored to stir it out of the place and to give it some small blows with it and the Light seemed to brush up and move from side to side as a turkey cock when he spreads his tail but went not out of the place. which perceiving this deponent Laid it on with his stick with all his might he thinks he gave her at least forty blows. and so was a going away and Leave it but as he was going his heels were struck up and he Laid on his back on the ground and was sliding into a deep place (as to him seemed) but taking hold of some brush or bushes and so recovered himself and having Lost his coat which he had upon his Arm went back to the Light saw his coat and took it up and went home without any more disturbance there.

he farther say he do not know any such pit to be in the place that he was sliding into. he also saith that when he did strike at the Light she did certainly feel a substance with his stick.

he further saith that after striking it and his recovering himself and going on his way as aforesaid when he had gone about 5 or 6 rod he Saw Susanna Martin then wife of George Martin of Amesbury standing on his Left hand as the lights had done there she stood and Looked upon him and turned her face after him as he went along but said nothing nor did nothing to this Deponent, but that he went home as aforesaid only he again over went his own house but knowing the ground that he was upon returned and found his own house but being then seized with fear could not speak till his wife spoke to him at the door and was in such condition that his family was afraid of him. which story being carried to the Town the next day it was upon inquiry understood (, that the said Goodwife Martin was in such a miserable case and in such pain that they swabbed her body (as was reported). This deponent further saith that these things being noised abroad Major Pike sent for this deponent and had an account of the case, but seemed to be troubled that this deponent had not told him of it in season that she might have been viewed to have seen what her ail was. John Pressey aforesaid made oath to the truth of what is written in these two sides of the paper the eleventh day of May Anno Dom 1692.

before me   ROBT. PIKE Assist.

Jurat in Curia.

John Pressey & Mary Pressey v. S. Martin.

The deposition of John Pressey aged 53 and Mary his wife: aged 46 or thereabouts testifying saith

That some years after that the said John Pressey had given his evidence against the said Susanna Martin she the said Martin came and took these deponents to do about it and reviled them with many foul words saying we had took a false oath and that we should never prosper and that we should never prosper for our so doing particularly that we should never have but two cows and that if we were never so likely to have more yet we should never obtain it.

we do further testify that from that time to this day we have never exceeded that number but something or other has prevented it, tho never so likely (to obtain it) though they had used all ordinary means for obtaining it by hiring cows of others that were not their own. this for twenty years' space

John Pressey made oath to the truth of all that is above written at my house in Salisbury the eleventh day of May Ano Domino 1692.

before me   ROBT. PIKE Assist

Mary Pressey testifieth to all the above Except Susanna her threatening of the not raising above two cows.

Jurat in Curia by both.

Bernard Peach v. S. Martin.

The deposition of Bernard Peach aged 43 or thereabouts, who testifying saith. That about six or seven years past this deponent Living at the house of Jacob Morell in Salisbury being in bed on a Lord's Day night he heard a scrabbling at the window he this deponent saw, Susanna Martin wife of George Martin of Amesbury come in at the window and Jumped Down upon the floor she was in her hood and scarf and the same dress that she was in before at meeting the same day. being come in she was coming up towards this deponent's face but turned back to his feet and took hold of them and drew up his body into a hoop and Lay upon him about an hour and half or 2 hours in all which time this deponent could not stir nor speak but feeling himself beginning to be Loosened or Lightened he beginning to strive he put out his hand among the clothes and took hold of her hand and brought it up to his mouth and bit three of the fingers (as he Judge) to the breaking of the bones which Done the said Martin went out of the Chamber down the stairs and out of the door.

And as soon as she went away this deponent called to the people of the house and told them what was done and that she said Martin was now gone out of the door this deponent did also follow her, but the people did not see her (as they said) but without the door there was a bucket of   on the left hand side and there was a drop of blood on the handle too more upon the snow for there was a little flight of snow and there were the print of her two feet. about a foot without the threshold but no more Footing did appear.

2. he further deposeth that some time after this as he supposeth about 3 weeks after after the said Martin desired this deponent to come and husk corn at her house the next Lord's Day night say that if I did not come it were better that I did. but this deponent did not go being then Living with N . . . Osgood of the said Salisbury and that night Lodged in the barn upon the hay and about an hour or 2 in the night the said Susanna Martin and another came out of the shop into the barn and one of them said here he is and then came towards this deponent, he having a quarter staff made a blow at them but the roof of the barn prevented it and they went away but this deponent followed them and as they were going toward the window made another blow at them and struck them both down but away they went out at the shop window and this deponent saw no more of them. and the Rumor went that the said Martin had a broken hand at that time but the deponent cannot speak to that upon his own knowledge.

Sworn May the eleventh 1692.

before me   ROBT PIKE   Assist.

Jarvis Ring v. S. Martin.

Jarvis Ring of Salisbury maketh oath as followeth

That about seven or eight years ago he had been several times afflicted in the night time by somebody or something coming up upon him when he was in bed and Did sorely afflict by Laying upon him and he could neither move nor speak while it was upon him but sometimes made a kind of noise that folks did hear him and come up to him and as soon as anybody came it would be gone this it did for a long time before and since but he did never see anybody clearly but one time but one time in the night it came upon me as at other times and I did then see the person of Susanna Martin of Amesbury I this deponent did perfectly see her and she came to this deponent and took him by the hand and bit him by the finger by force and then came and Lay upon him awhile as formerly and after a while went

away the print of the bite is yet to be seen on the little finger of his right
hand for it was hard to heal (he further saith) That several times he was
asleep when it came But at that time when bit his finger he was as fairly
awake as ever he was and plainly saw her shape and felt her teeth as aforesaid.

Sworn by Jarvis Ring abovesaid May the 13th 1692.

before me   ROBT. PIKE   Assit at Salisbury.

Jurat in Curia.

Joseph Ring v. S. Martin.

The deposition of Joseph Ring at Salisbury aged 27 years being sworn
saith. That about the Latter end of September last being in the wood, with
his brother Jarvis Ring hewing of timber his brother went home with his
team and left this deponent alone to finish the hewing of the piece for him.
for his brother to carry when he came again but as soon as his brother was
gone there came to this deponent the appearance of Thomas Hardy of the
great Island at Patascataway and by some impulse he was forced to follow
him to the house of   tucker [(?)] which was deserted and was about half
a mile from the place he was at work in) and in that house did appear Susanna Martin of Amesbury and the aforesaid Hardy and another female person which the deponent did not know, there they had a good fire and drink
it seemed to be cider there continued most part of the night said Martin
being then in her natural shape and talking as she used to do, but toward
the morning the said Martin went from the fire made a noise and turned
into the shape of a black hog and went away and so did the other two persons go away and this deponent was strangely carried away also and the first
place he knew was by Samuel wood's house in Amesbury.

Sworn by Joseph Ring May the 13th 1692.

before me   ROBT PIKE   Assist.

Jurat in Curia

Joseph Ring v. S. Martin.

Joseph Ring of Salisbury aged 27 years having been strangely handled
for the space of almost two year maketh this Relation upon oath as followeth, viz,

That in the month of June next after Casco Bay fort was taken this
deponent coming between Sandy Beach and hampton Town met with Thomas
Hardy of Great Island and a company of several other creatures with him
which said Hardy demanded of this deponent two shillings and with that
dreadful noise and hideous shapes of these creatures and fireball this deponent was almost frighted out of his wits and in about an half an hour
(or indeed he could not judge of the time) they left him and he came to
hampton. About ten days after as the deponent came from Boston between
this deponent was overtaken by a company of people on horseback who
passed by him and after they were passed by him The aforesaid Thomas

Hardy turned about his horse . . . and came back to this deponent with his horse in hand and desired this deponent to go to Mrs White's and drink with him which being refused he turned away to the Company and they all came up together such a weth [i.e., with so many horses] that it seemed impossible escape being trod down by them but they went all past and then appeared no more.

About Oct following coming from hampton in Salisbury pine plain a company of horses with men and women upon them overtook this deponent and the aforesaid Hardy being one of them came to this deponent as before and demanded his 2 s of him an[d] threatened to tear him in pieces to whom this deponent made no answer and so he and the rest went away and Left this deponent.

After this this deponent had divers strange appearances which did force him away with them into unknown places where he saw meetings and feastings and   and many strange sights and from August Last he was Dumb and could not speak till this Last April. he also relates that there did use to come to him a man that did present him a book to which he would have him set his hand with promise of anything that he would have and there were presented all Delectable things persons And places Imaginable., but he refusing it, would usually and with most dreadful shapes noises and screeching that almost scared him out of his wits and this was the usual manner of proceeding with him and one time the book was brought and a pen offered him to his apprehension there was blood in the Ink horn but he never touched the pen. he further say that they never told him what he should write nor he could not speak to ask them what he should write. he farther say in several their merry meetings he have seen Susanna Martin appear among them.

And that day that his speech came to him again which was about the end of April last as he was in bed she did stand by his bed's side and pinched him.

Joseph Ring abovesaid made oath of the truth of all that is above written this 13th day of May 1692.

before me   ROBT PIKE Assist.

Jurat in Curia the substance of it viva voce.

It is to be understood that the matter about that two shillings demanded of said Ring was this, viz, That when Casco was assaulted before it was taken, Capt Cedric Walt was going from Great Island in Patascataway with a party for their relief of which party said Ring was one and said Hardy coming up into the Room where said Ring   before they sailed and played at Shovelboard or some such like game and urged said Ring play, said Ring told him he had no money and said Hardy Lent him 2 s and then said Ring played with him said Hardy who won his money away from him again so he could not then pay him

this account was by said Ring given to me

ROBT PIKE Ast.

John Kimball v. S. Martin.

The deposition of John Kimball of Amesbury aged 45 or upwards testi-fying saith. That about 23 years ago this deponent being about to remove from newbury to Amesbury having bought a piece of land of George Martin of Amesbury for which he was to pay him in cash or goods upon a certain day in March next following and when the Day of payment was come Martin and his wife came for the pay and the said Kimball offered them the choice of three cows and other cattle but did reserve two cows which they were not free to part with they being the first that ever they had, and Martin him-self was satisfied with other pay but Susanna his wife understanding from this deponent and his wife that they would not part with one of these 2 cows the said Susanna Martin said (you had been as good you had) for she will never do you any more good (and so it came to pass) for the next April following that very Cow lay in the fair dry yard with her head to her side (but stark dead) and when she was floaed [flayed?] no Impediment did ap-pear in her for she was a stout Lusty Cow.

and in a little while after another cow died and then an ox, and then other cattle to the value of 30£ that spring.

Sworn by John Kimball may the 16 1692.

before   ROBT. PIKE. Assist.

Jurat in Curia.

John Kimball of Amesbury afore mentioned further deposeth That the same year after he was come to Live at Amesbury and was Dwelling in the house of Edmund Elliot he was needed to get a Dog and hearing that the wife of said George Martin had a bitch that had whelps and this deponent went to her to get one of her but she not letting him have his choice he did not absolutely agree for any but said he heard one Blesdell had a bitch by which he may supply   but if not there was no one else he would have heod [?] of her price.

but being upon that account at said blesdell's and marked the whelp that I agreed for, George Martin coming by asked me whether I would not have one of his wife's whelps to which this deponent made answer on the nega-tive.

The same day Edmond Elliot said that he was at the house of the said Martins and heard the said Martin. Asked his wife why this deponent were not to have one of her puppies and she said he was then said he he have got one at Goodman blesdell's and he saw him choose it and mark it (to which his said wife said) If I Live I'll give him puppies enough.

within a few days after this I this deponent coming from his Intended house in the woods to Edmond Elliot's house where I dwelt about the sun-set or presently after and there did arise a little black cloud in the n. w and a few drops of Rain and the wind blew pretty hard in going between the house of John wood and the meeting house, this said deponent came by several stumps of trees by the wayside he by Impulse he can give no reason of that made him tumble over the stumps one after another through though he had his ax upon his shoulder which put him in Danger and made him resolved to avoid the next but could not.

And when he came a little below the meeting house there did appear a little thing like a puppy of a darkish color it shot between my Legs forwards and backwards as one that were Distract the hay and this deponent being free from all fear used all possible endeavors to cut it with his ax but could not hurt it and as he was this [thus?] belaboring with his ax the puppy gave a little Jump from him & seemed to go into the ground.

in a little further going there did appear a black puppy somewhat bigger than the first but as black as a coal to his apprehension which came against him with such violence as its quick motions did exceed his motions of his ax. Do what he could and it flew at his belly and away and then at his throat and over his shoulder one way and go off and up at it again another way and with such quickness seized and violence did it assault him as if it would tear out his throat or his belly while he was without fear. but at last I felt my heart to fail and sink under it that I thought my life was going out and I recovered myself and gave a start up and ran to the fence and calling upon God and naming the name Jesus Christ and then it invisibly away my moaning is it looked that out but this deponent made it not known to anybody for fretting his wife.

The next morning Edmond Elliot (as he told abroad and in his own house) said that he going toward the house of said Martin to Look his oxen went in to light his pipe and the said Martin's wife Asked him where kimball was (said Elliot said abed with with his wife for aught he knew) (said she) they say he was frighted Last night) with what said Elliot she said with puppies Elliot replied that he heard nothing of it and Asked where she heard of it and she said about the Town which story said Elliot having told it was all the Town over when this deponent came home at night for he had been all day alone in the woods at work at his frame work.

John Kimball made oath to the truth of all that is written on both sides of this paper May the 16th 1692.

before me   ROBT PIKE Assist.

Jurat in Curia.

John Allen v. S. Martin.

The deposition of Lt. John Allen of Salisbury aged 45 years testifying saith That in or about the year   this deponent was hauling timber for Mr George Carr for building a vessel at Amesbury at Mr. Goodwin's building place and having Done and about to go home Susanna Martin the wife of George Martin desired this deponent to cart staves for them which this deponent refused to do because of his oxen which were weak and needed now to get flesh but she seemed to be discontent (and as James Freeze and others then present told this deponent) (that she said) I had been as good I had (for my oxen should never do me much more service) upon which this deponent said Dost threaten me thou old witch or words to that effect resolving to throw her into a brook that was fast by which to avoid she flew over the bridge and so escaped., but as he was going home one of his oxen tired that he was forced to unyoke him to get him home. And after they were come home, put the said oxen to Salisbury beach where several other oxen where cattle usually are put where they had Long range of meadow to feed on and where cattle did use to get flesh, but in a few days all the oxen upon the beach we found by their tracks were gone to the mouth of the River merrimack but not returned from whence we thought they were run into the said river but the next day sending to Plum Island found their tracks there to be come ashore which tracks they followed to the other end of said Island and a considerable way back again and then sat down which being apprized by those that sought them they did use all Imaginable Gentleness to them to some acquaintance which some of them seemed to attend but all on a sudden away they all ran with such violence as if they their motion had been diabolical till they came near the mouth of merrimack river and then turned to the right hand and ran right into the sea all but two old oxen (which had before Left their Company) and all the rest went to sea as far as they could see them, and then one of them came back again with such swiftness as was amazing to the beholders who stood ready to Im[?] him and help his tired carcass up, but Letting him Loose away he ran up into the Island and from there through the marshes up into newbury town and so up into their woods and there was after a while found about hartechok[?] river over against Amesbury. so that of: 14: good oxen only that was saved the rest were all cast up some at Cape ann some in one place and some in other of they they only had their hides, he further saith that the abovesaid James Freeze did often move the prosecuting of the said Susanna Martin in the case *being* confident that she was a witch.

Lt. John Allen made oath to the truth of all that is above written June the 7th 1692.

before me   ROBT PIKE Assist.

Jurat in Curia.

Joseph Knight v. S. Martin.

The Deposition of Joseph knight aged about 40 years

This Deponent do testify and say that on the 20th Day of October or thereabouts in the year of our Lord 1686 Nathaniel Clark Junior of Newbury together with this Deponent going out into the woods together to fetch up horses there met with Susanna Martin of Amesbury with a little Dog running by her side and in my sight she took up said Dog under her arm but coming up near to her she had a Keg or a half firkin under the same arm, this deponent then looked her in the face and told her that that keg was a little Dog but now Nathaniel Clark said so it was and then passing from her we found our horses and brought them to a small causeway but could not get them over, but there being a small knoll of land near our horses ran round about it the greatest part of that day we often bringing them up to the Causeway but then they turned to that knoll and Ran about it the same way but at length there Came a young man with a yoke of oxen to go over the Causeway who with some difficulty got them over for although the Causeway was very good yet one of the oxen hung back as though he were frighted but at length were forced over and then we got over our horses.

Joseph knight owned this his testimony to be the truth on his oath before the Jurors of Inquest this 29 of June 1692.

Elizabeth Clark v. S. Martin.

Elizabeth Clark who then was the wife of the abovesaid Nathaniel Clark do testify that when my said Husband Nathaniel Clark came home he told me this deponent the matter mentioned in Joseph knight's testimony and he related to me the whole of the matter and all the Circumstances related in said testimony excepting that my husband told Joseph knight that the Keg under Goodwife Martin's arm was or had been a Dog. This deponent do further testify that Goodwife Martin abovesaid came to our house the same day mentioned in Joseph knight's testimony before my husband came home and coming into the house our dog bit her by the leg as she said whereupon she being angry said that he was a churl like his master.

Elizabeth Clark owned this her testimony to be the truth: on the oath which she had taken before the Jury for Inquest. this 29 of June. 1692.

Robert Downer v. S. Martin.

The deposition of Robert Downer of Salisbury aged 52 years who testify and say.

That several years ago Susanna Martin the then wife of George Martin being brought to Court for a witch the said Downer having some words with her (she at that time attending Mrs. Light at Salisbury) This deponent among other things told her he believed that she was a witch by what was said or witnessed against her at which she seemed not well affected said that a she devil would fetch him away shortly at which this deponent was not much moved but at night as he lay in his bed in his own house alone there came at his window the likeness of a cat and by and by come up to his bed took fast hold of his throat and Lay hard upon him a Considerable while and was like to throttle him at Length he minded what Susanna Martin had threatened him with the Day before he strove what he could and said avoid thou she devil in the name of the father and the son and the holy Ghost and then it Let him go and slumped down upon the floor and went out at window again.

he further saith that the next morning before ever he had said anything of it some of that family asked him about it (as from her own)

Mary Andrews v. S. Martin.

Mrs. Mary Andrews aged 40 years testify that she did hear the said Susanna Martin threaten or tell the said Robt Downer that a she devil would fetch him away shortly she further saith that from some of her father's family she did hear that what the said Su Martin told them how said Downer was served that night that he was afflicted as abovesaid.

Moses Pike v. S. Martin.

Moses Pike aged 26:years or more testify that he did hear Susanna Martin tell how Ro Downer was handled and as he remembers it was the next day after it was done at night.

Sworn by Robt Downer. Mrs Mary Allen and Moses Pike June 30. 1692.
before me   ROBT PIKE   Assist.

Tho. Putnam v. S. Martin.

The deposition of Tho: Putnam aged 40 years and   aged 38 years who testify and say that we have been conversant with the afflicted persons or the most of them, as namely Mary Walcott Mercy lewis Eliz hubbard Abigail Williams and Sarah Vibber Ann Putnam Jun. and have often heard the aforementioned persons complain of Susanna Martin of Amesbury torturing them and we have seen the marks of several bites and pinch which they said Susanna martin did hurt them with and also on the 2 day of May 1692 being the day of the Examination of Susanna Martin the aforenamed persons were most grievously tortured during the time of her examination for upon the glance of her eyes they were stricken down or almost choke and upon the motion of her finger we took notice they were afflicted and if she did but clench her hands or hold her head aside the afflicted persons aforementioned were most grievously tortured in like manner and several times since we have seen them tortured complain of Susanna Martin for hurting them.

THOMAS PUTNAM.

Samuel Parris, N Ingersoll & Tho. Putnam v. S. Martin.

The Deposition of Sam Parris aged about 39 years and Nathaniel Ingersoll aged about fifty and eight years and also Tho: Putnam aged about forty years all of Salem. testifieth and saith that Abigail Williams Mercy Lewis Mary Walcott Susanna Sheldon and John Indian were much afflicted at the examination of Susanna Martin of Amesbury widow, before the honored Magistrates the' 2' May' 1692. and that Goody Vibber (who before had not accused her) and some others of the afflicted then and there testified that there was a black man whispering in her ear and also that the said Vibber Abigail Williams and Mary Walcott and John Indian could not come near said Martin whereupon in all they were ordered by the magistrates to attempt it and their agonies and tortures they charged said Martin as the cause of and also we further saw that when the said Martin bit her lips they were bitten and when the afflicted were ordered to go towards her they were knocked down.

Jurat in Curia.

Elizabeth Hubbard v. Susanna Martin.

The Deposition of Elizabeth Hubbard aged about 17 years. who testifieth and saith that I have often seen the apparition of Susanna Martin amongst the witches, but she did not hurt me till the: 2 day of May being the day of her examination, but then she did afflict me most grievously during the time of her examination for if she did but look personally upon me she would strike me down or almost choke me and several times since the apparition of Susanna Martin has most grievously afflicted me also on the day of her examination I saw the apparition of Susanna Martin go and afflict and almost choke Mary Walcott Mercy lewis Abigail Williams and Ann putnam Junr.

MARK

Eliz.   Hubbard.

Mercy Lewis v. S. Martin.

The Deposition of Mercy lewis aged about 19 years who testifieth and said that in the latter end of April 1692 there appeared to me the Apparition of a short old woman which told me her name was Goody Martin and that she came from Amesbury who did most grievously torment me by biting and pinching me urging me vehemently to write in her book but on the 2 May 1692 being the day of her examination Susanna Martin did torment and afflict me most grievously in the time of her examination for when she looked upon me personally she would strike me down on [or] almost choke me and several times since the Apparition of Susanna Martin has most grievously afflicted me by pinching and almost choking me to death urging me to write in her book and also on the day of her examination I saw the Apparition of Susanna Martin go and hurt the bodies of Mary Walcott Elizabeth Hubbard Abigail Williams and Ann Putnam Junr.

Mercy lewis.

Sarah Vibber v. S. Martin.

The Deposition of Sarah vibber aged about 36 years who testifieth and saith. that on the 2 May 1692. the Apparition of Susanna Martin of Amesbury did most grievously torment me during the time of her examination for if she did but look personally upon me she would strike me down or almost choke me and also the same day I saw the Apparition of Susanna Martin most grievously afflict the bodies of Mary Walcott Mercy lewis, and Ann Putnam by pinching and almost choking them and several times since the Apparition of Susanna Martin has most grievously afflicted me by beating and pinching me and almost choking me to death. and that she believes the said Martin is a witch and that she is bewitched by her.

Jurat in Curia.

Ann Putnam Jr. v. S. Martin.

The deposition of Ann Putnam Junr who testifieth and saith some time in April 1692. there appeared to me the Apparition of an old short woman that told her her name was Martin and that she came from Amesbury who did Immediately afflict me urging me to write in her book but on the 2 May 1692. being the day of her examination Susanna Martin did most grievously afflict me during the time of her examination for when she did but look personally upon she would strike me down or almost choke and several times since the Apparition of Susanna Martin has most grievously afflicted me by pinching me and almost choking me urging me vehemently to write in her book also on the the day of her Examination I saw the Apparition of Susanna Martin go and afflict the bodies of Mary Walcott Mercy lewis Elizabeth Hubbard and Abigail Williams.

John Atkinson v. S. Martin.

John Atkinson aged fifty six years or thereabouts: Testifieth that some time about five years since, one of the sons of Susanna Martin Senior of Amesbury Exchanged a cow of his with me For a cow which I bought of Mr Wells the minister which cow he took From Mr Wells his house, About a week after I went to the house of Susanna Martin to receive the cow of the young man her son when I came to bring the cow home not-with-standing hamstringing of her and halting her she was so mad that we could scarce get her along, but she broke all the ropes Fastened to her we put the halter two or three times round a tree which she broke and ran away and when she came down to the Ferry we were forced to run up to our waists in water she was so fierce but after with much ado we got her into the boat she was so tame as any creature whatsoever. and further this Deponent Saith that Susanna Martin Muttered and was unwilling this deponent should have the Cow.
          Jurat in Curia.

Sarah Atkinson v. S. Martin.

Sarah Atkinson aged forty eight years or thereabouts testifieth that some time in the spring of the year about eighteen years since Susanna Martin came unto our house at Newbury from Amesbury in an Extraordinary dirty season when it was not fit for any Person to travel she then came on foot when she came into our house I asked her whether she came from Amesbury a Foot she said she did I asked her how she could come in this time a Foot and bid my children make way For her to come to the fire to dry herself she replied she was as dry as I was and turned her coats on Side and I could not perceive that the Sole of her shoes were wet I was startled at it that she should come so dry and told her that I should have been wet up to my knees if I should have come so Far on Foot she replied that she scorned to have a drabbled tail.
          Jurat in Curia.

JOHN PROCTOR

Indictment vs. John Proctor No. 1.[10]

Anne Regis et Reginee Willm: et Mariee. nunc: Anglice etc. Quarto. Essex. ss.

The Jurors for for our Sovereign Lord and Lady the King and Queen presents, That John Proctor of Salem Husbandman, in the County of Essex. the eleventh day of April in the fourth year of the Reign of our Sovereign Lord and Lady, William and Mary by the Grace of God of England Scotland France and Ireland King and Queen defenders of the Faith etc. And divers other days and times as well before as after Certain detestable acts called witchcraft and sorceries wickedly and Feloniously hath used Practiced and exercised all and within the township of Salem in the County of Essex. aforesaid, in upon and against one Mary Walcott of Salem Village in the County of Essex. Singlewoman. by which said wicked arts, the said Mary Walcott the 11th day April in the year abovesaid and Divers other Days and times as well before as after was and is tortured. afflicted Pincd Consumed wasted tormented against the peace of our Sovereign Lord and Lady the King and Queen and against the form of the Statute in that case made and provided.

Witnesses Mary Walcott Jurat
    Mercy Lewis. Jurat. Ann Putnam Jurat.

Abigail Williams v. John Proctor.

1692. Apr. 4. *Abig Williams.* complained of Goodman *Proctor* and cried out what are you come to, are you come to you can pinch as well as your wife and more to that purpose.

[Apr.] 6. At night she complained of Goodman Proctor again, and beat upon her breast and cried he pinched her.

The like I hear at Thomas Putnam's house.

[Apr.] 12. Day. when the marshall was sent up to inquire of John Proctor and the others, and I was writing somewhat thereof as above I met with nothing but interruptions by reason of fits upon John Indian and Abigail, and Mary Walcott happening to come in just before, they one and another cried out there is Goodman Proctor very often, and Abigail said there is Goodman Proctor in the magistrate's lap. at the same time Mary Walcott was sitting by a-knitting, we asked her if she saw Goodman Proctor, (for

[10] In all, there were three indictments against John Proctor.

51

Abigail was immediately seized with a fit) but she was deaf and dumb, yet still a-knitting. then Mary recovered herself and confirmed what Abigail had said that Goodman Proctor she saw in the magistrate's lap, Then John cried out to the Dog under the table to come away for Goodman Proctor was upon his back; then he cried out of Goody Cloyce, O you old witch, and fell immediately into a violent fit that 3 men and the marshall could not without exceeding difficulty hold him. In which fit Mary Walcott that was knitting and well composed, said there was Goodman Proctor and his wife and Goody Cloyce helping of him, but so great were the interruptions of John and Abigail by fits while we were observing these things to notify them, that we were fain to send them both away that I might have liberty to write this without disturbance, Mary Walcott abiding composed and knitting whilst I was writing and the two others sent away, yet by and by whilst I was writing Mary Walcott said there Goody Cloyce has pinched me now

Note Mary Walcott never saw Proctor nor his wife till last night coming from the examination at Salem and then she saw Goody Proctor behind her brother Jonathan all the way from the widow Gedney's to Phillips', where Jonathan made a little stay, But this day and time I have been writing this, she saw them many times.

Note Just now as soon as I had made an end of reading this to the Marshall, Mary Walcott immediately cried O yonder is Goodman Proctor and his wife and Goody Nurse and Goody Cory and Goody Cloyce and Good's child and then said O Goodman Proctor is going to choke me and immediately she was choked.

Monday 11th III [May] ditto. Lt. Nathaniel Ingersoll declared that John Proctor told Joseph Pope, that if he had John Indian in his Custody he would soon beat the devil out of him, and so said several others.

Examination of Mary Warren.

The Examination of Mary Warren, At a Court held at Salem Village by.

JOHN HAWTHORNE
JONATHAN CORWIN } Esqrs.

As soon as she was coming toward the bar, the afflicted fell into fits.

Mary Warren, you stand he[re] charged with sundry acts of witchcraft, what do you say for yourself are you guilty or not?.

I am innocent.

Hath she hurt you (speaking to the sufferers) some were dumb. Betty Hubbard testified against her and then said Hubbard fell into a violent fit.

You were a little while ago an afflicted person, now you are an afflicter: How comes this to pass.?.

I look up to God and take it to be a great mercy of God.

What, do you take it to be a great mercy to afflict others?

Betty Hubbard testified that a little after this Mary was well she the said Mary, said that the afflicted persons did but dissemble.

Now they were all but John Indian grievously afflicted and Mrs Pope also who was not afflicted before hitherto this day, and after a few moments, John Indian fell into a violent fit also.

Well here was one just now, that was a tormentor in her apparition, and she owns that she had made a league with the Devil.

Now Mary Warren fell into a fit, and some of the afflicted cried out that she was going to confess, but Goody Cory and Proctor and his wife came in in their apparition and struck her down and said she should tell nothing.

Mary Warren continued a good space in a fit, that she did neither see, nor hear, nor speak.

Afterwards she started up, and said I will speak and cried out, Oh! I am sorry for it, I am sorry for it, and wringed her hands, and fell a little while into a fit again and then came to speak, but immediately her teeth were set, and then she fell into a violent fit and cried out, oh Lord help me! Oh Good Lord save me!

And then afterwards cried again, I will tell I will tell and then fell into a dead fit again.

And afterwards cried I will tell, they did, they did they did and then fell into a violent fit again.

After a little recovery she cried I will tell they brought me to it and then fell into a fit again which fits continuing she was ordered to be had out, and the next to be brought in, viz. Bridget Bishop

Sometime afterwards she was called in again but immediately taken with fits, for awhile,

Have you signed the Devil's book?

No.

Have you not touched it?

No.

Then she fell into fits again and was sent forth for air,

After a considerable space she was brought in again but could not give account of things by reason of fits and so sent forth,

Mary Warren called in afterwards in private, before magistrates and ministers.

She said I shall not speak a word: but I will I will speak Satan.—she saith she will kill me. Oh! she says she owes me a spite and will claw me off.

Avoid Satan, for the name of God Avoid and then fell into fits again: and cried will ye, I will prevent ye in the Name of God—

Tell us, how far have you yielded?

A fit interrupts her again.

What did they say you should do and you should be well?

Then her lips were bit so that she could not speak so she was sent away.

Note that not one of the sufferers was afflicted during her examination after once she began to confess though they were tormented before.

Salem Village April 19th. 1692.

Mr Samuel Parris being desired to take in writing of Mary Warren, hath delivered it as aforesaid. And upon hearing the same and seeing what we did then see together with the charge of the afflicted persons then present. We committed said Mary Warren.

JOHN HAWTHORNE
JONATHAN CORWIN } Assistants.

Mary Warren's Examination in Salem Prison.

She Testifies that Her Master Proctor was always very averse to putting up Bills for public prayer.

Q. Did you not know it was the Devil's book when you signed?

A. No. But I thought it was no good book.

Q. after you had a Mark in the Book, what did you think then?

A. Then I thought it was the Devil's book.

Q. How did you come to know your Master and Mistress were witches

A. The Sabbath eve after I had put up my note for thanks in public, my Mistress appeared, to me and pulled me out of the bed, and told me that she was a witch and had put her hand to the book she told me this in her bodily person, and that this examinant might have known she was a witch, if She had but minded what Books she read in.

Q. What did she say to you before you tormented the children?

A. the night after she told me she was a witch she in person told me this Examinant, that myself and her son John would quickly be brought out for witches.

This Examinant saith that Giles Cory in apparition told her the night before, that the Magistrates were going up to the farm, to bring down more witches to torment her, moreover being in a dreadful fit in the prison, she charged it on Giles Cory who, was then in close prison affirming that he came into the Room where she was and afflicting her charged her not to Come into the other Room while he was examining, But being sent for, and he Commanded to look upon her, He no sooner turned his face to her, but she fell into a dreadful fit again, and upon her Recovery Charged him to his face with being the procurer of it. Moreover the said Cory in prison formerly threatened her that he would fit her for it, because he told her she had caused her Master to ask more for a piece of Meadow than he was willing to give she likewise in her fit in the other room before she had seen Giles Cory in person charging him with afflicting of her, described him in all his garments, both of hat, Coat and the color of them, with a Cord about his waist, and a white Cap on his head and in Chains, as several then in company can affirm.

Mary Warren's Examination April 21. 1692.

Being Asked by the Honored Magistrates whether the bible that then was Showed her: was the book: that was brought: to her to touch and that she saw the flourish in, answered no she see she was deceived.

being asked whether she had not told Mercy Lewis that she had signed to a book: Answered: no:

she was Asked whether her Mistress had brought a book to her to sign, Answered her Mistress brought none, but her Master brought one, being Asked whether she signed to it, answered, not unless putting her finger to it was signing.

being Asked whether she did not see a spot where she had put her finger, Answered, there was a spot.

she was Asked what color the spot was. Answered: black,

She was Asked whether her master did not threaten her to run the hot tongs down her throat if she did not sign. Answered that her Master threatened her to burn her out of her fit

being asked whether she had made a mark in the book. Answered she made no mark but with her top of her finger.

She was asked what she dipped her finger in when it made the mark: Answered in nothing but her mouth.

She was asked whether her finger was wet when she touched the book with it. Answered she knew not that it was wet or whether it was wet with sweat or with Cider that she had been drinking of she knew not: but her finger did make a mark and the mark was black.

she was asked whether any but her Master and Mistress was with her; when she was threatened with the hot tongs answered none but them.

She said her Master put her hand to the book and her finger made a black spot which made her tremble then she said she was undone body and soul and cried out grievously she was told her[e] that it was he[r] own Voluntary act she would have denied it but she was told the devil could have done nothing: if she had not yielded and that she for ease to her body not for any good to her soul: had done it with this she much grieved and cried out, she said her Master & Mistress threatened to drown her and to make her run through the hedges.

she was asked whether she had not seen her Master & Mistress since she came to prison answered she thought she saw her Master and dare say it was he, she was asked what he said to her, answered nothing.

After a fit she cried out, I will tell: I will tell: thou wicked creature it is you stopped my mouth: but I will confess the little that I have to confess, being asked who she would tell of whether goodwife Proctor or no:: answered O Betty Proctor it is she: it is she: I lived with last. she then cried out it shall be known, thou wretch; hast thou undone me body and soul, she said also she wishes she had made me make a thorough league.

she was again asked what her finger was blacked with when she touched the book.

Answered. she knew not that her finger was black till she see it black the book, and after she had put her finger to the book, she eat, bread and butter and her finger blacked the bread and butter also.

being asked: what her mistress now said to her: when she complained of her mistress, she said her mistress bid her not tell there that her mistress was a witch.

Coming out of another fit said she would tell she would tell she said her master now bid her not tell, that he had sometimes gone: to make away with himself for her master had told her that he had been about sometimes to make away with himself because of his wife's quarreling with him, being asked how she knew: goodwife proctor was a witch she coming out of a fit said she would tell she would tell and she said her mistress proctor said she might know she was a witch if she harkened to what she used to read. she said her mistress had many books and her mistress carried one book with her to Reading when she went to see her sister.

being asked whether she knew her mistress to be a witch before she touched the book, and how she knew it: she said her mistress told her she had set her hand to the devil's book that same night: that: I was thrown out of bed: said she: which was the same night after she had a note of thanksgiving: put up at the meeting house.

she said her mistress came to her: her body: not her shape as far as she knew, she affirmed her mistress was a witch. being asked whether she had seen any of the witches since she came to prison. said she had seen goodman cory and Sarah Good they brought the book to her to Sign,

but she would not own that she knew her master to be a witch or wizzard. being asked whether she did not know her finger would make a mark if she touched the book with it. she answered no but her master and mistress asked her to read and she said the first word she read was Moses: the next word she could not tell what it was but her Master and Mistress bid her if she could not pronounce the word she should touch the book.

being asked why she would not tell the whole truth. she said she had formerly not told all the truth because she was threatened to be torn in pieces, if she did, but now she would and had told the truth.

being asked whether she did not suspect it was the devil's book that she touched. answered she did not suspect it before she see her finger blacked it.

she was asked why: she yielded to do as she did: answered that her master said if she would not: when she was in her fit she should run into the fire or water if she would and destroy herself.

being asked whether she had not been instrumental to afflict the afflicted persons. Answered no but when she heard they were afflicted in her shape she began to fear it was the devil.

being asked whether she had images to stick pins or thorns into to hurt people with, answered, no.

She was asked whether the devil never asked her consent to hurt in her shape, answered, no. she had her Master and Mistress tell of images and of sticking of thorns in them to hurt people with.

she was asked whether she knew of any images in the house, said no.

being asked if she knew of any ointment they had in the house she said her Mistress [an]ointed her once for some ail[ment] she had. but it was with ointment that came from Mrs Bassett of Lynn the color of it was greenish she was asked how it smelt, said very ugly to her

she said when: she touched the book she went to put her finger to another line but still her finger went to the same place where her finger had blacked

Mr Noyes told her she had then touched the book twice and asked her whether she did not suspect it to be the devil's book before she touched it the second time: she said she feared it was no good book, being asked what she meant by no good book, she said a book to deceive.

Mary Warren's Examination May 12th. 1692.

Q. Whether you did not know that it was the Devil's book when you signed.

A. I did not know it then but I know it now to be sure it was the Devil's book, in the first place to be sure I did set my hand to the devil's book: I have considered of it since you were here last and it was the devil's book that my Master Proctor brought to me and he told me if I would set my hand to that book I should believe and I did set my hand to it but . . . it was done with my finger. he brought the book and told me if I would take the book and touch it that I should be well and I thought then that it was the Devil's book.

Q. Was there not your consent to hurt the children when you were hurt?

A. No Sir. but when I was afflicted my master Proctor was in the Room and said if you are afflicted I wish they were more afflicted and you and all: I said Master what makes you say so. He answered, because you go to bring out Innocent persons, I told him that that could not be. and whether the Devil took advantage at that I know not to afflict them and one night talking about them I said I did not care though they were tormented if ye charged me

Q. Did you ever see any puppets?

A. Yes once I saw one made of cloth in Mistress proctor's hand

Q. Who was it like, or which of the Children was it for?

A. I cannot tell, whether for Ann Putnam or Abigail Williams for one of them it was I am sure, it was in my mistress's hand.

Q. What did you stick into the puppet?

A. I did stick in a pin about the neck of it as it was in proctor's hand

Q. How many more did you see afterwards?

A. I do not remember that ever I saw any more, yes I remember one and that Goody parker brought brought a puppet unto me of Mercy Lewis and she gave me another and I stuck it somewhere about the waist and she appeared once more to me in the prison and she said to me what are you got here? and she told me that she was coming here herself. I had another person that appeared to me, it was Goody Pudeator and said she was coming to see me there. it was in apparition and she brought me a puppet it was like to Mary Walcott and it was a piece of stick that she brought me to stick into it. and somewhere about her arms I stuck it in.

Q. Where did she bring it to you?

A. up at Proctor's. Goody Proctor told me she had been a witch these 12 years and more; and pudeator told me that she had done damage and told me that she had hurt James Cloyce's child taking it out of the mother's hand.

Q. Who brought the last to you?

A. my mistress and when she brought it, she brought it in her own person and her husband with his own hands brought me the book to Sign and he brought me an Image which looked yellow and I believe it was for Abigail Williams being like her and I put a thing like a thorn into it this was done by his bodily person after I had signed. the night after I had signed the book while she was thus confessing Parker appeared and bit her extremely on her arms as she affirmed unto us.

Q. Who have you seen more?

A. Nurse and Cloyce and Good's child after I had signed

Q. What said they to you?.

A. They said that I should never tell of them nor anything about them and I have seen Goody Good herself.

Q. Was that true of Giles Cory that you saw him that he afflicted you the other day.?.

A. Yes. I have seen him often and he hurts me very much and Goody Oliver hath appeared to me and afflicted me and brought the Book to tempt me and I have seen Goody Cory. the first night I was taken I saw as I thought the Apparition of Goody Cory and catched at it as I thought and caught my master in my lap though I did not see my master in the place at the time, upon which my master said it is nobody, but I it is my shadow that you see, but my master was not before me that I could discern but Catching at the apparition that looked like Goody Cory I caught hold of my master and pulled him down into my lap; upon which he said I see there is no heed to any of your talkings, for you are all possessed with the Devil for it is nothing but my shape; I have seen Goody Cory at my master's house in person, and she told me that I should be condemned for a witch as well as she cry out and bring out all.

Q. was this before you had signed?

A. Yes before I had my fits

Q. Now tell the truth about the Mountebank what writing was that.

A. I do not know. I asked her what it was about but she would not tell me saying she had promised not to let anybody see it.

Q. Well, but who did you see more?

A. I don't know any more

Q. How long hath your Master and Mistress been witches?

A. I don't know they never told me

Q. What likeness or appearance have you had to bewitch you?

A. They never gave me anything. while I was reading this over upon the coming in of Mr Higginson and Mr Hale as soon as I read the name parker she immediately Fell into dreadful fits. as she affirmed after her fit was over by the appearance of Goody Parker. and Mr Hawthorne presently but naming Goody Pudeator she also appeared and tormented her very much and Goody Parker in the time of her examination in one of Warren's fits told this examinant that she had bewitched the examinant's sister and was the cause of her dumbness as also that she had lately killed a man aboard a vessel and told me that his name was Michael Chapleman aboard the vessel in the harbor after they were come to anchor and that he died with a pain in his side and that she had done it by striking something into his side and that she had struck this examinant's sister dumb that she should never speak more and Goody Pudeator at the same time appeared and told this examinant that she had thrown John Turner off of a cherry tree and almost killed him and Goody Parker said that she had cast away Capt Price's ketch Thomas Westgate master, and Venus Colefox in it and presently told her that John Lapshorne was lost in it and and that they were Foundered in the sea, and she saith that Goody Pudeator told her that she went up to Mr Corwin's house to bewitch his mare that he should not go up to the Farms to examine the witches also Mr Burroughs appearing at the same time and afflicting her told her that he went to tie Mr Hawthorne's horse's legs when he went last to Boston and that he tried to bewitch him though he could not his horse Goody Pudeator told her that she killed her husband by giving him something whereby he fell sick and died. it was she told her about 7 or 10 years since and Goody parker told her that she was Instrumental to drown Orne's son in the harbor also she said she did bewitch John Scarlet's boy to death as his master was carrying him out to sea so that he was forced to bring him back again, also Burroughs told her that he killed his wife off of Cape Ann. Parker told her also that Margaret Jacobs was a witness against her and did charge her yesterday upon her (that is Jacobs') examination.

Return of Seaching Committee
v. John Proctor and John Willard.

We whose names underwritten having searched the bodies of John Proctor senior and John Willard now in the Jail and do not find anything to farther suspect them.

Dated June 2. 1692.

N Roudel . . . John Rogers, Joshua Rea Junior, John Cooke, J. Barton Surgeon, John Gyles, William Hyne, Ezekiel Cheever.

The morning after the examination of Goody Nurse Sam Sibley met John Proctor about Mr Phillips' we called to said Sibley as he was going to said Phillips' and asked how the folks did at the village. He answered he heard they were very bad last night, but he had heard nothing this morning. Proctor replied he was going to fetch home his jade, he left her there last night and had rather given 40 c [crowns?] than let her come up, said Sibley asked why he talked so. Proctor replied if they were let alone sir. we should all be devils and witches quickly they should rather be had to the whipping post, but he would fetch his jade home and thrust the Devil out of her and more to the like purpose [than] crying hang them, hang them. And also added that when she was first taken with fits he kept her close to the wheel and threatened to thrash her, and then she had no more fits till the next day he was gone forth and then she must have her fits again forsooth etc.

Jurat in Curia.

Proctor owns he meant Mary Warren.

Attested.   ST. SEWALL. Cler.

Abigail Hobbs's Examination No. 3.

Examination of Abigail Hobbs *before their* Majesties' Justices June 29 1692

Saith that on Friday last John Proctor Senior being in a Room with her alone told her that she had better to afflict than be afflicted and that she should not be hanged & but Enjoined her to afflict Ann Putnam and per-suaded her to Set her hand to the Book and Guided her hand personally to do it and after this his appearance brought me a puppet and a Thorn which I stuck into the puppet to afflict said Ann Putnam a friday.

Sarah Vibber v. John Proctor.

The deposition of Sarah Vibber aged about 36 years who testifieth and saith, that on the 3 June 1692. Jno: Proctor: senior: came to me and did most grievously. torment me by pinching pricking and almost pressing me to death urging me to drink drink as red as blood, which I refusing he did torture me with variety of tortures and immediately he vanished away also on the same day I saw Jno Proctor most grievously torture Susanna Sheldon by clapping his hands on her throat and almost choking her, also several times since Jno Proctor senior has most grievously tortured me a great many times with a variety of tortures,

Sarah Vibber owned this her testimony to be the truth on her oath be-fore the Jurors of Inquest this 30: of June. 1692.

Jurat in Curia.

Elizabeth Hubbard v. Jno. Proctor.

The deposition of Elizabeth Hubbard aged about 17 years, who testifieth and saith that I never saw the Apparition of Jno: Proctor senior before the day of his examination which was the 11th April. 1692. but since that the Apparition of Jno Proctor senior has most grievously afflicted me, a great many times by pinching pricking and beating me almost choking me to death urging me vehemently to writ[e] in his book.

Eliz. HER MARK Hubbard
Jurat in Curia.

Ann Putnam Jr. v. Jno Proctor.

The deposition of Ann Putnam Junior who testifieth and saith I have often seen the Apparition of Jno Proctor senior. Amongst the witches but he did not do me much hurt till a little before his examination which was on the 11th of April 1692. And then he set upon me most grievously and did torture me most dreadfully, also in the time of his examination he afflicted me very much, and several times since the Apparition of John Proctor senior, has most grievously tortured me by pinching and almost choking me urging me vehemently to writ[e] in his book. also on the day of his examination I saw the apparition of Jno: Proctor senior go and afflict and most grievously torture the bodies of Mistress Pope. Mary Walcott Mercy Lewis. Abigail Williams and Jno Indian and he and his wife and Sarah Cloyce kept Elizabeth Hubbard speechless all the time of their examination.

Ann HER MARK Putnam

Ann Putnam owned what is above written upon oath before and unto the Grand inquest on the 30th Day of June 1692.

Sam: Parris Nathaniel Ingersoll. and Thomas Putnam v. Jno Proctor.

The deposition of Sam. Parris. aged about 39 years and Nathaniel Ingersoll. aged about fifty and eight years and also. Thomas Putnam aged about forty years all of Salem.

testifieth and saith that divers of the afflicted by witchcraft were much tortured at the examination of John Proctor of Salem. Farmer. before the honored Magistrates the 11th April 1692. And particularly when Mr Joseph Pope's wife was several times afflicted Ann Putnam junior. and Abigail Williams testified that it was by John Proctor aforesaid and his wife Elizabeth and also when Mercy Lewis was much afflicted at the same examination, said Ann witnessed that it was by said Proctor and his wife and Goody Cloyce also when Goody Vibber was much afflicted Abig: Williams just before cried out there is Goodman Proctor going to hurt Goody Vibber, and also said Abigail cried out there is Goodman Proctor going to hurt Mary Walcott and immediately Mary Walcott was seized with a violent fit

Mary Warren v. John Proctor.

The deposition of Mary Warren aged 20 years he[re] testifieth. I have seen the apparition of John Proctor senior among the witches and he hath often tortured me by pinching me and biting me and choking me, and pressing me on my Stomach till the blood came out of my mouth and also I saw him torture Mis Pope and Mercy lewis and John Indian upon the day of his examination and he hath also tempted me to write in his book. and to eat bread which he brought to me, which I refusing to do, Jno Proctor did most grievously torture me with variety of tortures, almost Ready to kill me.

Mary Warren owned the above written upon her oath before and unto the Grand Inquest on the 30 Day of June 1692

James Holton v. John Proctor.

James Holton testifieth and said that as soon as Mary Walcott and Elizabeth Hubbard was afflicted that at that same time I had ease of my pains. Jurat in Curia.

John Proctor's Petition to the Ministers of Boston.

SALEM-Prison, July 23, 1692.

Mr. [probably Increase] *Mather, Mr. Allen,*
Mr. Moody, Mr. Willard, and
Mr. Bailey.
Reverend Gentlemen.

The innocency of our Case with the Enmity of our Accusers and our Judges, and Jury, whom nothing but our Innocent Blood will serve their turn, having Condemned us already before our Trials, being so much incensed and engaged against us by the Devil, makes us bold to Beg and Implore your Favorable Assistance of this our Humble Petition to his Excellency, That if it be possible our Innocent Blood may be spared, which undoubtedly otherwise will be shed, if the Lord doth not mercifully step in. The Magistrates, Ministers, Juries, and all the People in general, being so much enraged and incensed against us by the Delusion of the Devil, which we can term no other, by reason we know in our own Consciences, we are all Innocent Persons. Here are five Persons who have lately confessed themselves to be Witches, and do accuse some of us, of being along with them at a Sacrament, since we were committed into close Prison, which we know to be Lies. Two of the 5 are (Carrier's Sons) Young-men, who would not confess anything till they tied them Neck and Heels till the Blood was ready to come out of their Noses, and 'tis credibly believed and reported this was the occasion of making them confess that [which] they never did, by reason they said one had been a Witch a Month, and another five Weeks, and that their Mother had made them so, who has been confined here this nine Weeks. My son William Proctor, when he was examin'd, because he would not confess that he was Guilty, when he was Innocent, they tied him Neck and Heels till the Blood gushed out at his Nose, and would have kept him so 24 Hours, if one more Merciful than the rest, had not taken pity on him, and caused him to be unbound. These actions are very like the Popish Cruelties. They have already undone us in our Estates, and that will not serve their turns, without our Innocent Bloods. If it cannot be granted that we can have our Trials at Boston, we humbly beg that you would endeavor to have these Magistrates changed, and others in their rooms, begging also and beseeching you would be pleased to be here, if not all, some of you at our Trials, hoping thereby you may be the means of saving the shedding our Innocent Bloods, desiring your Prayers to the Lord in our behalf, we rest your Poor Afflicted Servants,

JOHN PROCTOR, etc.

Petition in Favor of Jno. Proctor and Wife.

The Humble and Sincere Declaration of us Subscribers Inhabitants in Ipswich on the behalf of our Neighbors Jno Proctor and his wife now in Trouble and under Suspicion of Witchcraft.

To the Honorable Court of Assistants now sitting In Boston.
Honored and Right Worshipful

The foresaid John Proctor. may have great reason to Justify the Divine Sovereignty of God under those severe Remarks of Providence upon his Peace and Honor under a due reflection upon his life past And so the best of us have reason to Adore the Great Pity and Indulgence of God's Providence that we are not exposed to the utmost shame that the Devil can Invent under the permissions of Sovereignty though not for that sin forenamed yet [?] for our many Transgressions for we do at present suppose it may be A Method within the Severer But Just Transactions of the Infinite Majesty of God that he sometimes may permit Satan to personate, Dissemble and thereby abuse innocents, and such as Do in the fear of God Defy the Devil and all his works. The Great Rage he is permitted to attempt holy Job with The abuse he does the famous Samuel in Disquieting his silent Dust by Shadowing his venerable person in answer to the charms of Witchcraft. and other instances from Good hands may be Argued Besides, the unsearchable footsteps of God's Judgments, that are brought to Light every morning that Astonish our weaker Reasons, To teach us Adoration Trembling and Dependence etc. But.

We must not Trouble your Honors by Being Tedious, Therefore we being smitten with the Notice of what hath happened, we Reckon it within the Duties of our Charity, that Teacheth us to do as we would be done by; to offer thus much for the Clearing of our Neighbor's Innocency: viz: That we never had the least knowledge of such a Nefarious wickedness, in our said Neighbors, since they have been within our acquaintance. Neither do we remember any such thoughts in us concerning them, or any action by them. or either of them. Directly tending that way no more than might be in the lives of any other persons, of the Clearest Reputation as to any such Evils. What God may have left them to, we cannot go into God's pavilions Clothed with Clouds of Darkness, Round About.

But as to what we have ever seen or heard of them upon our consciences we Judge them Innocent of the crime objected.

His Breeding hath been amongst us and was of Religious Parents in our place, and by reason of Relations and Properties within our Town hath had constant intercourse with us.

We speak upon our personal acquaintance and observations: and so leave our neighbors and this our Testimony on their behalf to the wise thoughts of your Honors. etc.

Subscribe etc.

[32 signatures.]

Petition in favor of John Proctor and Elizabeth Proctor.

We whose names are underwritten having several years known John Proctor and his wife do testify that we never heard or understood that they were ever suspected to be guilty of the crime now charged upon them and several of us being their near neighbors do testify that to our apprehension they lived christian life in their family and were ever ready to help such as stood in need of their help.

[20 signatures, including James Holton.]

[It is possible that the following testimony in favor of Elizabeth Proctor was not given until some time after John Proctor had been executed. Although the two had been accused at the same time and then convicted, Elizabeth had won a reprieve allowing her to live until her baby was born.]

Samuel Barton and John Houghton for Eliz: Proctor.

the testimony of Samuel Barton aged 28 years, or thereabouts who testifieth and saith that I being at Thomas Putnam's a-helping to attend the afflicted Folks I heard them talking who the children complained of and I heard them tell Mercy lewis that she cried out of Goody Proctor and Mercy lewis said that she did not cry out of Goody Proctor nor nobody, she said she did say there she is, but did not tell them who and Thomas Putnam and his wife and others, told her that she cried out of Goody Proctor and Mercy lewis said if she did it was when she was out in her head for she said she saw nobody, this being the 20 of March in the year 1691-92

John Houghton aged 23. testifieth and saith I this deponent was present at the same time above written, and I heard Thomas Putnam and his wife say that Mercy Lewis saw or named the wife of John Proctor in her fit and we heard the said Mercy Lewis affirm that she never said that ever she saw her.

Daniel Elliott for Elizabeth Proctor.

the testimony of Daniel Elliott, aged 27 years or thereabouts who testifieth and saith that I being at the house of lieutenant Ingersoll on the 28 of March, in the year 1692 there being present, one of the afflicted persons which cried out and said there's Goody Proctor William Raiment being there present, told the girl he believed she lied for he saw nothing then Goody ingersoll told the girl she told a lie for there was nothing then the girl said that she did it for sport they must have some sport.

GEORGE BURROUGHS

Examination of George Burroughs.

The examination of Geo: Burroughs 9 May, 1692.

By the
Honoured ⎰ William Stoughton
          John Hawthorne
          Sam. Sewall,
          Jonath. Corwin ⎱ Esqrs.

Being asked when he partook of the Lord's supper, he being (as he said) in full communion at Roxbury.

He answered is [it] was so long since he could not tell: yet he owned he was at meeting one Sab: at Boston part of the day, and the other a[t] Charlestown part of a Sab: when that sacrament happened to be at both, yet did not partake of either. He denied that his house as [at] Casco was haunted, yet he owned there were Toads. He denied that he made his wife swear, that she could not write to his father Ruck without his approbation of her letter to her Father. He owned that none of his children, but the eldest was Baptized The above was in private none of the Bewitched being present, At his entry into the Room many (if not all of the Bewitched) were grievously tortured.

1. Sus. Sheldon testified that Burroughs' two wives appeared in their winding sheets, and said that man killed them.

He was bid to look upon Sus. Sheldon,

He looked back and knocked down all (or most), of the afflicted who stood behind him.

Sus: Sheldon . . [one line gone] the soldiers

2. Mary Lewis' deposition going to be read and he looked upon her and she fell into a dreadful and tedious fit,

3. Mary Walcott
4 Eliz Hubbard ⎰ Testimony going to be read
   Susan Sheldon ⎱ and they all fell into fits

   Susan Sheldon ⎰ affirmed each of them that
5 Ann Putnam junior ⎱ he brought the Book
                      and would have them write.

Being asked what he thought of these things. He answered it was an amazing and humbling Providence, but he understood nothing of it and he

65

said (some of you may observe, that) when they begin to name my name, they cannot name it.

Ann Putnam junior Susan Sheldon	Testified that his 2 wives & 2, Children were destroyed by him.

The Bewitched were so tortured that Authority ordered them to be taken away some of them.

6. Sarah Vibber testified that he had hurt her, though she had not seen him personally before as she knew.

Abig. Hobbs. Deliverance Hobbs Eleazar Kezer	Testimony read

Capt Willard Jno Brown Jno Wheldon	Testimony about his great strength and the Gun.

Capt Putnam testified about the Gun.

Capt Wormwood testified about the Gun and the Molasses He denied that about the molasses About the Gun he said he took it before the lock and rested it upon his breast.

John Brown testified about a bbl Cider.

He denied that his family was affrighted by a white calf in his house

Capt Putnam testified that he made his wife enter into a covenant. 11 May 1692.

Abig: Hobbs in prison affirmed that Geo. Burroughs in his shape appeared to her, and urged her to set her hand to the Book, which she did, and after-wards in his own person he acknowledged to her, that he had made her set her hand to the Book.

Examination of Deliverance Hobbs.

(1) The Examination of Deliverance Hobbs 22 Apr. 1692. At a court held at Salem village by

JOHN HAWTHORNE JONAH CORWIN	Esqrs.

Mercy Lewis do you know her that stands at the Bar (for the Magistrates had privately ordered who should be brought in and not suffered he[r] name to be mentioned) Do you know her? speaking to another: but both were struck dumb.

Ann Putnam junior said it was Goody Hobbs and she hath hurt her much.

John Indian said he had seen her, & she choke him.

Mary Walcott said, yesterday was the first time that she saw her i. c. [in court?] as a Tormenter

Why do you hurt these persons?

It is unknown to me.

How come you to commit acts of witchcraft?

I know nothing of it.

It is you or your appearance, how comes this about? Tell us the truth.

I cannot tell.

Tell us what you know in this case. Who hurts them if you do not?

There are a great many Persons hurts us all.

But it is your appearance.

I do not know it.

Have not you consented to it, that they should be hurt?

No in the sight of God, and man, as I shall answer another day

It is said you were afflicted, how came that about?

I have seen sundry sights.

What sights.

Last Lord's day in this meeting house and out of the door, I saw a great many birds cats and dogs, and heard a voice say come away.

What have you seen since?

The shapes of several persons.

What did they say?

Nothing.

What neither the birds, nor persons?

No.

What persons did you see?

Goody Wildes and the shape of Mercy Lewis.

What is that? Did either of them hurt you?

None but Goody Wildes, who tore me almost to pieces.

Where was you then?

In bed

Was not the book brought to you to sign?

No.

Where were you not threatened by anybody, if you did not sign the book?

No, by nobody.

What were you tempted to under you[r] affliction?

I was not tempted at all.

Is it not a solemn thing, that last Lord's day you were tormented, & now you are become a tormentor, so that you have changed sides, how comes this to pass?

Abig: Williams and Ann Putnam junior cry out there is Goody Hobbs upon the Beam, she is not at the Bar, they cannot see her there: though there she stood.

What do you say to this, that though you are at the bar in person, yet they see your appearance upon the beam, & whereas a few days past you were tormented, now you are become a Tormentor? Tell us how this change comes. Tell true.

I have done nothing.

What have you resolved you will not confess? Hath anybody threatened you if you do confess? You can tell how this change comes.

She looked upon John Indian, & then another, & then they fell into fits. Tell us us the reason of this change: Tell us the truth. What have you done?

I cannot speak.

What do you say? What have you done?

I cannot tell.

Have you signed to any book?

It is very lately then.

When was it?

The night before the last.

Will the Lord open your heart to confess the truth. Who brought the book to you?

It was Goody Wildes.

What did you make your mark with in the book?

Pen and ink.

Who brought the Pen and Ink?

They that brought the book, Goody Wildes.

Did they threaten you if you did not sign?

Yes, to tear me in pieces.

Was there any else in company?

No, Sir.

What did you afflict others by? Did they bring images?

Yes.

Who brought the images?

Goody Wildes and Goody Osborne.

What did you put into those images.

Pins, Sir.

Well tell us who have you seen of this company?

None but those two.

Have you not seen many?

No. I heard last night a kind of Thundering.

How many images did you use?

But two.

Nay here is more afflicted by you, You said more, Well tell us the truth. Recollect yourself.

I am amazed.

can you remember how many were brought?

Not well, but several were brought.

Did they not bring the image of John Nichols his child?

Yes.

Did not you hurt that child?

Yes.

Where be those images, at your house?

No, they carried them away again.

When?

They carried some then & some since.
Was it Goody Wildes in body, or appearance?
In appearance.
Was there any man with them?
Yes a tall black man with an highcrowned hat.
Do you know no more of them?
No. Sir.

Note. All the sufferers free from affliction during her examination after once she began to confess, though at sundry times they were much afflicted till then.

Note. . . .

Examination of Deliverance Hobbs.

The first Examination of Deliverance Hobbs in prison. She continued in the free acknowledging herself to be a Covenant Witch, and further Confesseth She was warned to a meeting yesterday morning, and that there was present Proctor and his Wife, Goody Nurse, Giles Cory and his Wife, Goody Bishop alias Oliver, and mr Burroughs was the Preacher, and pressed them to bewitch all in the Village, telling them they should do it gradually and not all at once, assuring them they should prevail. He administered the sacrament unto them at the same time with Red Bread, and Red Wine like Blood, she affirms she saw Osborne, Sarah Good, Goody Wildes; Goody Nurse, and Goody Wildes distributed the bread and Wine, and a Man in a long crowned white Hat, sat next the Minister and they sat seemingly at a Table, and They filled out the wine in Tankards, The Notice of this meeting was given her by Goody wildes. She herself affirms did not nor would not Eat or drink, but all the Rest did who were there present, therefore they threatened to torment her. The meeting was in the Pasture by Mr Parris's House, and she saw when Abigail Williams ran out speak with them: But that Time Abigail was come a little distance from the House. This Examinant was struck blind, so that she saw not with whom Abigail spoke She further saith, that Goody Wildes to prevail with her to sign, told her that if she would put her hand to the book she would give her some Clothes, and would not afflict her any more—Her daughter Abigail Hobbs being brought in at the same time while her mother was present was immediately taken with a dreadful fit, and her mother being asked who it was that hurt her daughter answered it was Goodman Cory and she saw him and the gentlewoman of Boston striving to break her Daughter's neck.

Abigail Hobbs's Examination No. 2.[11]

Abigail Hobbs's Examination at Salem Prison May 12 1692

Q. Did Mr Burroughs bring you any of the puppets of his wives to stick pins into

A. I do not remember that he did

Q. Did he of any of his children or of the Eastward Soldiers

A. No.

Q. Have you known of any that have been killed by witchcraft

A. No. No-Body.

Q. How came you to speak of Mr Burroughs' wives yesterday.

A. I don't know.

Q. Is that true about Davis's Son of Casco and of those of the village?

A. Yes it is true.

Q. What service did he put you upon? and who are they you afflicted

A. I cannot tell who, neither do I know whether they died

Q. Were they strangers to you that Burroughs would have you afflict.

A. Yes

Q. and were they afflicted accordingly

A. Yes.

Q. Can't you name some of them?

A. No I cannot remember them.

Q. Where did they live?

A. At the Eastward.

Q. have any vessels been cast away by you?

A. I do not know.

Q. Have you consented to the afflicting any other besides those at the village?

A. Yes.

Q. Who were they?

A. I cannot tell But it was of such who Lived at the fort side of the river about half a mile from the fort toward Capt Brackett.

Q. What was the hurt you give to them by consent?

A. I don't know.

Q. was there anything brought to you like them?

A. Yes.

Q. what did you stick into them

A. Thorns.

Q. did some of them die

A. Yes. one of them was Mary Laurence that died.

Q. Where

Q. where did you stick the thorns?

A. I do not know

Q. was it about the middle of her body?

A. Yes and I stuck it right in.

[11] For Abigail Hobbs's testimony about the witches' sabbath, see p. 10.

q. what provoked you, had she displeased you?

a. Yes by some words she spoke of me.

q. who brought the image to you?

a. it was Mr Burroughs.

q. How did he bring it to you?

a. In his own person bodily.

q. where did he bring it to you?

a. abroad a little way off from our house.

q. and what did he say to you then?

a. he told me he was angry with that Family.

q. how many years Since was it?

a. Before this Indian war.

q. How did you know Mr Burroughs was a witch?

a. I don't know. She owned again she had made two Covenants with the Devil first for two years and after that for four years and she confesseth herself to have been a witch these six years

q. did the maid complain of pain about the place you stuck the thorn in.?

a. Yes but how long she Lived I don't know

q. How do you know Burroughs was Angry with Laurence's Family?

a. Because he told me so.

q. where did any other live that you afflicted?

a. Just by the other toward James Andrews' and they died also.

q. How many were they more than one?

a. Yes.

q. And who brought those puppets to you?

a. Mr Burroughs.

q. What did you stick into them?

a. Pins. and he gave them to me.

q. Did you keep those puppets?

a. No he carried them away with him

q. Was he there himself with you in Bodily person?

a. Yes and so he was when he appeared to tempt me to set my hand to the Book he then appeared in person and I felt his hand at the same time.

q. Were they men women or children you killed?

a. They were both Boys and Girls.

q. Was you angry with them yourself?

a. Yes though I don't know why now.

q. Did you know Mr. Burroughs' wife?

a. Yes.

q. Did you know of any puppets pricked to kill her?

a. No I don't.

q. Have you seen several witches at the Eastward?

a. Yes, But I don't know who they were.

Ann Foster's Confession.

The examination and Confession of Ann Foster at Salem Village 15 July 1692. after a while Ann Foster confessed that the devil appeared to her in the shape of a bird at several Times, such a bird as she never saw the like before, and that she had had this gift (viz. of striking the afflicted down with her eye) ever since, and being asked why she thought that bird was the devil she answered because he came white and vanished away black and that the devil told her that she should have this gift and that she must believe him and told her she should have prosperity, and she said that he had appeared to her three times and was always as a bird, and the last time was about half a year since, and sat upon a table had two legs & great eyes and that it was the second time of his appearance that he promised her prosperity and that it was Carrier's wife about three weeks ago that came and persuaded her to hurt these people.

16 July. 1692. Ann Foster Examined confessed that it was Goody Carrier that made her a witch that she came to her in person about Six years ago & told her if she would not be a witch the devil should tear her in pieces and carry her away at which time she promised to Serve the devil, that she had bewitched a hog of John Lovejoy's to death and that she had hurt some persons in Salem Village, that goody Carrier came to her and would have her bewitch two children of Andrew Allen's and that she had then two puppets made and stuck pins in them to bewitch the said children by which one of them died the other very sick, that she was at the meeting of the witches at Salem Village, that Goody Carrier came and told her of the meeting and would have her go, so they got upon Sticks and went said Journey and being there did see Mr Burroughs the minister who spoke to them all, and this was about two months ago that ther[e] was then twenty five persons meet together, that she tied a knot in a Rage and threw it into the fire to hurt Timo. Swan and that she did hurt the rest that complained of her by squeezing puppets like them and so almost choked them.

18 July 1692. Ann Foster Examined confessed that the devil in shape of a man appeared to her with Goody carrier about six year since when they made her a witch and that she promised to serve the devil two years, upon which the Devil promised her prosperity and many things but never performed it, that she and martha Carrier did both ride on a stick or pole when they went to the witch meeting at Salem Village and that the stick broke: as they were carried in the air above the tops of the trees, and they fell but she did hang fast about the neck of Goody Carrier and were presently at the village, that she was then much hurt of her Leg, she further saith that she heard some of the witches say, that there was three hundred and five in the whole Country and that they would ruin that place the Village, also saith ther[e] was was present at that meeting two men besides mr Burroughs the minister and one of them had gray hair, she saith that she formerly frequented the public meeting to worship god. but the devil had such power over her that she could not profit there and that was her undoing: she saith that about three or four years ago Martha Carrier told her

she would bewitch James Hobbs's child to death and the child died in twenty four hours.

21. July: 92. Ann Foster Examined Owned her former confession being read to her and further confessed that the discourse amongst the witches at the meeting at Salem village was that they would afflict there to set up the Devil's Kingdom. This confession is true as witness my hand:

the mark of
Ann Foster

View of body of Geo Burroughs.

We whose names are under written having received an order from the sheriff for to search the bodies of George Burroughs and George Jacobs we find nothing upon the body of the above said burroughs but what is natural, but upon the body of George Jacobs we find 3 teats which according to the best of our Judgments we think is not natural for we run a pin through 2 of them and he was not sensible of it. one of them being within his mouth upon the Inside of his right cheek and 2nd upon his right shoulder blade an[d] a 3rd upon his right hip.

Ed. Welch sworn	Tom flint Jurat
Will. Gill sworn.	Tom West sworn
Zeb. Hill Jurat	Sam Morgan sworn
John Bare Jurat.	

Samuel Webber v. Geo Burroughs.

Samuel Webber aged about 36 years Testifieth and saith that about seven or eight Years ago I lived at Casco Bay and George Burroughs was then Minister there, and having heard much of the great strength of him said Burroughs; he Coming to our house we were in discourse about the same and he then told me that he had put his fingers into the Bung of a Barrel of Molasses and lifted it up, and carried it Round him and set it down again. Salem August 2d 1692.

Jurat in Curia.   SAMUEL WEBBER.

Ann Putnam v. Geo Burroughs.

The Deposition of Ann putnam who testifieth and saith that on 20th of April 1692 at evening she saw the Apparition of a minister at which she was grievously affrighted and cried out oh dreadful: dreadful here is a minister com[e], what are Ministers witches to: whence com[e] you and What is your name for I will complain of you though you be A minister: if you be a wizard: and Immediately i was tortured by him being Racked and almost choked by him: and he tempted me to write in his book which I Refused with loud out cries and said I would not write in his book though he tore me all to pieces but told him that it was a dreadful thing: that he which was a Minister that should teach children to fear God should com[e] to persuade poor creatures to give their souls to the devil: Oh, dreadful dreadful, tell me your name that I may know who you are: then again he tortured me and urged me to write in his book: which I Refused: and then presently he told me that his name was George Burroughs and that he had had three wives: and that he had bewitched the Two first of them to death; and that he killed Mistress Lawson because she was so unwilling to go from the village and also killed Mr Lawson's child because he went to the eastward with Sir Edmon[d Andros] and preached so to the soldiers and that he had bewitched a great many soldiers to death at the eastward when Sir Edmon was there, and that he had made Abigail Hobbs a witch and several witches more: and he has continued ever since; by times tempting me to write in his book and grievously torturing me by beating pinching and almost choking me several times a day and he also told me that he was above a witch he was a conjurer.

Jurat in Curia.

Thomas Putnam, Peter Prescott, Robert Morrell and Ezekiel Cheever v. Geo Burroughs.

we whose names are under written being present with Ann putnam at the time above mentioned heard her declare what is above written what she said she saw and heard from the Apparition of Mr George Burroughs and also beheld her tortures and perceived her hellish temptations by her loud out cries I will not I will not write though you torment me all days of my life, and being conversant with her ever since have seen her tortured and complaining that Mr Burroughs hurt her, and tempts her to write in his book,

Thomas putnam   peter prescott
Robert Morrell,

Ann Putnam declared her above written evidence to be the truth before the Jury of Inquest. August 3. 92. upon her oath.

Ezekiel Cheever made oath to the latter part of this paper. Jurat in Curia.

Ann Putnam v. Geo Burroughs.

The deposition of Ann putnam who testifieth and saith that on the 3th of may 1692, at evening I saw the Apparition of Mr George Burroughs who grievously tortured me and urged me to write in his book which I refused then he told me that his Two first wives would appear to me presently and tell me a great many lies but I should not believe them, then Immediately appeared to me the form of Two women in winding sheets and napkins about their heads, at which I was greatly affrighted, and they turned their faces towards Mr Burroughs and looked very red and angry and told him that he had been a cruel man to them, and that their blood did cry for vengeance against him: and also told him that they should be clothed with white Robes in heaven, when he should be cast into hell, and immediately he vanished away, and as soon as he was gone the Two women turned their faces towards me and looked as pale as a white wall: and told me that they were Mr Burroughs' Two first wives and that he had murdered them: and one told me that she was his first wife and he stabbed her under the left Arm and put a piece of sealing wax on the wound and she pulled aside the winding sheet, and showed me the place and also told me that she was in the house Mr parris now lived where it was done, and the other told me that Mr Burroughs and that wife which he hath now killed her in the vessel as she was coming to see her friends because they would have one another: and they both charged me that I should tell these things to the Magistrates before Mr Burroughs' face and if he did not own them they did not know but they should appear there: this morning. also Mistress Lawson and her daughter Ann appeared to me whom I knew, and told me that Mr Burroughs murdered them, this morning also appeared to me another woman in a winding sheet and told me that she was goodman Fuller's first wife and Mr Burroughs killed her because there was some difference between her husband and him, also on the 9th may during the time of his examination he did most grievously torment and afflict mary Walcott mercy lewis Eliz. Hubbard and Abigail williams by pinching pricking and choking them. Jurat in Curia.

Edward Putnam and Thomas Putnam v. Geo Burroughs.

we whose names are under written being present with ann putnam at the times above mentioned, saw her tortured and heard her refuse to write in the book also heard her declare what is above written: what she said she saw and heard from the Apparition of Mr George Burroughs and from those which accused him for murdering of them.

Edward putnam   Thomas putnam

Ann putnam owned this her testimony to be the truth upon her oath before the Jurors of Inquest this 3d of August 92.

Mercy Lewis v. Geo Burroughs.

the deposition of mercy Lewis who testifieth and saith that on the 7th of may 1692. at evening I saw the apparition of Mr George Burroughs whom i very well knew which did grievously torture me and urged me to write in his book and then he brought to me a new fashion book which he did not use to bring and told me I might write in that book: for that was a book that was in his study when I lived with them: but I told him I did not believe him for I had been often in his study but I never saw that book there: but he told me that he had several books in his study, which I never saw in his study and he could raise the devil: and now had bewitched Mr. Shepard's daughter and I asked him how he could go to bewitch her now he was kept at Salem; and he told me that the devil was his servant, and he sent him in his shape to do it, then he again tortured me most dreadfully and threatened

to kill me for he said I should not witness against him also he told me that
he had made Abigail Hobbs a witch and several more then again he did most
dreadfully torture me as if he would have racked me all to pieces and urged
me to write in his book or else he would kill me but I told him I hoped my
life was not in the power of his hand and that I would not write tho he did
kill me: the next night he told me I should not see his Two wives if he could
help it because I should not witness against him: this 9th may mr Burroughs
carried me up to an exceeding high mountain and showed me all the Kingdoms of the earth and told me that he would give them all to me if I would
write in his book, and if I would not he would throw me down and break
my neck: but I told him they were none of his to give and I would not write
if he throwed me down on 100 pitchforks: also on the 9th may being the time
of his examination mr. George Burroughs did most dreadfully torment me:
and also several times since.

mercy lewis upon her oath did own this her testimony to be the truth before the Jurors for Inquest; august 3: 92.

Thomas Putnam Edward Putnam v. Geo Burroughs.

we whose names are under written being present heard mercy lewis declare what is above written what she said she saw and heard from the Apparition of Mr George Burroughs and also beheld her tortures which we cannot
express for some times we were ready to fear that every joint of her body was
ready to be displaced: also we perceived her hellish temptations by her loud
out cries mr Burroughs I will not write in your book though you do kill me.

Thomas putnam   Edward Putnam.
Jurat in Curia.

Simon Willard v. Geo Burroughs.

The Deposition of Simon Willard aged about forty two years saith I being at the house of Mr Robert Lawrence at Falmouth in Casco Bay in September 1689 said Mr Lawrence was commending Mr George Burroughs his
strength: saying that we none of us could do what he could do: for said Mr
Burroughs can hold out this gun with one hand; Mr. Burroughs being there:
said I held my hand here behind the lock and took it up, and held it out,
I said deponent saw Mr Burroughs put his hand on the gun: to show us:
how he held it and where he held his hand, and saying there he held his
hand when he held said gun out: but I saw him not hold it out then, said
gun was about seven foot barrel and very heavy I then tried to hold out said
gun with both hands, but could not do it long enough to take sight.

SIMON WILLARD

Simon willard owned to the Jury of inquest, that the above written evidence is the truth,
August 3: 1692,
                                                    Jurat in Curia.

Wm Wormall v. Geo Burroughs.

Capt William Wormall Sworn to the above and that he saw him Raise it from the ground, himself.

Jurat in Curia.

The Deposition of Simon Willard aged about 42 years saith I being at Saco in the year 1689 some in Capt Ed Sarjant's garrison was speaking of mr George Burroughs his great strength saying he could take a barrel of molasses out of a Canoe or boat alone, and that he could take it in his hands or arms out of the Canoe or boat and carry it and set it on the shore and mr Burroughs being there said that he had carried one barrel of molasses or cider out of a canoe that had like to have done him a displeasure: said mr Burroughs intimated as if he did not want strength to do it but the disadvantage of the shore was such, that his foot slipping in the sand: he had liked to have strained his leg.

SIMON WILLARD

Simon Willard owned to the Jury of inquest, that the above written evidence is the truth.

Jurat in Curia.

Sarah Vibber v. Geo Burroughs.

The deposition of sarah vibber who testifieth and saith that on the 9th day of may 1692. as I was agoing to Salem village I saw the apparition of a little man like a minister with a black coat on and he pinched me by the arm and bid me go along with him but I told him I would not but when I came to the village I saw there Mr George Burroughs or his Appearance most grievously torment and afflict mary walcott mercy lewis Elizabeth Hubbard Ann putnam and abigail williams by pinching twisting & almost choking them to death also several times since mr George Burroughs or his Appearance has most grievously tormented me with variety of tortures and I believe in my heart that mr George Burroughs is a dreadful wizzard and that he has most grievously tormented me and the above mentioned persons by his acts of witchcraft.

Sarah Vibber declared to the Jury of inquest that the above written evidence is the truth. August 3: 1692. the which she owned on her oath

Jurat in Curia.

Elizabeth Hubbard v. Geo Burroughs.

May the 9. 1692. Elizabeth hubbard aged about 17 years saith that the last second day at night: There appeared a little black beard man to me in blackish apparel I asked him his name and he told me his name was burroughs, Then he took a book out of his pocket: and opened it and bid me

set my hand to it I told him I would not; the lines in this book was red as
blood, then he pinched me twice and went away: The next morning he appeared to me again and told me he was above a wizzard; for he was a conjurer and so went away but since that he hath appeared to me every day &
night very often and urged me very much to set my hand to his book, and
to run away telling me if I would do so I should be well and that I should
need fear nobody: and withal tormented me several ways every time he came
except that time he told me he was a conjurer: This night he asked me very
much to set my hand to his book or else he said he would kill me; withal
torturing me very much by biting and pinching squeezing my body and running pins into me, also on the 9th may 1692. being the time of his examination mr George Burroughs or his Appearance did most grievously afflict and
torment the bodies of mary walcott mercy lewis Ann putnam and Abigail
williams for if he did but look upon them he would strike them down or
almost choke them to death also several times since he has most dreadfully
afflicted and tormented me with variety of torments and I believe in my heart
that mr George Burroughs is a dreadful wizzard and that he has very often
tormented me and also the above named persons by his acts of witchcraft.

Jurat in Curia.

Eliz. Hubbard declared the above written evidence to be the truth, upon
her oath, that she had taken: this she owned before the Jury of inquest:
August 3. 1692.

Hannah Harris v. Geo Burroughs.

The deposition of Hannah Harris Aged twenty seven years or thereabouts
Testifieth and saith that she lived at the house of George Burroughs at falmouth and the above said hannah harris many times hath taken notice that
when she hath had any Discourse with the above said burroughs' wife when
the above said burroughs was from home that upon his Return he hath often
scolded wife and told her that he knew what they said when he was abroad
and further saith that upon a time when his wife had Lain In Not above
one week that he fell out with his wife and kept her by Discourse at the Door
till she fell sick In the place and grew worse at night so that the above said
hannah harris was afraid she would die and they called In their Neighbors
and the above said burroughs' Daughter told One of the women that was
there the cause of her mother's Illness and the above said burroughs chid his
Daughter for telling and the above said burroughs came to the above said
hannah harris and told her If that his wife Did otherwise than well she should
not tell of it & the above said hannah harris told him that she would not be
confined to any such thing.

Jurat in Curia.

Benjamin Hutchinson v. Geo Burroughs.

Benjamin hutchinson said that on the 21st april 92. Abigail Williams said that there was a little black minister that Lived at Casco bay he told me so and said that he had killed 3 wives two for himself and one for mr Losen and that he had made nine witches in this place and said that he could hold out the heaviest gun that is in Casco bay with one hand which no man can Case hold out with both hands this Is about a 11 o'clock and I ask her where about this little man stood said she just where the Cart wheel went along I had a 3 grained iron fork in my hand and I threw it where she said he stood and she presently fell in a little fit and when it was over Said She you have torn his coat for I heard it tear whereabouts said I on one side said she, then we come into the house of lieutenant Ingersoll and I went into the great room and abigail come in and said there he stands I said where where and presently drawed my rapier but he immediately was gone as she said then said she there is a gray cat then i said whereabouts doth she stand there said she there then I struck with my rapier then she fell in a fit and when it was over she said you killed her and immediately Sarah good come and carried her away, this was about 12 o'clock. The same day after lecture in the said: Ingersoll's chamber abigail williams mary walcott said that goody hobbs of topsell [Topsfield] bit mary walcott by the foot then both falling into a fit as soon as it was over the said william hobbs and his wife go both of them a long the table the said Hutchinson took his rapier stabbed goody hobbs on the side as abigail williams and mary walcott said the said abigail and mar[y] said the room was full of them then the said hutchinson & Ely putnam stabbed with their rapiers at a venter [woman, i.e., a witch's specter] then said mary and abigail you have killed a great black woman of Stoningtown and an Indian that come with her for the floor is all covered with blood then the said mary and abigail looked out of doors and said the[y] saw a great company of them on a hill & there was three of them lay dead the black woman and the indian and one more that the[y] knew not.

This being about 4 o'clock in the afternoon.

Susanna Sheldon v. Geo Burroughs.

The Complaint of Susanna Sheldon against mr burroughs which brought a book to me and told me if i would not set my hand to it he would tear me to pieces i told him i would not then he told me he would starve me to death then the next morning he told me he could not starve me to death, but he would choke me that my victuals should do me but little good then he told me his name was burroughs which had preached at the village the last night he came to me and asked me whether i would go to the village tomorrow to witness against him i asked him if he was examined then he told he was then i told him i would go then he told me he would kill me before morning then he appeared to me at the house of nathaniel ingersoll and told me he had been the death of three children at the eastward and had killed two of his wives the first he smothered and the second he choked and killed two of his own children.

Thomas Greenslett v. Geo Burroughs.

Tho Greenslett aged about forty years being deposed Testifieth that about the first breaking out of the last Indian war being at the house of Capt Joshua Scotts at Black point, he saw mr George Burroughs who was lately executed at Salem lift a gun of six foot Barrel or thereabouts putting the fore finger of his right hand into the muzzle of said gun and that he held it out at arm's end only with that finger, and further this deponent testifieth that at the same time he saw the said Burroughs Take up a full barrel of molasses with but two of fingers of one of his hands in the bung and carry it from the stage head to the door at the end of the stage without letting it down and that Lieutenant Richard Hunniwell and John Greenslett were then present and some others that are dead.

> Thomas Greenslett
> his   mark. Jurat.

Major Brown, Thomas Ruck, Thomas Evans, Sarah Wilson, Martha Tyler & als v. Geo Burroughs.

Memorandum in mr George Burroughs' Trial besides the written Evidences that was Sworn Several who gave theirs by word of mouth Major Brown holding out a heavy Gun with one hand.

Thomas Ruck of his sudden coming in after them and that he could tell his thoughts.

Thomas Evans that he carried out Barrels Molasses and meat etc. out of a canoe whilst his mate went to the fort for hands to help out with them Sarah Wilson Confessed that the night before mr Burroughs was Executed that there was a great meeting of the witches Nigh Sargeant Chandler's that mr Bur. was there and they had the Sacrament and after they had done he took leave and bid them Stand to their faith, and not own anything.

Martha Tyler saith the same with Sarah Wilson & Several others.

CONTEMPORARY COMMENT

DEODAT LAWSON

A Brief and True Narrative . . .

Deodat Lawson had been the minister at Salem Village from 1684 to 1688. It seems that he escaped the usual bitterness which the parishioners of Salem Village came to express against their other ministers in this decade. Lawson revisited Salem Village soon after the first afflictions in 1692, and he wrote the first printed account of the examinations and the behavior of the afflicted.

Collected by Deodat Lawson.
Boston, Printed for Benjamin Harris and are to be Sold at his Shop, over-against the Old-Meeting-House. 1692.

On the Nineteenth day of March last I went to Salem Village, and lodged at Nathaniel Ingersoll's near to the Minister Mr. P[arris]'s house, and presently after I came into my Lodging Capt. Walcott's Daughter Mary came to Lieut. Ingersoll's and spoke to me, but, suddenly after as she stood by the door, was bitten, so that she cried out of her Wrist, and looking on it with a Candle, we saw apparently the marks of Teeth both upper and lower set, on each side of her wrist.

In the beginning of the Evening, I went to give Mr. P. a visit. When I was there, his Kins-woman, Abigail Williams, (about 12 years of age,) had a grievous fit; she was at first hurried with Violence to and fro in the room, (though Mrs. Ingersoll endeavored to hold her,) sometimes making as if she would fly, stretching up her arms as high as she could, and crying "Whish, Whish, Whish!" several times; Presently after she said there was Goodw. N[urse]. and said, "Do you not see her? Why there she stands!" And the said Goodw. N. offered her The Book, but she was resolved she would not take it, saying Often, "I won't, I won't, I won't, take it, I do not know what Book it is: I am sure it is none of God's Book, it is the Devil's Book, for aught I know." After that, she run to the Fire, and begun to throw Fire Brands, about the house; and run against the Back, as if she would run up Chimney, and, as they said, she had attempted to go into the Fire in other Fits.

On Lord's Day, the Twentieth of March, there were sundry of the afflicted Persons at Meeting, as, Mrs. Pope, and Goodwife Vibber, Abigail Williams, Mary Walcott, Mercy Lewis, and Doctor Griggs's Maid. There was also at Meeting, Goodwife C[ory]. (who was afterward Examined on suspicion of being a Witch:) They had several Sore Fits, in the time of Public Worship, which did something interrupt me in my First Prayer; being so unusual. After

83

Psalm was Sung, Abigail Williams said to me, "Now stand up, and Name your Text": And after it was read, she said, "It is a long Text." In the beginning of Sermon, Mrs. Pope, a Woman afflicted, said to me, "Now there is enough of that." And in the afternoon, Abigail Williams upon my referring to my Doctrine said to me, "I know no Doctrine you had, If you did name one, I have forgot it."

In Sermon time when Goodw. C was present in the Meeting-house Ab. W. called out, "Look where Goodw. C sits on the Beam suckling her Yellow bird betwixt her fingers"! Ann Putnam another Girl afflicted said there was a Yellow-bird sat on my hat as it hung on the Pin in the Pulpit: but those that were by, restrained her from speaking loud about it.

. . . . .

. . . The Magistrates and Ministers also did inform me, that they apprehended a child of Sarah G[ood]. and Examined it, being between 4 and 5 years of Age, And as to matter of Fact, they did Unanimously affirm, that when this Child did but cast its eye upon the afflicted persons, they were tormented, and they held her Head, and yet so many as her eye could fix upon were afflicted. Which they did several times make careful observation of: the afflicted complained, they had often been Bitten by this child, and produced the marks of a small set of teeth, accordingly, this was also committed to Salem Prison; the child looked hale, and well as other Children. I saw it at Lieut. Ingersoll's. . . .

On the 25th of March, (as Capt. Stephen Sewall, of Salem, did afterwards inform me) Eliza. Parris had sore Fits, at his house, which much troubled himself, and his wife, so as he told me they were almost discouraged. She related, that the great Black Man came to her, and told her, if she would be ruled by him, she should have whatsoever she desired, and go to a Golden City. She relating this to Mrs. Sewall, she told the child, it was the Devil, and he was a Liar from the Beginning, and bid her tell him so, if he came again: which she did accordingly, at the next coming to her, in her fits.

On the 26th of March, Mr. Hawthorne, Mr. Corwin, and Mr. Higginson were at the Prison-Keeper's House, to Examine the Child [Dorcas Good], and it told them there, it had a little Snake that used to Suck on the lowest Joint of it[s] Fore-Finger; and when they inquired where, pointing to other places, it told them, not there, but there, pointing on the Lowest point of Fore-Finger; where they Observed a deep Red Spot, about the Bigness of a Flea-bite, they asked who gave it that Snake? whether the great Black man, it said no, its Mother gave it.

The 31 of March there was a Public Fast kept at Salem on account of these Afflicted Persons. And Abigail Williams said, that the Witches had a Sacrament that day at an house in the Village, and that they had Red Bread and Red Drink. The first of April, Mercy Lewis, Thomas Putnam's Maid, in her fit, said, they did eat Red Bread like Man's Flesh, and would have had her eat some: but she would not; but turned away her head, and Spit at them, and said, "I will not Eat, I will not Drink, it is Blood," etc. She said, "That is not the Bread of Life, that is not the Water of Life; Christ gives the Bread of Life, I will have none of it!" This first of April also Mercy Lewis aforesaid saw in her fit a White man and was with him in a Glorious Place, which had no Candles nor Sun, yet was full of Light and Brightness; where was a great Multitude in White glittering Robes, and they Sung the Song in the fifth of Revelation the Ninth verse, and the 110 Psalm, and the 149 Psalm; and said with herself, "How long shall I stay here? let me be along with you": She was loth to leave this place, and grieved that she could tarry no longer. This Whiteman [white man] hath appeared several times to some of them, and given them notice how long it should be before they had another Fit, which was sometimes a day, or day and half, or more or less: it hath fallen out accordingly.

. . . . .

Remarks of things more than ordinary about the Afflicted Persons.

1. They are in their Fits tempted to be Witches, are showed the List of the Names of others, and are tortured, because they will not yield to Subscribe, or meddle with, or touch the Book, and are promised to have present Relief if they would do it.

2. They did in the Assembly mutually Cure each other, even with a Touch of their Hand, when Strangled, and otherwise Tortured; and would endeavor to get to their Afflicted, to Relieve them.

3. They did also foretell when another's Fit was a-coming, and would say, "Look at her! she will have a Fit presently," which fell out accordingly, as many can bear witness, that heard and saw it.

4. That at the same time, when the Accused Person was present, the Afflicted Persons saw her Likeness in other places of the Meeting-House, suckling her Familiar, sometimes in one place and posture, and sometimes in another.

5. That their Motions in their Fits are Preternatural, both as to the manner, which is so strange as a well person could not Screw their Body into; and as to the violence also it is preternatural, being much beyond the Ordinary force of the same person when they are in their right mind.

6. The eyes of some of them in their fits are exceeding fast closed, and if you ask a question they can give no answer, and I do believe they cannot hear at that time, yet do they plainly converse with the Appearances, as if they did discourse with real persons.

7. They are utterly pressed against any persons Praying with them, and told by the appearances, they shall not go to Prayer, so Tho. Putnam's wife was told, I should not Pray; but she said, I should: and after I had done, reasoned with the Appearance, "Did not I say he should go to Prayer?"

8. The forementioned Mary W[alcott].[1] being a little better at ease, the Afflicted persons said, she had signed the book; and that was the reason she was better. Told me by Edward Putnam.

[1] Lawson may mean Mary Warren. He has not mentioned her before, but she was accused after becoming "a little better at ease."

Remarks concerning the Accused.

1. For introduction to the discovery of those that afflicted them, It is reported Mr. Parris Indian Man and Woman made a Cake of Rye Meal, and the Children's water, baked it in the Ashes, and gave it to a Dog, since which they have discovered, and seen particular persons hurting of them.

2. In Time of Examination, they seemed little affected, though all the Spectators were much grieved to see it.

3. Natural Actions in them produced Preternatural actions in the Afflicted, so that they are their own Image without any Puppets of Wax or otherwise.

4. That they are accused to have a Company about 23 or 24 and they did Muster in Arms, as it seemed to the Afflicted Persons.

5. Since they were confined, the Persons have not been so much Afflicted with their appearing to them, Biting or Pinching of them, etc.

6. They are reported by the Afflicted Persons to keep days of Fast and days of Thanksgiving, and Sacraments; Satan endeavors to Transform himself to an Angel of Light, and to make his Kingdom and Administrations to resemble those of our Lord Jesus Christ.

7. Satan Rages Principally amongst the Visible Subjects of Christ's Kingdom [2] and makes use (at least in appearance) of some of them to Afflict others; that Christ's Kingdom may be divided against itself, and so be weakened. . . .

9. Some of the most solid Afflicted Persons do affirm the same things concerning seeing the accused out of their Fits as well as in them.

10. The Witches had a Fast, and told one of the Afflicted Girls, she must not Eat, because it was Fast Day, she said, she would: they told her they would Choke her then; which when she did eat, was endeavored.

[2] I.e., those whose outward conduct supported their own assertion that they had experienced the influx of God's grace. These "elect" were church members.

Excerpts from the

DIARY OF SAMUEL SEWALL

The following excerpts are reprinted from Samuel Sewall's Diary, *1674-1700, Collections of the Massachusetts Historical Society,* Fifth Series, Vol. V.

Tuesday, Jan. 26, 1691-92. News comes to Town by Robin Orchard, of Dolberry's being arrived at Cape Cod; Sir William Phips made Governor of the Province of New England. Foy (in whom went Mr. Lee) taken into France; Quelch and Bant also. Six weeks' passage from Plymouth. This day, almost at the same Time, news was brought of an Attack made by the Indians on York.

April 11th 1692. Went to Salem, where, in the Meeting-house, the persons accused of Witchcraft were examined; was a very great Assembly; 'twas awful to see how the afflicted persons were agitated. Mr. Noyes pray'd at the beginning, and Mr. Higginson concluded. [In the margin, *"Vae, Vae, Vae, Witchcraft."*]

Thursday, Aug 4. At Salem, Mr. Waterhouse brings the news of the desolation at Jamaica, June 7th. 1700 persons kill'd, besides the Loss of Houses and Goods by the Earthquake.

Augt 19th 1692. . . .

This day [in the margin, "Doleful Witchcraft!"] George Burroughs, John Willard, Jno Proctor, Martha Carrier and George Jacobs were executed at Salem, a very great number of Spectators being present. Mr. Cotton Mather was there, Mr. Sims, Hale, Noyes, Cheever, etc. All of them said they were innocent, Carrier and all. Mr. Mather says they all died by a Righteous Sentence. Mr. Burroughs by his Speech, Prayer, protestation of his Innocence, did much move unthinking persons, which occasions their speaking hardly concerning his being executed.

Aug 25. Fast at the old [First] Church, respecting the Witchcraft, Drought, etc.

Monday, Sept. 19, 1692. About noon, at Salem, Giles Cory was press'd to death for standing Mute; much pains was used with him two days, one after another, by the Court and Capt. Gardner of Nantucket who had been of his acquaintance: but all in vain.

Sept. 20. Now I hear from Salem that about 18 years ago, he was suspected to have stamped and press'd a man to death, but was cleared. Twas not remembered till Ann Putnam was told of it by said Cory's Specter the Sabbath-day night before the Execution.

Sept. 21. A petition is sent to Town in behalf of Dorcas Hoar, who now confesses: Accordingly an order is sent to the Sheriff to forbear her Execution, notwithstanding her being in the Warrant to die tomorrow. This is the first condemned person who has confess'd.

Thursday, Sept. 22, 1692. William Stoughton, Esq., John Hawthorne, Esq., Mr. Cotton Mather, and Capt. John Higginson, with my Brother St[ephen]., were at our house, speaking about publishing some Trials of the Witches. . . .

Oct. 11, 1692. . . . Read Mr. Willard's Epistle to Mr. Mather's book, as to Cases of Conscience touching Witchcraft.

Saturday, Oct. 15th. Went to Cambridge and visited Mr. Danforth, and discoursed with Him about the Witchcraft; thinks there cannot be a procedure in the Court except there be some better consent of Ministers and People. Told me of the woman's coming into his house last Sabbath-day sennight at Even.

Oct. 26, 1692. A Bill is sent in about calling a Fast, and Convocation of Ministers, that may be led in the right way as to the Witchcrafts. The season and manner of doing it, is such, that the Court of Oyer and Terminer count themselves thereby dismissed. 29 Nos. and 33 yeas to the Bill. Capt. Bradstreet and Lieut. True, Wm Hutchins and several other interested persons there, in the affirmative.

Oct. 28th Lieut. Governor coming over the Cause[wa]y is, by reason of the high Tide, so wet, that is fain to go to bed till sends for dry clothes to Dorchester; In the Afternoon, as had done several times before, desired to have the advice of the Governor and Council as to the sitting of the Court of Oyer and Terminer next week; said should move it no more; great silence, as if should say do not go.

Oct. 29. Mr. Russell asked whether the Court of Oyer and Terminer should sit, expressing some fear of Inconvenience by its fall. Governor said it must fall. Lieut. Governor not in Town today. . . .

Nov. 22, 1692. I prayed that God would pardon all my Sinful Wanderings, and direct me for the future. That God would bless the Assembly in their debates, and that would choose and assist our Judges, etc., and save New England as to Enemies and Witchcrafts, and vindicate the late Judges, consisting with his Justice and Holiness, etc., with Fasting. . . .

Copy of a Letter to Major Nathaniel Saltonstall Esq. at Haverhill, March, 3. 1692-93. . . .

SIR, Not seeing you in the Assembly, to speak to you and for the reason forementioned, I am put upon writing my Salutations to Mr. Ward, yourself, and good Lady: and telling, that I have sympathized with you and your family, as to the report that went of some being afflicted by a person in your shape, and that I fully believe the Letter asserting your Innocence. Allow me also to intimate that I was grieved upon this day was fortnight, when I heard and saw that you had drunk to excess; so that your head and hand were rendered less useful than at other times. You may remember, you were sitting in the South-side of the Council-chamber, on the bench; I drew near to you, and inquired concerning Mr. Ward; you answer'd, He was better, which made you so merry: you also told me of the breaking up of the Ice of the River Merrimack, having received the account from your son Cotton. That is the time I intend. Let me entreat you, Sir, to break off this practice (so 'tis rumored to be) not as the River; but obstinately and perpetually to refuse the Yoke. As to your being denied a Judge's place by the Governor, I no ways influenc'd Him in the matter, neither do I know who did. And I was surpris'd to hear any Talk of the North Regiment of Essex being put under any other Major. Don't furnish your Enemies with Arms. I mention this that you may believe, I write not of prejudice but Kindness; and out of a sense of Duty, as indeed I do. Take it in good part from him who desires your everlasting welfare, S. S.

Dece. 21. [1696] A very great Snow is on the Ground. I go in the morn to Mr. Willard, to entreat him to choose his own time to come and pray with little Sarah: He comes a little before night, and prays very fully and well. Mr. Mather, the President, had prayed with her in the time of the Court's sitting. Dec. 22. being Catechising day, I give Mr. Willard a note to pray for my daughter publicly, which he did. Note, this morn Madam Eliza Bellingham came to our house and upbraided me with setting my hand to pass Mr. Wharton's account to the Court, where he obtain'd a Judgment for Eustace's farm. I was wheedled and hector'd into that business, and have all along been uneasy in the remembrance of it: and now there is one come who will not spare to lay load. The Lord take away my filthy garments, and give me change of Raiment. This day I remove poor little Sarah into my Bed-chamber, where about Break of Day Dec. 23, she gives up the Ghost in Nurse Cowell's Arms. Born, Nov. 21. 1694. Neither I nor my wife were by: Nurse not expecting so sudden a change, and having promis'd to call us. I thought of Christ's Words, could you not watch with me one hour! and would fain have sat up with her: but fear of my wife's illness, who is very valetudinarious, made me to lodge with her in the new Hall, where was call'd by Jane's Cry, to take notice of my dead daughter. Nurse did long and pathetically ask our pardon that she had not call'd us, and said she was surprised. Thus this very fair day is rendered foul to us by reason of the general Sorrow and Tears in the family. Master Cheever was here the evening before, I desir'd him to pray for my daughter. The Chapter read in course on Dec. 23. m. was Deut. 22. which made me sadly reflect that I had not been so thoroughly tender of my daughter; nor so effectually careful of her Defence and preservation as I should have been. The good Lord pity and pardon and help for the future as to those God has still left me.

December 24. Sam. recites to me in Latin, Mat. 12. from the 6th to the end of the 12th v. The 7th verse [3] did awfully bring to mind the Salem Tragedy.

[3] "If ye had known what this meaneth, I will have mercy and not sacrifice, ye would not have condemned the guiltless."

Petition Put Up By Mr. Sewall on the Fast Day, January 14, 1697.

Copy of the Bill I put up on the Fast day; giving it to Mr. Willard as he pass'd by, and standing up at the reading of it, and bowing when finished; in the Afternoon.

Samuel Sewall, sensible of the reiterated strokes of God upon himself and family; and being sensible, that as to the Guilt contracted upon the opening of the late Commission of Oyer and Terminer at Salem (to which the order for this Day relates) he is, upon many accounts, more concerned than any that he knows of, Desires to take the Blame and shame of it, Asking pardon of men, And especially desiring prayers that God, who has an Unlimited Authority, would pardon that sin and all other his sins; personal and Relative: And according to his infinite Benignity, and Sovereignty, Not Visit the sin of him, or of any other, upon himself or any of his, nor upon the Land: But that He would powerfully defend him against all Temptations to Sin, for the future; and vouchsafe him the efficacious, saving Conduct of his Word and Spirit.

Letters of

GOVERNOR PHIPS

Sir William Phips, the governor under the new charter, did not ar-
rive in Boston until May 14, 1692, and he spent most of the sum-
mer "in the Eastern part of the country," leading the fight against
the French and Indians. The two letters which follow were published
in Calendars of State Papers, America and West Indies, 1689-1692,
1693-1696. Notice the changed tone of the second letter in the sec-
tion diagnosing the afflictions.

Letter to William Blathwayt, Clerk of the Privy Council.

When I first arrived I found this Province miserably harrassed with a
most Horrible witchcraft or Possession of Devils which had broke in upon
several Towns, some scores of poor people were taken with preternatural torments some scalded with brimstone some had pins stuck in their flesh others
hurried into the fire and water and some dragged out of their houses and
carried over the tops of trees and hills for many Miles together; it hath been
represented to me much like that of Sweden about thirty years ago, and there
were many committed to prison upon suspicion of Witchcraft before my arrival. The loud cries and clamors of the friends of the afflicted people with the
advice of the Deputy Governor and many others prevailed with me to give
a Commission of Oyer and Terminer for discovering what witchcraft might
be at the bottom or whether it were not a possession. The chief Judge in this
Commission was the Deputy Governor and the rest were persons of the best
prudence and figure that could then be pitched upon. When the Court came
to sit at Salem in the County of Essex they convicted more than twenty persons of being guilty of witchcraft, some of the convicted were such as confessed their Guilt, the Court as I understand began their proceedings with the
accusations of the afflicted and then went upon other human evidences to
strengthen that. I was almost the whole time of the proceeding abroad in the
service of Their Majesties in the Eastern part of the Country and depended
upon the Judgment of the Court as to a right method of proceeding in cases
of Witchcraft but when I came home I found many persons in a strange ferment of dissatisfaction which was increased by some hot Spirits that blew up
the flame, but on inquiring into the matter I found that the Devil had taken
upon him the name and shape of several persons who were doubtless innocent
and to my certain knowledge of good reputation for which cause I have now

91

forbidden the committing of any more that shall be accused without unavoidable necessity, and those that have been committed I would shelter from any Proceedings against them wherein there may be the least suspicion of any wrong to be done unto the Innocent. I would also wait for any particular directions or commands if their Majesties please to give me any for the fuller ordering this perplexed affair. I have also put a stop to the printing of any discourses one way or other, that may increase the needless disputes of people upon this occasion, because I saw a likelihood of kindling an inextinguishable flame if I should admit any public and open Contests and I have grieved to see that some who should have done their Majesties and this Province better service have so far taken Counsel of Passion as to desire the precipitancy of these matters, these things have been improved by some to give me many interruptions in their Majesties' service and in truth none of my vexations have been greater than this, than that their Majesties' service has been hereby unhappily clogged, and the Persons who have made so ill improvement of these matters here are seeking to turn it all upon me, but I hereby declare that as soon as I came from fighting against their Majesties' Enemies and understood what danger some of their innocent subjects might be exposed to, if the evidence of the afflicted persons only did prevail either to the committing or trying any of them, I did before any application was made unto me about it put a stop to the proceedings of the Court and they are now stopped till their Majesties' pleasure be known. Sir I beg pardon for giving you all this trouble, the reason is because I know my enemies are seeking to turn it all upon me and I take this liberty because I depend upon your friendship, and desire you will please to give a true understanding of the matter if anything of this kind be urged or made use of against me. Because the justness of my proceeding herein will be a sufficient defense. Sir

I am with all imaginable respect

Your most humble Servt

WILLIAM PHIPS.

Dated at Boston
    the 12th of october 1692.

Letter to the Earl of Nottingham.

Boston in New England Febry 21st, 1692-93.

May it please your Lordship.

By the Capn. of the *Samuel and Henry* I gave an account that at my arrival here I found the Prisons full of people committed upon suspicion of witchcraft and that continual complaints were made to me that many persons were grievously tormented by witches and that they cried out upon several persons by name, as the cause of their torments. The number of these complaints increasing every day, by advice of the Lieut. Govr. and the Council I gave a Commission of Oyer and Terminer to try the suspected witches and at that time the generality of the People represented the matter to me as real witchcraft and gave very strange instances of the same. The first in Commission was the Lieut. Govr. and the rest persons of the best prudence and figure that could then be pitched upon and I depended upon the Court for a right method of proceeding in cases of witchcraft. At that time I went to command the army at the Eastern part of the Province, for the French and Indians had made an attack upon some of our Frontier Towns. I continued there for some time but when I returned I found people much dissatisfied at the proceedings of the Court, for about Twenty persons were condemned and executed of which number some were thought by many persons to be innocent. The Court still proceeded in the same method of trying them, which was by the evidence of the afflicted persons who when they were brought into the Court as soon as the suspected witches looked upon them instantly fell to the ground in strange agonies and grievous torments, but when touched by them upon the arm or some other part of their flesh they immediately revived and came to themselves, upon [which] they made oath that the Prisoner at the Bar did afflict them and that they saw their shape or specter come from their bodies which put them to such pains and torments: When I inquired into the matter I was informed by the Judges that they begun with this, but had human testimony against such as were condemned and undoubted proof of their being witches, but at length I found that the Devil did take upon him the shape of Innocent persons and some were accused of whose innocency I was well assured and many considerable persons of unblameable life and conversation were cried out upon as witches and wizzards. The Deputy Govr. notwithstanding persisted vigorously in the same method, to the great dissatisfaction and disturbance of the people, until I put an end to the Court and stopped the proceedings, which I did because I saw many innocent persons might otherwise perish and at that time I thought it my duty to give an account thereof that their Majesties' pleasure might be signified, hoping that for the better ordering thereof the Judges learned in the law in England might give such rules and directions as have been practiced in England for proceedings in so difficult and so nice a point; When I put an end to the Court there were at least fifty persons in prison in great misery by reason of the extreme cold and their poverty, most of them having only specter evidence against them, and their mittimusses being defective, I caused some of them to be let out upon bail and put the Judges upon considering of a way to relieve others and prevent them from perishing in prison, upon which some of them were convinced and acknowledged that their former proceedings were too violent and not grounded upon a right foundation but that if they might sit again, they would proceed after another method, and whereas Mr. Increase Mathew [Mather] and several other Divines did give it as their Judgment that the Devil might afflict in the shape of an innocent person and that the look and the touch of the suspected persons was not sufficient proof against them, these things had not the same stress laid upon them as before, and upon this consideration I permitted a special Superior Court to be held at Salem in the County of Essex on the third day of January, the Lieut. Govr. being Chief Judge. Their method of proceeding being altered, all that were brought to trial to the number of fifty two, were cleared saving three, and I was informed by the King's Attorney General that some of the cleared and the condemned were under the same circumstances or that there was the same reason to clear the three condemned as the rest according to his Judgment. The Deputy Govr. signed a Warrant for their speedy execution and also of five others who were condemned at the former Court of Oyer and terminer, but considering how the matter had been managed I sent a reprieve whereby the execution was stopped until their Maj. pleasure be signified and declared. The Lieut. Gov. upon this occasion was enraged and filled with passionate anger and refused to sit upon the bench in a Superior Court then held at Charlestown, and indeed hath from the beginning hurried on these matters with great precipitancy and by his warrant hath caused the estates, goods and chattels of the executed to be seized and disposed of without my knowledge or consent. The stop put to the first method of proceedings hath dissipated the black cloud that threatened this Province with destruction; for whereas this delusion of the Devil did spread and its dismal effects touched the lives and estates of many of their Majesties' Subjects and the reputation of some of the principal persons here, and indeed unhappily clogged and interrupted their Majesties' affairs which hath been a great vexation to me, I have no new complaints but people's minds before divided and distracted by differing opinions concerning this matter are now well composed.

I am
Your Lordship's most faithful
humble Servant
WILLIAM PHIPS

Confession of

WILLIAM BARKER

William Barker of Andover was one of the many confessors whose detailed testimony convinced the judges that a vast diabolical plot threatened Salem Village and all of Massachusetts. John Hale reprinted this confession in his Modest Inquiry into . . . Witchcraft, Boston, 1702.

God having called me to Confess my sin and Apostasy in that fall in giving the Devil advantage over me appearing to me like a Black, in the evening to set my hand to his Book, as I have owned to my shame. He told me that I should not want so doing. At Salem Village, there being a little off the Meeting-House, about an hundred five Blades, some with Rapiers by their side, which was called and might be more for aught I know by B[ishop]. and Bu[rroughs]. and the Trumpet sounded, and Bread and Wine which they called the Sacrament, but I had none; being carried over all on a Stick, never being at any other Meeting. I being at Cart a Saturday last, all the day, of Hay and English Corn, the Devil brought my Shape to Salem, and did afflict M. S. and R. F. by clutching my Hand; and a Sabbath day my Shape afflicted A. M. and at night afflicted M. S. and A. M. E. I. and A. F. have been my Enticers to this great abomination, as one have owned and charged her to her Sister with the same. And the design was to Destroy Salem Village, and to begin at the Minister's House, and to destroy the Church of God, and to set up Satan's Kingdom, and then all will be well. And now I hope God in some measure has made me something sensible of my sin and apostasy, begging pardon of God, and of the Honorable Magistrates and all God's people, hoping and promising by the help of God, to set to my heart and hand to do what in me lieth to destroy such wicked worship, humbly begging the prayers of all God's People for me, I may walk humbly under this great affliction and that I may procure to myself, the sure mercies of David, and the blessing of Abraham.

COTTON MATHER

A Discourse on Witchcraft

In the winter of 1688-1689, after Goodwife Glover of Boston was hanged for bewitching John Goodwin's children, Cotton Mather preached a sermon on witchcraft, describing the crime and discussing the problems it forced on the people. This sermon presents, as well as any single work could present, the orthodox Puritan's attitude toward witchcraft in the last decade of the seventeenth century. Cotton published this sermon in his Memorable Providences, Relating to Witchcrafts and Possessions, *Boston, 1689.*

I. Sam. XV. 23.
Rebellion is as the Sin of Witchcraft.

. . . . .

Prop. I.

Such an Hellish thing there is as *Witchcraft* in the World. There are Two things which will be desired for the advantage of this Assertion. It should *first* be showed,

WHAT *Witchcraft* is.

My Hearers will not expect from me an accurate *definition* of the *vile Thing;* since the Grace of God has given me the Happiness to speak without *Experience* of it. But from Accounts both by *Reading* and *Hearing* I have learn'd to describe it so.

WITCHCRAFT is the doing of *strange* (and for the most part *ill*) things by the help of *evil Spirits, covenanting* with (and usually *Representing* of) the woeful Children of Men.

This is the *Diabolical Art* that *Witches* are notorious for.

First, *Witches* are the Doers of *strange* Things. They cannot indeed perform any proper *Miracles;* those are things to be done only by the *Favorites* and *Ambassadors* of the LORD. But *Wonders* are often produced by them, though chiefly such Wonders as the Apostle calls in 2 *Thes.* 2. 9. *Lying Wonders.* There are *wonderful Storms* in the *great* World, and *wonderful Wounds* in the *little* World, often effected by these *evil Causes.* They do things which transcend the ordinary *course* of Nature, and which puzzle the ordinary *Sense* of Mankind. Some *strange* things are done by them in a way of *Real Production.* They do really *Torment,* they do really *Afflict* those that their Spite shall extend unto. Other *strange* things are done by them in a way of *Crafty Illusion.* They do

96

craftily make of the *Air*, the *Figures* and *Colors* of things that never can be truly created by them. All men might *see*, but, I believe, no man could *feel* some of the Things which the *Magicians* of *Egypt*, exhibited of old.

Secondly, They are not only *strange* things, but *ill* things, that *Witches* are the Doers of. In this regard also they are not the Authors of *Miracles:* those are things *commonly* done for the *good* of Man, *always* done for the *praise* of GOD. But of these *Hell-hounds* it may in a special manner be said, as in *Psal.* 52. 3. *Thou lovest evil more than good.* For the most part they labor to rob *Man* of his *Ease* or his *Wealth;* they labor to wrong *God* of his *Glory*. There is mention of Creatures that they call *White Witches*, which do only *Good-Turns* for their Neighbors. I suspect that there are none of that sort; but rather think, *There is none that doeth good no, not one.* If they *do good*, it is only that they *may do hurt*.

Thirdly, It is by virtue of *evil Spirits* that *Witches* do what they do. We read in *Ephes.* 22. about the *Prince of the power of the Air*. There is confined unto the *Atmosphere* of our *Air* a vast *Power*, or *Army* of *Evil Spirits*, under the Government of a Prince who employs them in a continual Opposition to the Designs of GOD: The Name of that *Leviathan* who is the *Grand Seignior of Hell*, we find in the Scripture to be *Beelzebub*. Under the Command of that mighty Tyrant, there are vast *Legions* and *Myriads* of *Devils*, whose *businesses* and *accomplishments* are not all the same. Every one has his *Post*, and his *Work;* and they are all glad of an opportunity to be *mischievous* in the World. These are they by whom *Witches* do exert their devilish and malignant rage upon their *Neighbors:* And especially Two Acts concur hereunto. The *First* is, Their *Covenanting* with the Witches. There is a most hellish *League* made between them, with various *Rites* and *Ceremonies*. The *Witches* promise to serve the *Devils*, and the *Devils* promise to *help* the Witches; *how?* It is not convenient to be related. The *Second* is, Their *Representing* of the Witches. And hereby indeed these are drawn into *Snares* and *Cords* of Death. The *Devils*, when they go upon the Errands of the *Witches*, do bear their Names; and hence do *Harms* too come to be carried from the *Devils* to the *Witches*. We need not suppose such a wild thing as the *Transforming* of those Wretches into *Brutes* or *Birds*, as we too often do.

It should next be proved THAT Witchcraft *is*.

The *Being* of such a thing is denied by many that place a *great part* of their *small wit* in deriding the Stories that are told of it. Their chief Argument is, that they never *saw* any Witches, therefore there are *none*. Just as if you or I should say, we never met with any *Robbers* on the Road, therefore there was never any *Padding* there.

Indeed the *Devils* are loath to have true Notions of *Witches* entertained with us. I have beheld them to put out the Eyes of an Enchanted Child, when a Book that proves, *There is Witchcraft*, was laid before her. But there are especially two Demonstrations that Evince the Being of that Infernal mysterious thing.

First, We have the Testimony of *Scripture* for it. We find *Witchcrafts* often mentioned, sometimes by way of *Assertion*, sometimes by way of *Allu-*

sion, in the Oracles of God. Besides that, We have there the History of divers *Witches* in these infallible and inspired Writings. Particularly, the Instance of the *Witch* at *Endor,* in I *Sam.* 28. 7. is so plain and full that *Witchcraft* itself is not a more amazing thing than any *Dispute* about the Being of it, after this. The Advocates of *Witches* must use more *Tricks* to make Nonsense of the *Bible,* than ever the *Witch* of *Endor* used in her Magical Incantations, if they would Evade the Force of that Famous History. They that will believe no *Witches,* do imagine that *Jugglers* only are meant by them whom the Sacred Writ calleth so. But what do they think of that Law in *Exod.* 22. 18. *Thou shalt not suffer a Witch to live?* Methinks 'tis a little too hard to punish every silly *Juggler* with so great severity.

Secondly, We have the *Testimony* of *Experience* for it. What will those *Incredulous,* who must be the only *Ingenious* Men say to this? Many *Witches* have like those in *Acts* 19. 18. *Confessed and showed their Deeds.* We see those things done, that it is impossible any *Disease,* or any *Deceit* should procure. We see some hideous *Wretches* in hideous *Horrors* confessing, *That they did the Mischiefs.* This Confession is often made by them that are owners of as much Reason as the people that laugh at all *Conceit* of *Witchcraft:* The Exactest Scrutiny of Skillful Physicians cannot find any distraction in their minds. This *Confession* is often made by them that are apart one from another, and yet they *agree* in all the Circumstances of it. This *Confession* is often made by them that at the same time will produce the *Engines* and *Ensigns* of their *Hellish Trade,* and give the standers-by an *Ocular Conviction* of what they do, and how. There can be no Judgment left of any *Human Affairs,* if such *Confessions* must be Ridiculed: all the *Murders,* yea, and all the *Bargains* in the World must be mere *Imaginations* if such *Confessions* are of no Account.

Prop. II.

WITCHCRAFT is a most Monstrous and Horrid *Evil.* Indeed there is a vast Heap of Bloody Roaring Impieties contained in the *Bowels* of it. *Witchcraft,* is a Renouncing of *God,* and Advancing of a filthy *Devil* into the Throne of the Most High; 'tis the most nefandous *High-Treason* against the MAJESTY on High. *Witchcraft,* is a Renouncing of *Christ,* and preferring the Communion of a loathesome lying *Devil* before all the Salvation of the Lord Redeemer; 'tis a Trampling under foot that *Blood* which is more precious than *Hills* of *Silver,* or whole *Mountains* of *Gold.* There is in *Witchcraft,* a most explicit *Renouncing* of all that is *Holy,* and *Just* and *Good.* The *Law* given by *God,* the *Prayer* taught by *Christ,* the *Creed* left by the *Apostles,* is become *Abominable* where *Witchcraft* is Embraced: The very Reciting of those blessed things is commonly burdensome where *Witchcraft* is. All the *sure Mercies* of the *New Covenant,* and all the *just Duties* of it, are utterly abdicated by that *cursed Covenant* which *Witchcraft* is Constituted with. *Witchcraft* is a Siding with *Hell* against *Heaven* and *Earth;* and therefore a *Witch* is not to be endured in either of them. 'Tis a *Capital* Crime; and it is to be prosecuted as a piece of *Devilism* that would not not only deprive *God* and *Christ* of all His Honor, but also plunder Man of all his Comfort. *Witchcraft,* it's an impotent, but an impudent *Essay* to make an *Hell* of the Universe, and to allow Nothing but a *Tophet* in the World. *Witchcraft*—What shall I say of it! It is the furthest Effort of our *Original Sin;* and all that can make any Practice or Persons odious, is here in the *Exalt[at]ion* of it.

It was the speech of *Jehu* to *Joram,* in 2 *King.* 9. 22. *What peace, so long as the* Witchcrafts *of thy Mother are so many?* Truly, as *Witchcraft* would break the *Peace* of all Mankind, so 'tis a thing that should enjoy no *Peace* among the Children of *Adam.* Nothing too *vile* can be said of, nothing too hard can be done to such an horrible Iniquity as *Witchcraft* is.

. . . . .

The Improvement of these things now calls for our *Earnest Head;* and unto each of our Three Propositions, we may annex Applications agreeable thereunto. I begin with

The use of the *First* Proposition.

I. By way of INFORMATION.

There are especially Two *Inferences* to be drawn from this Position, *That, Such a thing there is as* Witchcraft *in the World.*

(*First,*) Since there are *Witches,* we are to suppose that there are *Devils* too. Those are the Objects that *Witches* converse withal. It was the Heresy of the Ancient *Sadducees* in *Act.* 23. 8. *The* Sadducees *do say, That there is neither Angel nor Spirit.* And there are multitudes of *Sadducees* yet in our days; *Fools,* that say, *Seeing is Believing;* and will *believe* nothing but what they *see.* A Devil, is in the Apprehension of those Mighty Acute Philosophers, no more than a *Quality,* or a *Distemper.* But, as *Paul* said unto Him of old, *King* Agrippa, *believest thou the Prophets?* Thus I would say, *Friend, believest thou the Scriptures?* I pray, What sort of things were they, of whom we read in *Jude 6. Angels that kept not their first Estate, but left their own Habitation, and be reserved in Chains unto the judgment of the great day.* What sort of things were they, who in *Matth.* 18. 16. *besought* our Lord, *If thou cast us out, suffer us to go into the Herd of Swine?* What thing was that, which in *Luk.* 4. 33. Cried out unto the Lord Jesus with a loud Voice, *Let us alone?* Surely, These things could be none but *Spiritual and rational Substances, full of all* Wickedness *against God, and* Enmity *against Man.* We shall come to have no *Christ* but a *Light within,* and no *Heaven* but a *Frame of Mind,* if the Scriptures must be expounded after the Rules of the modern *Sadducees.* Perhaps tho' the *Scriptures* are *Fables* to that sort of Men. Come then, thou *Sadducee,* What kind of thing is that which will so handle towardly, ingenuous, well-disposed persons, That if any *Devotions* be performed, they shall *roar* and *tear* unreasonably, and have such *Noises* and such *Tortures* in them, as not only to hinder themselves *wholly,* but others *too much* from joining in the Service; and strive to *kick* or *strike* the Minister in his Prayers, but have their *hands* or *feet* strangely stopped when they are just come at him, and yet be quiet before and after the *Worship?* That if any *Idle* or *Useless* Discourse be going, they shall be well, but at any *se-*

rious Discourse they shall be tormented in all their Limbs? That if a portion of the *Bible* be read, tho' they *see* and *hear* nothing of it, and tho', it may be, in *Greek* or *Hebrew* too, they shall fall into terrible Agonies, which will be over when the *Bible* is laid aside? That they shall be able to peruse whole *Pages* of *Evil Books,* but scarce a *Line* of a *good one?* That they shall *Move* and *Fly,* and *Tell secret things,* as no ordinary Mortals can? Let me ask, *Is not the hand of* Joab *in all this?* Or, is there not a *Devil* whose Agency must account for things that are so extravagant? I am now to tell you, *That these eyes of mine have beheld all these things,* and many other more, no less amazing. Christian, there are *Devils:* and so many of them too, that sometimes a *Legion* of them are spared for the vexation of *One Man.* The *Air* in which we breathe is full of them. Be sensible of this, you that *obey God:* there are Troops of *Tempters* on every side of thee. *Awake,* O Soul, Awake, those *Philistines* of Hell *are upon thee.* Upon the least affrightment in the dark, many simple people cry out, *The Devil! the Devil!* Alas, there are Devils thronging about thee every day. O let the thought of it make thee a careful and a watchful Man. And be sensible of this, you that *commit Sin:* the Lord Jesus hath said of you, *Ye will do the lusts of your father the* Devil. How often do many of you make a *Mock* and a *Jeer* of the Devil, while you are drudging for him? But know, that there are dreadful *Devils* to seize upon thy forlorn, forsaken Soul, at its departure hence. O become a new Man at the thought of this.

2. Since there are *Witches* and *Devils,* we may conclude that there are also *Immortal Souls. Devils* would never contract with *Witches* for their Souls if there were no such things to become a prey unto them. . . .

II. By way of *Exhortation.*

There is one thing to be now pressed upon us all.

Let us wisely endeavor to be preserved from the Molestations of all *Witchcraft* whatsoever. Since there is a thing so dangerous, *defend* yourselves, and *shelter* yourselves by all *right* means against the annoyance of it.

Consider the *Multitudes* of them, whom *Witchcraft* hath sometimes given *Trouble* to. Persons of *all sorts* have been racked and ruined by it; and not a *few* of them neither. It is hardly twenty years ago; that a whole Kingdom in *Europe* was alarmed by such potent *Witchcrafts.* that some hundreds of poor Children were invaded with them. Persons of great *Honor* have sometimes been cruelly *bewitched.* What lately befell a worthy *Knight* in *Scotland,* is well known unto the World. Persons of great *Virtue* too have been bewitched, even into their Graves. But four years are passed since a holy Man was killed in this doleful way, after the *Joy* as well as the *Grace* of God had been wonderfully filling of him. This Consideration should keep us from *censuring* of those that *Witchcraft* may give disturbance to: But it should put us on *studying* of our own security. *Suppose ye that the Enchanted Family in the Town, were sinners above all the Town, because they have suffered such things? I tell ye nay, but except ye repent, ye may all be so dealt withal.* The Father of *Lies* uttered an awful Truth when he said through the Mouth of a possessed Man, *If God would give me leave, I would find enough in the best of you all, to make you all mine.*

Consider also, the Misery of them whom *Witchcraft* may be *let loose* upon. If *David* thought it a sad thing to *fall into the hands of men,* what is it to *fall into the hands of Devils?* The Hands of *Turks,* of *Spaniards,* of *Indians,* are not so dreadful as those hands that *Witches* do their *works of Darkness* by. O what a direful thing is it, to be pricked with *Pins,* and stabbed with *Knives* all over, and to be filled all over with *broken Bones?* 'Tis impossible to reckon up the varieties of miseries which those Monsters inflict where they can have a blow. No less than *Death,* and that a languishing and a terrible *Death* will satisfy the Rage of those formidable Dragons. Indeed *Witchcraft* sometimes grows up into *Possession* itself: the Devils that are permitted to *torment,* at last do possess the *Bodies* of the *bewitched sufferers.* But who can bear the thoughts of that! who can forbear crying out, *O Lord, my flesh trembles for fear of Thee, and I am afraid of Thy Judgments.*

What shall then be done for our *Preservation?* Away with all *superstitious* Preservatives; about *those* confidences the Word of God is that in *Jer.* 2. 37. *Thou shalt not prosper in them.*

But there are three admirable *Amulets* that I can heartily recommend unto you all.

The First Preservative is, *A fervent* Prayer. Pour out that *Prayer* before the Lord, in *Psal.* 59. 2, 3. *Deliver me from the workers of* Iniquity, *and save me from the bloody ones; for lo, they lie in wait for my Soul.* And be much in Prayer every day. The Devils are *afraid* of our *Prayers;* they tremble and complain, and are in a sort of *Anguish* while our *Prayers* are going. There was a House of a Renowned Minister in *France* infested with *evil Spirits;* who tho' they had been very troublesome, yet when the good Man was betaking himself to prayer, they would say, *Now you are going to* Prayer, *I'll be gone.* Let us pray much, and we need fear nothing. Particularly, Let *Ejaculatory* Prayers be almost continually in our minds, and so we shall never lie open to the *fiery darts of the wicked one.*

The Second Preservative is, *A lively Faith.* The Psalmist well said, in *Psal.* 56. 2, 3. *Mine enemies would daily swallow me up; at what time I am afraid I will trust in thee.* Be not *afraid* of any *Devils;* if you are, turn the *Fear* into *Faith.* By *Faith* resign yourselves to the Custody of him that is *the keeper of* Israel. By *Faith* persuade yourselves that *he is able to keep what you have committed unto him.* Thus, run to the *Rock,* and there triumph over all the *powers of darkness.* Triumph and say, *The Lord is on my side; I will not fear what Hell can do unto me?* The Third Preservative is, *A Holy Life.* There was a very *Holy* Man of old, *a man, that feared God and eschewed evil;* and the Devils murmured, in *Job* 1. 10. *God has made an hedge about him.* The same have the Devils confessed, when they have plotted against other holy men. Do not thou break the Hedge of God's *Commandment,* and perhaps he will not let any break the Hedge of his *Providence,* by which thou art secured. The holy *Angels* are the Friends, the Guardians, the Companions, of all *holy men;* they may open their Eyes, and see *more with them than against them*. A *Camp,* an *Host of Angels* will fight against all the *Harpies* of Hell which may offer to devour a Saint of GOD.

Use these things as the *Shields* of the Lord; so you shall be *preserved in Christ Jesus* from the assaults of the *Destroyer*. Suppose now that any *Witches* may let fly their *Curses* at you, you are now like a *Bird* on the *Wing,* in such Heavenward Motions that they cannot hit you. Now the *Devils* and their Creatures cannot say of you, as the *Demon* said of the Christian Woman whom, at a *Stage-play* he took *Possession* of, and being asked, gave this reason of his taking her, *I found her on my own ground*.

We pass on to the USE of the *Second Proposition*.

And that must be a *Counsel* from God unto us all. Particularly, Since *Witchcraft* is an *Evil* so horrible.

I. To them that may be *Enticed* unto the Sin of Witchcraft: To them we say,

1. Take heed that you be not by any *Temptation* drawn into this *monstrous* and *horrid* Evil.

The best man that ever breathed was *tempted* hereunto; that man who was more than a *mere* Man, was assaulted by the *Chief Devil* of the *lowest Hell* with this Temptation in *Mat.* 4. 9. *Fall down and worship me*. But by the *Sword of the Spirit* our Lord kept him off. If any of you are by any Devil so solicited, thus *resist,* thus *repel* all the Motions of the *wicked one*. Don't give yourselves away to those Deceivers that will become *Tormentors* of your Souls in another World.

It may be the proposal of this Counsel may make some to say as he in 2 *King*. 8. 13. *What? Is thy Servant a Dog, that he should do this great thing?* I answer, Alas, we should every one of us be a *Dog* and a *Witch* too, if God should leave us to ourselves. It is the mere *Grace* of God, the *Chains* of which restrain us from bringing the *Chains of darkness* upon our Souls. The *Humble* and (therefore) *Holy* Martyr *Bradford,* when he heard of any wickedness committed in the Neighborhood, would lay his Hand on his *Breast* and say, *In this heart of mine, is that which would render me as wicked as the worst in the World, If God should leave me to myself*. When we see a forlorn wretch Executed for *Witchcraft,* you and I may say the same. They that are Witches now, once little dreamed of ever becoming so. *Let him that stands, take heed lest he fall*. If we would not fall into that *Horrible Pit,* Let us follow these Directions.

Direction I.

Avoid those *Ill-Frames* which are a Step to *Witchcraft*. There are especially Two ill Frames which do lead people on to the worst *Witchcraft* in the World. Shun a Frame of discontent. When persons are discontented with their own state; When persons through discontent at their *Poverty,* or at their *Misery,* shall be always murmuring and repining at the Providence of God, the Devils do then invite them to an *Agreement* with, and a Reliance on them for help. Downright *Witchcraft* is the upshot of it. We find in

Luk. 4. 2. our Lord *Hungered,* and then the Devil came in an audible or a visible manner to Him, tho' he had been more spiritually long before Assaulting of him. They are needy persons whom Devils make the most likely attempts upon. And some persons are not only *Hungry,* but *Angry* too; but then every *Fret,* every *Fume* is as it were a Call to the *Devils;* it calls to them, *come and help me.* Shun also a Frame of *Ill-Wishing.* There is a *Witchcraft* begun in the Imprecations of wicked people. Many profane persons will wish the Devil to take this and that, or, the Devil to do this and that; and when they call, at last he comes, or at least the Devil does what they wish. Observe this, We are by our Sins worthy to have Mischiefs befalling us every day; and the Devils are always ready to inflict what we deserve. I am also apt to think that the Devils are seldom able to hurt us in any of our *exterior* Concerns without a Commission from some of our *fellow-worms.* It is intimated in *Gen.* 4. 9. That every man is his *Brother's Keeper:* We are by our good wishes to *keep* our Brethren from the inroads of *Ill spirits.* But when *Foul-Mouthed* men shall wish harm unto their Neighbors, they give a Commission unto the Devils to perform what they desire; and if God should not mercifully prevent it, they would go through with it. Hear this, you that in wild passions will give everything to the *Devil:* Hear it, you that will bespeak a *Rot,* a *Pox,* and a *Plague* upon all that shall provoke you. I here Indict you as guilty of Hellish *Witchcraft* in the sight of God. 'Tis the little Wapping of *small Dogs* that stirs up the *Cruel Mastiffs* to fall upon the Sheep in the Field.

Direction II.

Avoid all those *Ill Charms* which are a *piece* of *Witchcraft.* . . .

. . . . .

There are manifold *Sorceries* practiced among them that make a profession of *Christianity,* against which I would this day bear a witness in the Name of the most holy Lord.

First, There are some that make use of wicked *Charms* for the *curing of Mischiefs.* It is too common a thing for persons to oppose *Witchcraft* itself with *Witchcraft.* When they suppose one to be *bewitched,* they do with Burning, and Bottles, and Horseshoes, and, I know not what, magical Ceremonies, endeavor his Relief. *Mark* what I say: To use any Remedy, the force of which depends upon the Compact of the *Devils* with the *Witches,* is to involve oneself in the cursed Compact: it is, as it were, to say, O Devil, *Thou hast agreed with such a person that they shall be exposed unto Torments by the use of such or such a Ceremony, we do now use the Ceremony, and expect thy blessing upon it.* This is the Language foamed out by this foolish *Magic.* Does not thy Conscience tremble at such iniquity and Impiety? This may be to heal a Body, but it is to destroy a Soul. These persons give themselves to the Devils to be delivered from the *Witches.* And the people that are eased and helped by such means, they say, do usually come to unhappy *Ends.* Let me say as in 2 *King.* 1. 3.

Is there not a God in Israel, *that you go to* Beelzebub? What? will not *Prayer* and *Faith* do, but must the *Black Art* be used against our Enemies?

2. Take heed that you do not *wrongfully accuse* any other person, of this horrid and Monstrous Evil. It is the Character of a godly man, in *Psal.* 15. 3. *He taketh not up a* Reproach *against his Neighbor.* What more dirty *Reproach* than that of *Witchcraft* can there be? Yet it is most readily cast upon *worthy* persons, when there is hardly a shadow of any Reason for it. An *Ill-look* or a *Cross word* will make a Witch with many people who may on more ground be counted so themselves. There has been a fearful deal of injury done in this way in this Town, to to the *good name* of the most credible persons in it. Persons of more Goodness and Esteem than any of their Calumnious Abusers have been defamed for *Witches* about this Country. *A Country full of Lies.* I beseech you let all *Backbiting,* and all *Evil-surmising* be put away from among you: Do not, on small grounds *Fly-blow* the *precious Ointment* of the *good-name* that thy Neighbor should have. On the least provocation, *I will never believe but such an one is a Witch*——that is presently the Sentence of some that might speak more wearily than so. Alas, thou mightst with as much Honesty break open the House, or take away the Purse of thy Neighbor: His *Good Name* is of more Account. They that indulge themselves in this Course of *Evil Judging,* are usually paid home for it before they Die; the just God sues them in an *Action of Defamation,* and makes *their* Names to be up too, before they leave the world.

We'll suppose the most probable Presumptions:

Suppose that a Person Bewitched should pretend to see the Apparition of such or such an one, yet this may be no infallible Argument of their being Naughty People. It seems possible that the Devils may so traduce the most *Innocent,* the most praise-worthy. Why may not *spiritual* Devils, as well as Devils *Incarnate* get leave to do it? There was at *Groton,* a while since, a very memorable Instance of such a thing, and what should hinder them than [i.e., that] can Imitate the *Angels of Light* but that they may likewise personate the Children of Light, in their Delusions?

2. To them that have been *seduced* into the Sin of *Witchcraft.* And under this Rank, there are two sorts of Persons to be addressed unto.

First, Let them that have been guilty of *Implicit Witchcraft,* now repent of their *Monstrous* and *Horrid* evil in it. I fear that I speak to some Scores that may lay their hands on their Mouths, and Cry, *Guilty, Guilty!* before the Lord, in this particular. Let these now Confess and bewail their own sin in the sight of God; and as it was said in *Hos.* 14. 8. *What have I any more to do with Idols?* Thus let them say, *What have I any more to do with* Devils? The things that you have done, have been *Payments of Respects unto Devils;* and it becomes you to *abhor yourselves in Dust and Ashes* for your folly. The great and terrible God says of you, as in *Deut.* 32. 21. *They have provoked me to Anger with their Vanities.* Let the things that did *provoke* Him to *Anger,* now *provoke* you to sorrow. Retire this Evening, and humble yourselves very deeply, in that you have been so *foolish and unwise.* Lament all your Acquaintance with *Hell;* and let your Acquaintance with *God* be more. Let your *Lamentations* be more than ever your *Divinations* were.

Let them that have been guilty of *Explicit* Witchcraft, now also repent of their *monstrous* and *horrid* evil in it. If any of you have (I hope none of you have) made an *Express Contract* with *Devils,* know that your promise is better *broke* than kept; it concerns you that you turn immediately from the *Power of Satan unto God.* Albeit your sin be beyond all expression or conception heinous, yet it is not unpardonable. We read of *Manasseh* in 2 *Chron.* 33. 6. *He used* Enchantments, *and used* Witchcraft, *and dealt with a* Familiar *Spirit, and wrought* much Evil *in the sight of the Lord.* But that *great* Wizzard found Mercy with *God,* upon his deep Humiliation for it: Such a *boundless* thing is the *Grace* of our God! The *Prey* of *Devils,* may become the *Joy* of *Angels:* The *Confederates* of *Hell,* may become the *Inhabitants* of *Heaven,* upon their sincere turning unto God. A *Witch* may be *penitent* in *this,* and *glorious* in *another* World. There was one *Hartford* here, who did with much brokenness of Heart *own* her *Witchcraft,* and *leave* her *Master,* and expire, depending on the *Free Grace* of God in Christ, and on that word of his, *Come to me, ye that labor and are heavy laden, and I will give you rest;* and on that, *There is a fountain open for sin and for uncleanness.* Come then, renounce the Slavery and the Interest of the Devils, renounce your mad *League* with 'em. Come and give up yourselves unto the *Lord Jesus Christ,* loathing yourselves exceedingly for your so siding with the black Enemies of his Throne. O come away from the *doleful* estate you are in. Come away from *serving* of the *Devils* that have ensnared your Souls. What *Wages* have you from those Hellish *Taskmasters?* Alas you are *here* among the *poor* and *vile,* and *ragged* Beggars upon Earth. When did Witchcraft ever make any person *Rich?* And *hereafter* you must be Objects for the intolerable *insolence* and cruelty of those *Cannibals,* and be *broken sore in the place of Dragons for evermore.* Betake yourselves then to Instant and Constant *Prayer,* and unto your old filthy Rulers now say, "Depart from me, ye Evil Spirits, for I will keep the Commandments of God."

But we must now conclude with the
    USE of the *Third* Proposition.

And *that* may be a *Caution* to every one of us. *This* in short, Since *Rebellion* is like *Witchcraft.*

O let us not make light of any Rebellion against the Almighty GOD. Particularly,

First, let not a *course* of Rebellion be followed by us. It is the *course* of unregenerate Men to be daily doing those things, for which *the wrath of God comes upon the Children of disobedience.* When God requires, *Repent of Sin,* they do *rebel* and reply, *No, I have loved Idols, and after them I will go.* When God requires, *Believe on Christ,* they do *rebel* and reply, *No, I will not have this Man to reign over me.* They *rebel* against all the divine Commands of *Love* to God, or *Love* to Man. They *rebel* against all the *Precepts* of the Lord, which are to be *esteemed concerning all things to be right.* And they *love every false way.* O Consider of this, ye strangers to the *new Birth;* Consider *what* you are doing, consider *where* you are going every day. I would now say, alluding to that in *Dan.* 4. 27. *O Soul, let my counsel be acceptable unto thee, and break off thy sins.* You have been doing of *Iniquity;* O now say, *I will do so no more.*

Consider, First, There is a sort of *Witchcraft* charged on you. You shall as undoubtedly perish as any *Witch* in the World, except you reform. Can you imagine that *an obstinate Witch* will have Admission into the *Kingdom of God?* Behold, and be astonished, ye unrenewed ones; as impossible it is for *you to see the Lord.* It is said in *Joh.* 3. 3. *Verily, verily, I say unto thee, except a man be born again, he cannot see the kingdom of God.* That *verily, verily,* which like a *flaming Sword,* stands to keep the vilest *Witches* out of Paradise, the *same* there is to keep every *unbeliever* out. . . .

. . . . .

Letter to John Richards

> *Although Cotton Mather was ill and could not attend the first trial (Bridget Bishop's) in Salem, he did reply to Judge John Richards' request for advice on the proper procedure for conducting a witchcraft trial. In this letter Cotton expressed the basic dilemma that went unsolved during the summer of 1692: how to protect the innocent who were accused and still act on the belief that an unconfessing "witch" could be justly convicted. This letter was printed in The Mather Papers, Collections of the Massachusetts Historical Society, Fourth Series, Vol. VIII.*

Boston. 31 day 3 m [May] 1692.

HONORABLE SIR, I could not have asked you as I now do to Excuse me from waiting upon you, with the utmost of my little skill & care to assist the noble service whereto you are called of God this week, the service of Encountering the Wicked Spirits in the high places of our Air, & of detecting & confounding of their confederates, were it not that I am Languishing under such an overthrow of my health as makes it very dubious that my company may prove more troublesome than serviceable: the least Excess of travel, or diet, or anything that may discompose me, would at this time threaten perhaps my life itself, as my friends advise me; & yet I hope before you can get far into that mysterious affair which is now before you, I may with God's blessing recover so far as to attend your desires, which to me always are commands. In the meantime, lest I should be guilty of any sinful omission in declining what no good man amongst us can decline, Even to do the best I can for the strengthening of your honorable hands in that work of God, whereto (I thank him) he hath so well fitted you, as well as called you, I thought it my duty briefly to offer you my poor thoughts on this astonishing occasion.

I. I am not without very lively hopes, that our good God will prosper you in that undertaking which he hath put you now upon: His people have been fasting & praying before him for your direction: & yourselves are persons whose Exemplary devotion disposeth you to such a dependence on the Wonderful Counselor, for his counsel in an affair thus full of wonder, as he doth usually answer with the most favorable assistances. You will easily pardon me that I do not back my thoughts with confirming Histories, it is not a sudden letter that will admit them: & it would be too like ostentation to produce them; nevertheless, I cannot for once forbear minding of the famous accidents at Mohra in Swedeland, where a fast was kept among the people of God, because of a stupendous Witchcraft, much like ours, making Havoc of the Kingdom, [and] was immediately [followed] with a remarkable Smile of God upon the endeavors of the Judges to discover & Extirpate the Authors of that Execrable witchcraft. Wherefore be Encouraged.

II. And yet I must most humbly beg you that in the Management of the affair in your most worthy hands, you do not lay more stress upon pure Specter testimony than it will bear. When you are satisfied or have good plain legal Evidence that the Demons which molest our poor neighbors, do indeed represent such & such people to the sufferers, though this be a presumption, yet I suppose you will not reckon it a conviction that the people so represented are witches to be immediately exterminated. It is very certain that the devils have sometimes represented the shapes of persons not only innocent, but also very virtuous. Though I believe that the just God then ordinarily provides a way for the Speedy vindication of the persons thus abused. Moreover I do suspect that persons who have too much indulged themselves in Malignant, Envious, malicious Ebullitions of their souls, may unhappily expose themselves to the Judgment of being represented by Devils, of whom they never had any vision, & with whom they have much less written any Covenant. I would say this: If upon the bare supposal of a poor creature's being represented by a Specter, too great a progress be made by the Authority in ruining a poor neighbor so represented, it may be that a door may be thereby opened for the Devils to obtain from the Courts in the invisible world a license to proceed unto most hideous desolations upon the repute & repose of such as have yet been Kept from the great transgression. If mankind have thus far once consented unto the Credit of Diabolical representations the Door is opened! Perhaps there are wise & good men, that may be ready to style him that shall advance this Caution, A Witch Advocate, but in the winding up this caution will certainly be wished for.

III. Though 'tis probable that the Devils may (though not often, yet sometimes) make most bloody invasions upon our Exterior Concerns, without any Witchcrafts of our fellow Creatures to empower them, & I do Expect, that as when our Lord was coming in his human Nature among us, there was a more sensible annoyance of the Destroyer upon our Human Nature, than at other times, thus it will be just before our Lord's coming again in his Human Nature. when he will also dispossess the Devils of their Aerial Region to make a new Heaven for his raised there: Nevertheless there is cause Enough to think that it is a horrible Witchcraft which hath given rise to the troubles wherewith Salem Village is at this day harassed: & the inde-

fatigable pains that are used for the tracing this Witchcraft are to be thank-
fully accepted, & applauded among all this people of God.

IV. Albeit the business of this Witchcraft be very much transacted upon
the Stage of Imagination, yet we Know, that, as in treason there is an imag-
ining which is a Capital Crime. & here also the business thus managed in
Imagination yet may not be called Imaginary. The Effects are dreadfully
real. Our dear neighbors are most really tormented. Really murdered, & really
acquainted with hidden things, which are afterwards proved plainly to have
been Realities. I say then, as that man is justly Executed for an Assassin,
who in the sight of man shall with a sword in his hand stab his neighbor
into the heart, so suppose a long train laid unto a barrel of Gunpowder under the floor where a neighbor is, & suppose a man with a match perhaps
in his mouth, out of sight, set fire unto the further end of the train, though
never so far off, this man also is to be treated as equally a malefactor. Our
neighbors at Salem Village, are blown up after a sort, with an infernal gunpowder, the train is laid in the laws of the Kingdom of Darkness limited
by God himself, now the question is, Who gives fire to this train? & by
what acts is the match applied? find out the persons that have done this
thing, & be their acts in doing it, either mental, or oral, or manual, or what
the Devil will, I say *abeant quo digni sunt* [Let them vanish where the
righteous are].

V. To determine a matter so much in the Dark as to Know the guilty
Employers of the Devils in this work of darkness, this is a work, this is a
labor. Now first a credible Confession of the guilty wretches is one of the
most hopeful ways of coming at them, & I say a credible confession, because
even confession itself sometimes is not credible. But a person of a Sagacity
many times thirty furlongs less than yours, will Easily perceive what Confession may be Credible, & what may be the result of only a delirious brain,
or a discontented heart. All the difficulty is, how to obtain this Confession.
For this I am far from urging the un-English method of torture, but instead thereof I propound these three things, first, Who can tell but when the
witches come upon their trials, they may be so forsaken, as to confess all.
The Almighty God having heard the appeals of our Cries to Heaven, may
so thunder strike their souls, as to make them show their Deeds. Moreover
the Devils themselves who aim at the entrapping of their own miserable
Clients, may treacherously depart from them in their Examinations, which
throws them into such toiling vexations they [that] they'll discover all. Besides, when you come solemnly in God's name, to Exhibit yourselves as his
Viceregents; & when you come to form a most awful type of the last Judgment, whereat the Devils of all things tremble most, even they also may be
smitten with such terrors as may contribute a little to their departure from
the miscreants whom they have entangled. An unexpected confession, is that
whereunto Witches are very often driven. Secondly, I am ready to think,
that there is usually some Expression or behavior, whereto the Devils do constantly oblige the Witches, as a Kind of Sacrament, upon their least failure
wherein the Witches presently lose the thus forfeited assistances of the Devils,
& all comes out. Please then to observe, if you can find any one constant

scheme of discourse or action, whereto the suspected seem religiously devoted, & (which may Easily be done by the common policies of conversation) cause them to transgress That, a confession will probably then come on apace. Thirdly, what Ever hath a tendency to put the witches into confusion, is likely to bring them unto Confession too. Here Cross & Swift Questions have their use, but besides them, for my part, I should not be unwilling, that an Experiment be made whether accused parties can repeat the Lord's prayer, or those other Systems of christianity, which it seems, the Devils often make the witches unable to repeat, without ridiculous Depravations or Amputations. The danger of this Experiment will be taken away, if you make no Evidence of it, but only put it to the use I mention, which is that of confounding the lisping Witches to give a reason why they cannot, Even with prompting, repeat those heavenly Composures. the like I would say of some other experiments only we may venture too far before we are aware.

VI. But what if no confession can be obtained, I say yet the case is far from desperate. For if there have been those words uttered by the witches, Either by way of threatening, or of Asking, or of Bragging, which rationally demonstrate such a Knowledge of the woeful circumstances attending the afflicted people, as could not be had, without some Diabolical Communion, the proof of such words is Enough to fix the guilt. Moreover I look upon wounds that have been given unto specters, & received by witches, as intimations broad enough, in concurrence with other things, to bring out the guilty. Though I am not fond of assaying to give such wounds, yet the proof such when given carries with it what is very palpable.

Once more, can there be no puppets found out? & here I would say thus much, I am thinking, that some witches make their own bodies to be their Puppets. If therefore you can find that when the witches do anything Easy, that is not needful (& it is needful that I put in that clause, "not needful," because it is possible that a prestidigital Demon may imitate what we do, though we are none of His) I say if you find the same thing, presently & hurtfully, & more violently done by any unseen hand, unto the bodies of the sufferers, hold them, for you have catched a Witch. I add, why should not Witch-marks be searched for? The properties, the qualities of those marks are described by divers weighty writers. I never saw any of those marks, but it is doubtless not impossible for a chiurgien [surgeon], when he sees them, to say what are magical, & if these become once apparent, it is apparent that these witches have gone so far in their wickedness as to admit most cursed Suckages, whereby the Devils have not only fetched out of them, it may be the Spirits of which they make vehicles, wherein they visit the afflicted, but also they have infused a venom into them which Exalts the malignity of their spirits as well as of their bodies: & it is likely, that by means of this ferment they would be found Buoyant (if the water-Ordeal were made upon them.)

VII. I begin to fear that the Devils do more easily proselyte poor mortals into witchcraft, than is commonly conceived. When a sinful child of man distempers himself with some Exorbitant motions in his mind (& it is to be feared the murmuring Frenzies of late prevailing in the country, have this way Exposed many to sore Temptations) a Devil then soon present himself unto him, & he demands are you willing that I should go do this or that for you? if the man once comply, the Devil hath him now in a most horrid snare, & by a permission from the just vengeance of God he visits the man with buffetings as well as allurements, till the forlorn man, at first only for the sake of quietness, but at length out of improved wickedness, will commission the Devil to do mischief as often as he requires it. And for this cause it is worth considering, whether there be a necessity always by Extirpations by Halter or fagot, [?] every wretched creature, that shall be hooked into some degrees of Witchcraft. What if some of the lesser Criminals, be only scourged with lesser punishments, & also put upon some solemn, open, Public & Explicit renunciation of the Devil? I am apt to think that the Devils would then cease afflicting the neighborhood whom these wretches have 'stoo'd [?] them upon, & perhaps they themselves would now suffer some impressions from the Devils, which if they do, they must be willing to bear, till the God that hears prayer deliver them. Or what if the death of some of the offenders were either diverted or inflicted, according to the success of such their renunciation.

But I find my free thoughts, thus freely laid before your Honor, begin to have too much freedom in them. I shall now therefore add no more, but my humble & most fervent Prayers to the God who gives wisdom liberally, that you & your Honorable Brethren may be furnished from on High, with all that wisdom, as well as Justice, which is requisite in the thorny affair before you. God will be with you. I am persuaded He will: & with that persuasion I Subscribe myself

Sir Your very devoted Servant,

C. MATHER.

The Return of Several Ministers Consulted

by his Excellency, and the Honorable Council, upon the present Witchcrafts in Salem Village.

This brief essay was probably written by Cotton Mather. Notice the similarity between its language and that in Cotton's letter to John Richards. The ministers' "Return" is reprinted from the London edition (1862) of Cotton Mather's The Wonders of the Invisible World.

Boston, June 15, 1692.

I. The afflicted State of our poor Neighbors, that are now suffering by Molestations from the Invisible World, we apprehend so deplorable, that we think their Condition calls for the utmost help of all Persons in their several Capacities. II. We cannot but with all Thankfulness acknowledge, the

Success which the merciful God has given unto the sedulous and assiduous Endeavors of our honorable Rulers, to detect the abominable Witchcrafts which have been committed in the Country; humbly praying that the discovery of these mysterious and mischievous Wickednesses, may be perfected. III. We judge that in the prosecution of these, and all such Witchcrafts, there is need of a very critical and exquisite Caution, lest by too much Credulity for things received only upon the Devil's Authority, there be a Door opened for a long Train of miserable Consequences, and Satan get an advantage over us, for we should not be ignorant of his Devices. IV. As in Complaints upon Witchcrafts, there may be Matters of Inquiry, which do not amount unto Matters of Presumption, and there may be Matters of Presumption which yet may not be reckoned Matters of *Conviction;* so 'tis necessary that all Proceedings thereabout be managed with an exceeding tenderness towards those that may be complained of; especially if they have been Persons formerly of an unblemished Reputation. V. When the first Inquiry is made into the Circumstances of such as may lie under any just Suspicion of Witchcrafts, we could wish that there may be admitted as little as is possible, of such Noise, Company, and Openness, as may too hastily expose them that are examined: and that there may nothing be used as a Test, for the Trial of the suspected, the Lawfulness whereof may be doubted among the People of God; but that the Directions given by such judicious Writers as *Perkins* and *Bernard,* be consulted in such a Case. VI. Presumptions whereupon Persons may be committed, and much more Convictions, whereupon Persons may be condemned as guilty of Witchcrafts, ought certainly to be more considerable, than barely the accused Person being represented by a Specter unto the Afflicted; inasmuch as 'tis an undoubted and a notorious thing, that a Demon may, by God's Permission, appear even to ill purposes, in the Shape of an innocent, yea, and a virtuous Man: Nor can we esteem Alterations made in the Sufferers, by a Look or Touch of the Accused to be an infallible Evidence of Guilt; but frequently liable to be abused by the Devil's Legerdemains. VII. We know not, whether some remarkable Affronts given to the Devils, by our disbelieving of those Testimonies, whose whole force and strength is from them alone, may not put a Period, unto the Progress of the dreadful Calamity begun upon us, in the Accusation of so many Persons, whereof we hope, some are yet clear from the great Transgression laid unto their Charge. VIII. Nevertheless, We cannot but humbly recommend unto the Government, the speedy and vigorous Prosecution of such as have rendered themselves obnoxious, according to the Direction given in the Laws of God, and the wholesome Statutes of the *English* Nation, for the Detection of Witchcrafts.

from

The Wonders of the Invisible World

*During the summer of 1692 Cotton Mather decided to prepare for
publication summaries of the trials of several witches. He finished
this book in October, 1692, and it was published in London the next
spring. This book,* The Wonders of the Invisible World, *included a
long sermon on witchcraft and accounts of five of the Salem trials.
His description of George Burroughs' trial is representative.*

I. The Trial of G[eorge]. B[urroughs]. At a Court of Oyer and Terminer, Held in Salem, 1692.

Glad should I have been, if I had never known the Name of this man;
or never had this occasion to mention so much as the first Letters of his Name.
But the Government requiring some Account of his Trial to be Inserted in
this Book, it becomes me with all Obedience to submit unto the Order.

I. This G. B. was indicted for Witch-crafts, and in the Prosecution of the
Charge against him, he was Accused by five or six of the Bewitched, as the
Author of their Miseries; he was Accused by eight of the Confessing Witches,
as being an Head Actor at some of their Hellish Rendezvous, and one who
had the promise of being a King in Satan's Kingdom, now going to be
Erected: he was Accused by nine persons for extraordinary Lifting, and such
Feats of Strength, as could not be done without a Diabolical Assistance. And
for other such Things he was Accused, until about Thirty Testimonies were
brought in against him; nor were these judged the half of what might have
been considered for his Conviction: however they were enough to fix the
Character of a Witch upon him, according to the Rules of Reasoning, by the
Judicious Gaule,[4] in that Case directed.

II. The Court being sensible, that the Testimonies of the Parties Bewitched
use to have a Room among the Suspicions or Presumptions, brought in against
one Indicted for Witchcraft, there were now heard the Testimonies of several
Persons, who were most notoriously Bewitched, and every day Tortured by
Invisible Hands, and these now all charged the Specters of G. B. to have a
share in their Torments. At the Examination of this G. B. the Bewitched People were grievously harassed with Preternatural Mischiefs, which could not
possibly be Dissembled; and they still ascribed it unto the Endeavors of G. B.
to kill them. And now upon his Trial, one of the Bewitched Persons testified,
That in her Agonies, a little Black hair'd man came to her, saying his Name
was B. and bidding her set her hand unto a Book which he show'd unto her;
and bragging that he was a Conjurer, above the ordinary Rank of Witches;

[4] John Gaule, *Select Cases of Conscience touching Witches and Witchcrafts*, London, 1646.

That he often persecuted her with the offer of that Book, saying, She should be well, and need fear nobody, if she would but Sign it; but he inflicted cruel Pains and Hurts upon her, because of her Denying so to do. The Testimonies of the other Sufferers concurred with these; and it was Remarkable, that whereas Biting was one of the ways which the Witches used for the vexing of the Sufferers, when they cried out of G. B. biting them, the print of the Teeth would be seen on the Flesh of the Complainers, and just such a set of Teeth as G. B.'s would then appear upon them, which could be distinguished from those of some other men's. Others of them testified, That in their Torments, G. B. tempted them to go unto a Sacrament, unto which they perceived him with a sound of Trumpet Summoning of other Witches, who quickly after the Sound would come from all Quarters unto the Rendezvous. One of them falling into a kind of Trance, afterwards affirmed, That G. B. had carried her into a very high Mountain, where he showed her mighty and glorious Kingdoms, and said, He would give them all to her, if she would write in his Book; but she told him, They were none of his to give; and refused the motions, enduring of much misery for that Refusal.

It cost the Court a wonderful deal of Trouble, to hear the Testimonies of the Sufferers; for when they were going to give in their Depositions, they would for a long time be taken with fits, that made them uncapable of saying anything. The Chief Judge asked the prisoner, who he thought hindered these witnesses from giving their testimonies? and he answered, He supposed it was the Devil. That Honorable person then replied, How comes the Devil so loath to have any Testimony borne against you? Which cast him into very great confusion.

III. It has been a frequent thing for the Bewitched people to be entertained with Apparitions of Ghosts of murdered people, at the same time that the Specters of the witches trouble them. These Ghosts do always affright the Beholders more than all the other spectral Representations; and when they exhibit themselves, they cry out, of being Murdered by the witchcrafts or other violences of the persons who are then in specter present. It is further considerable, that once or twice, these Apparitions have been seen by others at the very same time that they have shown themselves to the Bewitched; and seldom have there been these Apparitions but when something unusual and suspected had attended the Death of the party thus Appearing. Some that have been accused by these Apparitions, accosting of the Bewitched People, who had never heard a word of any such persons ever being in the world, have upon a fair examination freely and fully confessed the murders of those very persons, although these also did not know how the Apparitions had complained of them. Accordingly several of the Bewitched had given in their Testimony, that they had been troubled with the Apparitions of two women, who said that they were G. B.'s two wives, and that he had been the Death of them; and that the Magistrates must be told of it, before whom if B. upon his trial denied it, they did not know but that they should appear again in the Court. Now, G. B. had been infamous for the Barbarous usage of his two successive wives, all the Country over. Moreover, It was testified, the specter of G. B. threatening of the sufferers told them, he had killed (besides others) Mrs.

Lawson and her Daughter Ann. And it was noted, That these were the virtuous wife and Daughter of one at whom this G. B. might have a prejudice for his being serviceable at Salem-village, from whence himself had in Ill Terms removed some years before: and that when they died, which was long since, there were some odd circumstances about them, which made some of the Attendants there suspect something of witchcraft, though none Imagined from what Quarter it should come.

Well, G. B. being now upon his Trial, one of the Bewitched persons was cast into Horror at the Ghosts of B.'s two deceased wives then appearing before him, and crying for Vengeance against him. Hereupon several of the Bewitched persons were successively called in, who all not knowing what the former had seen and said, concurred in their Horror of the Apparition, which they affirmed that he had before him. But he, though much appalled, utterly denied that he discerned anything of it; nor was it any part of his Conviction.

IV. Judicious Writers have assigned it a great place in the Conviction of witches, when persons are Impeached by other Notorious witches, to be as Ill as themselves; especially, if the persons have been much noted for neglecting the Worship of God. Now, as there might have been Testimonies Enough of G. B.'s Antipathy to Prayer and the other Ordinances of God, though by his profession singularly obliged thereunto; so, there now came in against the prisoner the Testimonies of several persons, who confessed their own having been Horrible Witches, and ever since their confessions had been themselves terribly Tortured by the Devils and other Witches, even like the other Sufferers; and therein undergone the pains of many Deaths for their Confessions.

These now Testified, that G. B. had been at Witch-meetings with them; and that he was the Person who had Seduc'd and Compell'd them into the snares of Witchcraft: That he promised them Fine Clothes, for doing it; that he brought Puppets to them, and thorns to stick into those Puppets, for the afflicting of other People; And that he exhorted them, with the rest of the Crew, to bewitch all Salem-Village, but be sure to do it Gradually, if they would prevail in what they did.

When the Lancashire Witches were condemned, I don't Remember that there was any considerable further Evidence, than that of the Bewitched, and then that of some that confessed. We see so much already against G. B. But this being indeed not Enough, there were other things to render what had already been produced credible.

V. A famous Divine recites this among the Convictions of a Witch; The Testimony of the Party Bewitched, whether Pining or Dying; together with the Joint Oaths of Sufficient Persons that have seen certain Prodigious Pranks or Feats wrought by the party Accused. Now God had been pleased so to leave this G. B. that he had ensnared himself by several Instances, which he had formerly given of a Preternatural strength, and which were now produced against him. He was a very Puny man; yet he had often done things beyond the strength of a Giant. A Gun of about seven foot barrel, and so heavy that strong men could not steadily hold it out with both hands: there were several Testimonies, given in by Persons of Credit and Honor, that he made nothing of taking up such A Gun behind the Lock, with but one hand, and holding it out like a Pistol, at Arms-end. G. B. in his Vindication was so foolish as to say, That an Indian was there, and held it out at the same time: Whereas, none of the Spectators ever saw any such Indian; but they suppos'd the Black man (as the Witches call the Devil; and they generally say he resembles an Indian) might give him that Assistance. There was Evidence likewise brought in, that he made nothing of Taking up whole Barrels filled with Molasses or Cider, in very Disadvantageous Postures, and Carrying of them through the Difficultest Places out of a Canoe to the Shore.

Yea, there were Two Testimonies that G. B. with only putting the Fore-Finger of his Right hand into the Muzzle of an heavy Gun, a Fowling-piece of about six or seven foot Barrel, did Lift up the Gun, and hold it out at Arm's end; a Gun which the Deponents though strong men could not with both hands Lift up, and hold out at the Butt end, as is usual. Indeed, one of these Witnesses was over persuaded by some persons to be out of the way upon G. B.'s Trial; but he came afterwards with sorrow for his withdraw, and gave in his Testimony: Nor were either of these Witnesses made use of as evidences in the Trial.

VI. There came in several Testimonies relating to the Domestic Affairs of G. B. which had a very hard Aspect upon him; and not only proved him a very ill man; but also confirmed the Belief of the Character, which had been already fastened on him.

'Twas testified, That keeping his two Successive Wives in a strange kind of Slavery, he would when he came home from abroad pretend to tell the Talk which any had with them; That he has brought them to the point of Death, by his Harsh Dealings with his Wives, and then made the People about him to promise that in Case Death should happen, they would say nothing of it; That he used all means to make his Wives Write, Sign, Seal, and Swear a Covenant, never to Reveal any of his Secrets; That his Wives had privately complained unto the Neighbors about frightful Apparitions of Evil Spirits, with which their House was sometimes infested; and that many such things have been Whispered among the Neighborhood. There were also some other Testimonies, relating to the Death of People, whereby the Consciences of an Impartial Jury were convinced that G. B. had Bewitched the persons mentioned in the Complaints. But I am forced to omit several passages, in this, as well as in all the succeeding Trials, because the Scribes who took Notice of them, have not Supplied me.

VII. One Mr. Ruck, Brother in Law to this G. B., Testified, that G. B. and he himself, and his Sister, who was G. B.'s Wife, going out for Two or three Miles to gather Straw-Berries, Ruck with his Sister the Wife of G. B. Rode home very Softly, with G. B. on Foot in their Company. G. B. stepped aside a little into the Bushes; Whereupon they Halted and Hallooed for him. He not answering, they went away homewards, with a Quickened pace, without any expectation of seeing him in a considerable while; and yet when they were got near home, to their Astonishment they found him on foot with them, having a Basket of Straw-Berries. G. B. immediately then fell to chiding his Wife, on the account of what she had been speaking to her Brother, of him, on the Road: which when they wondered at, he said, He knew their thoughts.

Ruck being startled at that, made some Reply, intimating that the Devil himself did not know so far; but G. B. answered, My God makes known your Thoughts unto me. The prisoner now at the Bar had nothing to answer, unto what was thus Witnessed against him, that was worth considering. Only he said, Ruck and his Wife left a Man with him, when they left him. Which Ruck now affirm'd to be false; and when the Court asked G. B. What the Man's Name was? his countenance was much altered; nor could he say, who 'twas. But the Court began to think, that he then stepped aside, only that by the assistance of the Black Man, he might put on his Invisibility, and in that Fascinating Mist, gratify his own Jealous humor, to hear what they said of him. Which trick of rendering themselves Invisible, our Witches do in their confessions pretend that they sometimes are Masters of; and it is the more credible, because there is Demonstration that they often render many other things utterly Invisible.

VIII. Faltering, Faulty, unconstant, and contrary Answers upon Judicial and deliberate examination, are counted some unlucky symptoms of guilt, in all crimes, Especially in Witchcrafts. Now there never was a prisoner more Eminent for them, than G. B. both at his Examination and on his Trial. His Tergiversations, Contradictions, and Falsehoods, were very sensible: he had little to say, but that he had heard some things that he could not prove, Reflecting upon the Reputation of some of the witnesses. Only he gave in a paper to the Jury; wherein, although he had many times before granted, not only that there are Witches, but also that the present sufferings of the Country are the Effect of horrible Witchcrafts, yet he now goes to evince it, That there neither are, nor ever were Witches, that having made a compact with the Devil, Can send a Devil to Torment other people at a distance. This paper was Transcribed out of Ady;[5] which the Court presently knew, as soon as they heard it. But he said, he had taken none of it out of any Book; for which, his evasion afterwards was, that a Gentleman gave him the discourse in a manuscript, from whence he Transcribed it.

IX. The Jury brought him in guilty: But when he came to Die, he utterly denied the Fact, whereof he had been thus convicted.

[5] Thomas Ady, *A Candle in the Dark*, London, 1656. Ady argued that witches did not exist.

INCREASE MATHER

Cases of Conscience Concerning Evil Spirits Personating Men. . . .

As the number of accusations continued to increase during the summer of 1692, and as more and more "men of good conversation" were cried out upon, Increase Mather decided to write an essay defining admissible evidence for witchcraft trials. He read this essay to the Boston ministers on October 3, and fourteen ministers signed an approving introduction when the essay was published as a book. As we can see from the letters of Governor Phips, the ideas in Increase Mather's book played an important part in preventing further executions.

Christian Reader.

So Odious and Abominable is the Name of a Witch, to the Civilized, much more the Religious part of Mankind, that it is apt to grow up into a Scandal for any, so much as to enter some sober cautions against the over hasty suspecting, or too precipitant Judging of Persons on this account. But certainly, the more execrable the Crime is, the more critical care is to be used in the exposing of the Names, Liberties, and Lives of Men (especially of a Godly Conversation) to the imputation of it. The awful hand of God now upon us, in letting loose of evil Angels among us to perpetrate such horrid Mischiefs, and suffering of Hell's Instruments to do such fearful things as have been scarce heard of; hath put serious persons into deep Musings, and upon curious Inquiries what is to be done for the detecting and defeating of this tremendous design of the grand Adversary: And, tho' all that fear God are agreed, *That no evil is to be done, that good may come of it;* yet hath the Devil obtained not a little of his design, in the divisions of Reuben, about the application of this Rule.

That there are Devils and Witches, the Scripture asserts, and experience confirms, That they are common enemies of Mankind, and set upon mischief, is not to be doubted: That the Devil can (by Divine Permission) and often doth vex men in Body and Estate, without the Instrumentality of Witches, is undeniable: That he often hath, and delights to have the concurrence of Witches, and their consent in harming men, is consonant to his native Malice to Man, and too lamentably exemplified: That Witches, when detected and

117

convinced, ought to be exterminated and cut off, we have God's warrant for, *Exod*. 22. 18. Only the same God who hath said, *thou shalt not suffer a Witch to live;* hath also said, *at the Mouth of two Witnesses, or three Witnesses shall he that is worthy of Death, be put to Death: But at the Mouth of one Witness, he shall not be put to Death,* Deut. *17.* 6. Much debate is made about *what is* sufficient Conviction, and some have (in their Zeal) supposed that a less clear evidence ought to pass in this than in other Cases, supposing that else it will be hard (if possible) to bring such to condign Punishment, by reason of the close conveyances that there are between the Devil and Witches; but this is a very dangerous and unjustifiable tenet. Men serve God in doing their Duty, he never intended that all persons guilty of Capital Crimes should be discovered and punished by men in this Life, though they be never so curious in searching after Iniquity. It is therefore exceeding necessary that in such a day as this, men be informed what is Evidence and what is not. It concerns men in point of Charity; for tho' the most shining Professor may be secretly a most abominable Sinner, yet till he be detected, our Charity is bound to Judge according to what appears: and notwithstanding that a clear evidence must determine a case; yet presumptions must be weighed against presumptions, and Charity is not to be forgone as long as it has the most preponderating on its side. And it is of no less necessity in point of Justice; there are not only Testimonies required by God, which are to be credited according to the Rules given in his Word referring to witnesses: But there is also an Evidence supposed to be in the Testimony, which is thoroughly to be weighed, and if it do not infallibly prove the Crime against the person accused, it ought not to determine him guilty of it; for so a righteous Man may be Condemned unjustly. In the case of Witchcrafts we know that the Devil is the immediate Agent in the Mischief done, the consent or compact of the Witch is the thing to be Demonstrated.

Among many Arguments to evince this, that which is most under present debate, is that which refers to something vulgarly called *Specter Evidence,* and a certain sort of *Ordeal* or trial by the sight and touch. The principal Plea to justify the convictive Evidence in these, is fetched from the Consideration of the Wisdom and Righteousness of God in Governing the World, which they suppose would fail, if such things were permitted to befall an innocent person: but it is certain, that too resolute conclusions drawn from hence, are bold usurpations upon spotless *Sovereignty:* and tho' some things if suffered to be common, would subvert this Government, and disband, yea ruin Human Society; yet God doth sometimes suffer such things to evene, that we may thereby know how much we are beholden to him, for that restraint which he lays upon the Infernal Spirits, who would else reduce a World into a Chaos. That the Resolutions of such Cases as these is proper for the Servants of Christ in the Ministry cannot be denied; the seasonableness of doing it now, will be justified by the Consideration of the necessity there is at this time of a right Information of men's Judgments about these things, and the danger of their being misinformed.

The Reverend, Learned, and Judicious Author of the ensuing Cases, is too well known to need our Commendation: All that we are concerned in, is to *assert our hearty Consent to, and Concurrence with the substance of what is contained in the following Discourse:* And, with our hearty Request to God, that he would discover the depths of this Hellish Design; direct in the whole management of this Affair; prevent the taking any wrong steps in this dark way; and that he would in particular Bless these faithful Endeavors of his Servant to that end, we Commend it and you to his Divine Benediction.

William Hubbard, Samuel Phillips, Charles Morton, James Allen, Michael Wigglesworth, Samuel Whiting, *Sen.,* Samuel Willard, John Baily, Jabez Fox, Joseph Gerrish, Samuel Angier, John Wise, Joseph Capen, Nehemiah Walter.

Cases of Conscience Concerning Witchcrafts.

The First Case that I am desired to express my Judgment in, is this, *Whether it is not Possible for the Devil to impose on the imaginations of Persons Bewitched, and to cause them to Believe that an Innocent, yea that a Pious person does torment them, when the Devil himself doth it; or whether Satan may not appear in the Shape of an Innocent and Pious, as well as of a Nocent and Wicked Person, to Afflict such as suffer by Diabolical Molestations?*

The Answer to the Question must be Affirmative; Let the following Arguments be duly weighed in the Balance of the Sanctuary.

Argu. 1. There are several Scriptures from which we may infer the Possibility of what is Affirmed.

1. We find that the *Devil by the Instigation of the Witch at Endor appeared in the Likeness of the Prophet Samuel.* I am not ignorant that some have asserted that, which, if it were proved, would evert [i.e., overthrow] this Argument, *viz.* that it was the true and not a delusive *Samuel* which the Witch brought to converse with *Saul.* . . . Moreover, had it been the true *Samuel* from Heaven reprehending *Saul,* there is great Reason to believe, that he would not only have reproved him for his sin, in not executing Judgment on the *Amalekites;* as in Ver. 18. But for his Wickedness in consulting with Familiar Spirits: For which Sin it was in special that he died. 2 *Chron.* 10. 13. But inasmuch as there is not one word to testify against that Abomination, we may conclude that it was not real *Samuel* that appeared to *Saul:* and if it were the Devil in his likeness, the Argument seems very strong, that if the Devil may appear in the form of a Saint in Glory, much more is it possible for him to put on the likeness of the most Pious and Innocent Saint on Earth. There are, who acknowledge that a *Demon* may appear in the shape of a Godly Person, *But not as doing Evil.* Whereas the Devil in *Samuel's* likeness told a pernicious Lie, when he said, *Thou hath disquieted me.* It was not in the Power of *Saul,* nor of all the Devils in Hell, to disquiet a Soul in Heaven, where *Samuel* had been for Two years before this Apparition. Nor did the *Specter* speak true, when he said, *Thou and thy Sons shall be with me:* Tho' *Saul* himself at his Death went to be with the Devil, his Son *Jonathan* did not so. Besides, (which suits with the matter in hand) the Devil in *Samuel's* shape confirmed *Necromancy* and *Cursed Witchery.* He that can in the likeness of Saints encourage Witches to Familiarity with Hell, may possibly in the likeness of a Saint afflict a Bewitched Person. But this we see from Scripture, Satan may be permitted to do.

. . . . .

. . . It is evident from another Scripture, *viz.* that in 2 *Cor.* 11. 14. *For Satan himself is transformed into an Angel of Light.* He seems to be what he is not, and makes others seem to be what they are not. He represents evil men as good, and good men as evil.

. . . . .

. . . nor are these things to be wondered at, since the Holy Son of God himself was reputed a *Magician,* and one that had Familiarity with the greatest of Devils. The Blaspheming Pharisees said, *he casts out the Devils thro' the Prince of Devils,* Matth. 9. 34. There is then not the best Saint on Earth (Man or Woman) that can assure themselves that the Devil shall not cast such an Imputation upon them. *It is enough for the Disciple that he be as his Master, and the Servant as his Lord: If they have called the Master of the House Beelzebub, how much more them of his Household,* Matth. 10. 25. It is not for men to determine how far the Holy God may permit the wicked one to proceed in his Accusations. The sacred story of *Job* giveth us to understand, that the Lord whose ways are past finding out, does for wise and Holy Ends suffer Satan by immediate Operation (and consequently by Witchcraft), greatly to afflict innocent Persons, as in their Bodies and Estates, so in their Reputations. I shall mention but one Scripture more to confirm the Truth in hand: It is that in *Eccles.* 9. 2, 3. where it is said, *All things come alike to all, there is one event to the Righteous and to the Wicked, as is the Good, so is the Sinner, this is an evil amongst all things under the Sun, that there is one Event happeneth to all.* And in *Eccles.* 7. 15. 'tis said, *There is a just man that perisheth in his Righteousness.*

From hence we infer, that there is no outward Affliction whatsoever but may befall a good Man; now to be represented by Satan as a Tormentor of Bewitched or Possessed Persons, is a sore Affliction to a good man. To be tormented by Satan is a sore Affliction, yet nothing but what befell *Job,* and a Daughter of *Abraham,* whom we read of in the Gospel: To be represented by Satan as tormenting others, is an Affliction like the former; the Lord may bring such extraordinary Temptations on his own Children, to afflict and humble them, for some Sin they have been guilty of before him. . . .

Have we not known some that have bitterly censured all that have been complained of by bewitched Persons, saying it was impossible they should not be guilty; soon upon which themselves or some near Relations of theirs, have been to the lasting Infamy of their Families, accused after the same manner, and Personated by the Devil! Such tremendous Rebukes on a few, should make all men to be careful how they join with Satan in Condemning the Innocent.

. . . . .

. . . the Blood and Spirits of a Man, that is bitten with a Mad-Dog, are so envenomed, as that strange Impressions are thereby made on his Imagination: let him be brought into a Room where there is a Looking-Glass, and he will (if put upon it) not only say but swear that he sees a Dog, tho' in truth there is no Dog it may be within 20 Miles of him; and is it not then possible for the Dogs of Hell to poison the Imaginations of miserable Creatures, so as that they shall believe and swear that such Persons hurt them as never did so? I have heard of an Enchanted Pin, that has caused the Condemnation and Death of many scores of innocent Persons. There was a notorious *Witchfinder* in *Scotland,* that undertook by a Pin, to make an infallible Discovery of suspected Persons, whether they were Witches or not, if when the Pin was run an Inch or two into the Body of the accused Party no Blood appeared, nor any sense of Pain, then he declared them to be Witches; by means hereof my Author tells me no less then 300 persons were Condemned for Witches in that Kingdom. This Bloody Juggler . . . thrust a great Brass Pin two Inches into the Body of one, that some would in that way try whether there was Witchcraft in the Case or no: the accused Party was not in the least sensible of what was done, and therefore in danger of receiving the Punishment justly due for Witchcraft; only it so happened, that Colonel *Fenwick* (that worthy Gentleman, who many years since lived in *New-England*) was then the Military Governor in that Town; he sent for the Mayor and Magistrates advising them to be careful and cautious in their proceedings; for he told them, it might be an Enchanted Pin, which the Witchfinder made use of: Whereupon the Magistrates of the place ordered that he should make his Experiment with some other Pin as they should appoint: But that he would by no means be induced unto, which was a sufficient Discovery of the Knavery and Witchery of the Witchfinder. . . .

. . . . .

I have myself known several of whom I ought to think that they are now in Heaven, considering that they were of good Conversation, and reputed Pious by those that had the greatest Intimacy with them, of whom nevertheless, some complained that their Shapes appeared to them, and threatened them: Nor is this answered by saying, we do not know but those Persons might be Witches: We are bound by the Rule of Charity to think otherwise: And they that censure any, merely because such a sad Affliction as their being falsely represented by Satan has befallen them, do not do as they would be done by. I bless the Lord, it was never the portion allotted to me, nor to any Relation of mine to be thus abused: But no Man knoweth what may happen to him, since *there be just Men unto whom it happeneth according to the Work of the Wicked,* Eccles. 8. 14. But what needs more to be said, since there is one amongst ourselves whom no Man that knows him, can think him to be a Wizzard, whom yet some bewitched Persons complained of, that they are in his Shape tormented: And the Devils have of late accused some eminent Persons.

It is an awful thing which the Lord has done to convince some amongst us of their Error: This then I declare and testify, that to take away the Life of anyone, merely because a *Specter* or Devil, in a bewitched or possessed Person does accuse them, will bring the Guilt of innocent Blood on the Land, where such a thing shall be done: Mercy forbid that it should (and I trust that as it has not it never will be so), in *New-England*. What does such an Evidence amount unto more than this: Either such an one did afflict such an one, or the Devil in his likeness, or his Eyes were bewitched.

The things which have been mentioned make way for, and bring us unto the second Case, which is to come under our Consideration, *viz.*

If one bewitched is struck down at the Look or cast of the Eye of another, and after that recovered again by a Touch from the same Person, Is not this an infallible Proof, that the Person suspected and complained of is in League with the Devil?

. . . . .

. . . Now no Credit ought to be given to what *Demons* in such as are by them obsessed shall say. Our Saviour by his own unerring Example has taught us not to receive the Devil's Testimony in anything. . . . the Father of Lies is never to be believed: He will utter twenty great truths to make way for one lie: He will accuse twenty Witches, if he can but thereby bring one innocent Person into trouble: He mixeth Truths with Lies, that so those truths giving credit unto lies, Men may believe both, and so be deceived. . . .

. . . . .

As for that which concerns the Bewitched Persons being recovered out of their Agonies by the Touch of the suspected Party, it is various and fallible.

For sometimes the afflicted Person is made sick, (instead of being made whole) by the Touch of the Accused; sometimes the Power of Imagination is such, as that the Touch of a Person innocent and not accused shall have the same effect. It is related in the Account of the Trials of Witches at *Bury* in *Suffolk* 1664, during the time of the Trial, there were some Experiments made with the Persons afflicted, by bringing the accused to touch them, and it was observed that by the least Touch of one of the supposed Witches, they that were in their Fits, to all men's Apprehension wholly deprived of all Sense and Understandings, would suddenly shriek out and open their Hands.

Mr. Serjeant *Keeling* did not think that sufficient to Convict the Prisoners, for admitting that the Children were in truth Bewitched, yet (saith he) it cannot be applied to the Prisoners upon the Imagination only of the Parties afflicted; for if that might be allowed, no Person whatsoever can be in safety, for perhaps they might fancy another Person who might altogether be innocent in such matters: To avoid this Scruple it was privately desired by the Judge, that some Gentlemen there in Court would attend one of the distempered Persons in the farther part of the Hall, whilst she was in her Fits, and then to send for one of the Witches to try what would happen, which they did accordingly. One of them was conveyed from the Bar, and brought to the Afflicted Maid. They put an Apron before her Eyes, and then another person (not the Witch) touched her, which produced the same effect, as the Touch of the Witch did in the Court. Whereupon the Gentlemen returned much unsatisfied. . . .

. . . . .

4. *There are* [those] *that Question the Lawfulness of the Experiment.* For if this healing power in the Witch is not a Divine but a Diabolical Gift, it may be dangerous to meddle too much with it. If the Witch may be ordered to touch afflicted Persons in order to their healing or recovery out of a sick Fit, why may not the Diseased Person be as well ordered to touch the Witch for the same cause? And if to touch him, why not to scratch him and fetch Blood out of him, which is but an harder kind of touch? But as for this Mr. *Perkins* doubts not to call it *a Practice of Witchcraft.* It is not safe to meddle with any of the Devil's Sacraments or Institutions; *For my own part, I should be loath to say to a Man, that I knew or thought was a Witch, do you look on such a Person, and see if you can Witch them into a Fit, and there is such an afflicted Person do you take them by the Hand, and see if you can Witch them well again. If it is by virtue of some Contract with the Devil that witches have Power to do such without* [their judges'] *being too much concerned in that Hellish Covenant.* I take it to be . . . a solid Principle, . . . *That they who force another to do that which he cannot possibly do, but by virtue of a Compact with the Devil, have themselves implicitly Communion with the Diabolical Covenant.* The Devil is pleased and honored when any of his Institutions are made use of; this way of discovering Witches, is no better than that of putting the Urine of the afflicted Person into a Bottle, that so the Witch may be tormented and dis-covered: The Vanity and Superstition of which practice I have formerly showed, and testified against. . . .

5. *If the Testimony of a bewitched or possessed Person, is of validity as to what they see done to themselves, then it is so as to others, whom they see afflicted no less than themselves:* But what they affirm concerning others, is not to be taken for Evidence. Whence had they this Supernatural Sight? It must needs be either from Heaven or from Hell: If from Heaven, (as *Elisha's* Servant, and *Balaam's* Ass could discern Angels) let their Testimony be received: But if they had this Knowledge from Hell, tho' there may possibly be truth in what they affirm, they are not legal Witnesses: For the Law of God allows of no Revelation from any other Spirit but himself, *Isa.* 8. 19. It is a Sin against God to make use of the Devil's help to know that which cannot be otherwise known: And I testify against it, as a great Transgression, which may justly provoke the Holy One of *Israel,* to let loose Devils on the whole Land, *Luke* 4. 35. . . . The Persons, concerning whom the Question is, see things through Diabolical Mediums; on which account their Evidence is not mere human Testimony; and if it be in any part Diabolical, it is not to be owned as Authentic; for the Devil's Testimony ought not to be received neither in whole nor in part. . . .

6. It has always been said, that it is a difficult thing to find out Witches: But if the Representation of such a Person as afflicting, or the Look or Touch be an infallible proof of the guilt of Witchcraft in the Persons complained of, 'tis the easiest thing in the World to discover them; for it is done to our hand, and there needs no inquiry into the Matter.

7. *Let them* [that] *say this is an infallible Proof, produce any Word out of the Law of God which does in the least countenance that Assertion:* The

Word of God instructs Jurors and Judges to proceed upon clear human Testimony, *Deut.* 35. 30.[6] But the Word nowhere giveth us the least Intimation, that every one is a Witch, at whose look the bewitched Person shall fall into Fits; nor yet that any other means should be used for the discovery of Witches, than what may be used for the finding out of Murderers, Adulterers, and other Criminals.

8. Sometimes Antipathies in Nature have strange and unaccountable Effects. I have read of a Man that at the sight of his own Son, who was no Wizzard would fall into Fits. There are that find in their Natures an averseness to some Persons whom they never saw before. . . . It may proceed from Nature, and the Power of Imagination.

To conclude; Judicious *Casuists* have determined, that to make use of those Media to come to the Knowledge of any Matter, which have no such power in them by Nature, nor by Divine Institution is an Implicit going to the Devil to make a discovery: Now there is no natural Power in the Look or Touch of a Person to bewitch another; nor is this by Divine Institution the means whereby Witchcraft is discovered: Therefore it is an unwarrantable Practice.

We proceed now to the third Case proposed to Consideration; If the things which have been mentioned are not infallible Proofs of Guilt in the accused Party, it is then Queried, *Whether there are any Discoveries of this Crime, which Jurors and Judges may with a safe Conscience proceed upon to the Conviction and Condemnation of the Persons under Suspicion?*

Let me here premise Two things,

1. The Evidence in this Crime ought to be as clear as in any other Crimes of a Capital nature. The Word of God does nowhere intimate, that a less clear Evidence, or that fewer or other Witnesses may be taken as sufficient to convict a Man of Sorcery, which would not be enough to convict him were he charged with another evil worthy of Death, *Numb.* 35. 30. if we may not take the Oath of a distracted Person, or of a possessed Person in a Case of Murder, Theft, Felony of any sort, then neither may we do it in the Case of Witchcraft.

2. Let me premise this also, that there have been ways of trying Witches long used in many Nations, . . . which the righteous God never approved of. But which (as judicious Mr. *Perkins* expresseth it in plain *English*) were invented by the Devil, that so innocent Persons might be condemned, and some notorious Witches escape: . . . Of this sort is that of scratching the Witch, or seething the Urine of the Bewitched Person, or making a Witch-cake with that Urine: And that trial of putting their Hands into scalding Water, to see if it will not hurt them: And that of sticking an Awl under the Seat of the suspected Party. . . .

. . . . .

. . . If a Crime cannot be found out but by Miracle, it is not for any Judge on Earth to usurp that Judgment which is reserved for the Divine Throne.
. . . . .

[6] The relevant verse is *Numbers* 35. 30.

These things being premised, I answer the Question affirmatively; *There are Proofs for the Conviction of Witches which Jurors may with a safe Conscience proceed upon, so as to bring them in guilty.* The Scripture which saith, *Thou shalt not suffer a Witch to live,* clearly implies, that some in the World may be known and proved to be Witches: For until they be so, they may and must be suffered to live. . . .

Q. But then the Inquiry is, *What is sufficient Proof?*

. . . . .

1. *That a free and voluntary Confession of the Crime made by the Person suspected and accused after Examination, is a sufficient Ground of Conviction.*

Indeed, if Persons are Distracted, or under the Power of *Phrenetic Melancholy,* that alters the Case; but the Jurors that examine them, and their Neighbors that know them, may easily determine that Case; or if Confession be extorted, the Evidence is not so clear and convictive; but if any Persons out of Remorse of Conscience, or from a Touch of God in their Spirits, confess and show their Deeds, as the Converted Magicians in *Ephesus* did, *Acts* 19. 18, 19. nothing can be more clear. . . .

. . . But as for the Testimony of Confessing Witches against others, the case is not so clear as against themselves, they are not such credible Witnesses, as in a Case of Life and Death is to be desired: It is beyond dispute, that the Devil makes his Witches to dream strange things of themselves and others which are not so. . . . What Credit can be given to those that say they can turn Men into Horses? If so, they can as well turn Horses into Men; but all the Witches on Earth in Conjunction with all the Devils in Hell, can never make or unmake a rational Soul. . . . In a word, there is no more Reality in what many Witches confess of strange things seen or done by them, whilst Satan had them in his full Power, than there is in *Lucian's* ridiculous Fable of his being Bewitched into an *Ass,* and what strange Feats he then played; so that what such persons relate concerning Persons and Things at Witch-meetings, ought not to be received with too much Credulity.

. . . . .

2. *If two credible Persons shall affirm upon Oath that they have seen the party accused speaking such words, or doing things which none but such as have Familiarity with the Devil ever did or can do, that's a sufficient Ground for Conviction.*

. . . The Devil never assists men to do supernatural things undesired. When therefore such like things shall be testified against the accused Party not by *Specters* which are Devils in the Shape of Persons either living or dead, but by real men or women who may be credited; it is proof enough that such an one has that Conversation and Correspondence with the Devil, as that he or she, whoever they be, ought to be exterminated from amongst men. This notwithstanding I will add; It were better that ten suspected Witches should escape, than that one innocent Person should be Condemned; that is an old saying, and true, *Prestat reum nocentem absolvi, quam ex prohibitis Indiciis & illegitima probatione condemnari.* It is better that a

Guilty Person should be Absolved, than that he should without sufficient ground of Conviction be condemned. I had rather judge a Witch to be an honest woman, than judge an honest woman as a Witch. The Word of God directs men not to proceed to the execution of the most capital offenders, until such time as upon searching diligently, the matter is *found to be a Truth, and the thing certain,* Deut. 13. 14, 15.

. . . . .

Boston, New-England, Octob. 3. 1692.

Postscript.

The Design of the preceding *Dissertation,* is not to plead for Witch-crafts, or to appear as an Advocate for Witches. . . .

Nor is there designed any Reflection on those worthy Persons who have been concerned in the late Proceedings at *Salem:* They are wise and good Men, and have acted with all Fidelity according to their Light, and have out of tenderness declined the doing of some things, which in our own Judgments they were satisfied about: Having therefore so arduous a Case before them, Pity and Prayers rather than Censures are their due; on which account I am glad that there is published to the World (by my Son) a *Breviate of the Trials* of some who were lately executed, whereby I hope the thinking part of Mankind will be satisfied, that there was more than that which is called *Specter Evidence* for the Conviction of the Persons condemned. I was not myself present at any of the Trials, excepting one, *viz.* that of *George Burroughs;* had I been one of his Judges, I could not have acquitted him: For several Persons did upon Oath testify, that they saw him do such things as no Man that has not a Devil to be his Familiar could perform: And the Judges affirm, that they have not convicted anyone merely on the account of what *Specters* have said, or of what has been represented to the Eyes or Imaginations of the sick bewitched Persons. . . . It becomes those of my Profession to be very tender in Cases of Blood, and to imitate our Lord and Master, *Who came not to destroy the Lives of Men, but to save them.*

. . . . .

Some I hear have taken up a Notion, that the Book newly published by my Son, is contradictory to this of mine: 'Tis strange that such Imaginations should enter into the Minds of Men: I perused and approved of that Book before it was printed; and nothing but my Relation to him hindered me from recommending it to the World: But myself and Son agreed unto the humble Advice which twelve Ministers concurringly presented before his Excellency and Council,[7] respecting the present Difficulties, which let the World judge, whether there be anything in it dissentany from what is attested by either of us. . . .

[7] This was "The Return of Several Ministers" on June 15, reprinted on pp. 110-11.

Letter of

THOMAS BRATTLE

Thomas Brattle was a Boston merchant whose ability in mathematics and astronomy won him posthumous recognition by the Royal Society. He was a religious and political opponent of such orthodox Puritans as Cotton and Increase Mather. He did not publish his letter on witchcraft, although he may have intended it to circulate in manuscript form. It was addressed to a minister whose name we do not know. It was published in Narratives of the Witchcraft Cases, 1648- 1706, *ed. George L. Burr, New York, 1914. (See* Sibley, *Harvard Graduates, Vol. II, pp. 489-98.)*

October 8, 1692.

Reverend Sir,

Yours I received the other day, and am very ready to serve you to my utmost. I should be very loath to bring myself into any snare by my freedom with you. . . . Obedience to lawful authority I evermore accounted a great duty; and willingly I would not practice anything that might thwart and contradict such a principle. . . . Far, therefore, be it from me, to have anything to do with those men your letter mentions, whom you acknowledge to be men of a factious spirit, and never more in their element than when they are declaiming against men in public place, and contriving methods that tend to the disturbance of the common peace. . . . However, Sir, I never thought Judges infallible; but reckoned that they, as well as private men, might err; and that when they were guilty of erring, standers by, who possibly had not half their judgment, might, notwithstanding, be able to detect and behold their errors. . . .

First, as to the method which the Salem Justices do take in their examinations, it is truly this: A warrant being issued out to apprehend the persons that are charged and complained of by the afflicted children, (as they are called); said persons are brought before the Justices, (the afflicted being present.) The Justices ask the apprehended why they afflict those poor children; to which the apprehended answer, they do not afflict them. The Justices order the apprehended to look upon the said children, which accordingly they do; and at the time of that look, (I dare not say by that look, as the Salem Gentlemen do) the afflicted are cast into a fit. The apprehended are then blinded, and ordered to touch the afflicted; and at that touch, tho'

127

not by the touch, (as above) the afflicted ordinarily do come out of their fits. The afflicted persons then declare and affirm, that the apprehended have afflicted them; upon which the apprehended persons, tho' of never so good repute, are forthwith committed to prison, on suspicion for witchcraft. One of the Salem Justices was pleased to tell Mr. Alden, (when upon his examination) that truly he had been acquainted with him these many years; and had always accounted him a good man; but indeed now he should be obliged to change his opinion. This, there are more than one or two did hear, and are ready to swear to, if not in so many words, yet as to its natural and plain meaning. He saw reason to change his opinion of Mr. Alden, because that at the time he touched the poor child, the poor child came out of her fit. I suppose his Honor never made the experiment, whether there was not as much virtue in his own hand, as there was in Mr. Alden's, to cure by a touch. I know a man that will venture two to one with any Salemite whatever, that let the matter be duly managed, and the afflicted person shall come out of her fit upon the touch of the most religious hand in Salem. It is worthily noted by some, that at some times the afflicted will not presently come out of their fits upon the touch of the suspected; and then, forsooth, they are ordered by the Justices to grasp hard, harder yet, etc. insomuch that at length the afflicted come out of their fits; and the reason is very good, because that a touch of any hand, and process of time, will work the cure; infallibly they will do it, as experience teaches.

I cannot but condemn this method of the Justices, of making this touch of the hand a rule to discover witchcraft; because I am fully persuaded that it is sorcery, and a superstitious method, and that which we have no rule for, either from reason or religion. The Salem Justices, at least some of them, do assert, that the cure of the afflicted persons is a natural effect of this touch; . . .

I would fain know of these Salem Gentlemen, but as yet could never know, how it comes about, that if these apprehended persons are witches, and, by a look of the eye, do cast the afflicted into their fits by poisoning them, how it comes about, I say, that, by a look of their eye, they do not cast others into fits, and poison others by their looks; and in particular, tender, fearful women, who often are beheld by them, and as likely as any in the whole world to receive an ill impression from them. This Salem philosophy, some men may call the new philosophy; but I think it rather deserves the name of Salem superstition and sorcery, and it is not fit to be named in a land of such light as New-England is. I think the matter might be better solved another way; but I shall not make any attempt that way, further than to say, that these afflicted children, (as they are called,) do hold correspondence with the devil, even in the esteem and account of the S[alem]. G[entlemen]., for when the black man, *i.e.* (say these gentlemen,) the Devil, does appear to them, they ask him many questions, and accordingly give information to the inquirer; and if this is not holding correspondence with the devil, and something worse, I know not what is.

But furthermore, I would fain know of these Salem Justices what need there is of further proof and evidence to convict and condemn these apprehended persons, than this look and touch, if so be they are so certain that this falling down and arising up, when there is a look and a touch, are natural effects of the said look and touch, and so a perfect demonstration and proof of witchcraft in those persons. What can the Jury or Judges desire more, to convict any man of witchcraft, than a plain demonstration, that the said man is a witch? Now if this look and touch, circumstanced as before, be a plain demonstration, (as their Philosophy teaches,) what need they seek for further evidences, when, after all, it can be but a demonstration?

But let this pass with the S. G. for never so plain and natural a demonstration; yet certain is it, that the reasonable part of the world, when acquainted herewith, will laugh at the demonstration, and conclude that the said S. G. are actually possessed, at least, with ignorance and folly. . . .

Secondly, with respect to the confessors, (as they are improperly called,) or such as confess themselves to be witches, (the second thing you inquire into in your letter), there are now about fifty of them in Prison; many of which I have again and again seen and heard; and I cannot but tell you, that my faith is strong concerning them, that they are deluded, imposed upon, and under the influence of some evil spirit; and therefore unfit to be evidences either against themselves, or anyone else. I now speak of one sort of them, and of others afterward.

These confessors, (as they are called,) do very often contradict themselves, as inconsistently as is usual for any crazed, distempered person to do. This the S. G. do see and take notice of; and even the Judges themselves have, at some times, taken these confessors in flat lies, or contradictions, even in the Courts; By reason of which, one would have thought, that the Judges would have frowned upon the said confessors, discarded them, and not minded one tittle of any thing that they said; but instead thereof, (as sure as we are men,) the Judges vindicate these confessors, and salve their contradictions, by proclaiming, that the Devil takes away their memory, and imposes upon their brain. If this reflects anywhere, I am very sorry for it: I can but assure you, that, upon the word of an honest man, it is truth, and that I can bring you many credible persons to witness it, who have been eye and ear witnesses to these things. . . .

If the Devil does actually take away the memory of them at some times, certainly the Devil, at other times, may very reasonably be thought to affect their fancies, and to represent false ideas to their imagination. But now, if it be thus granted, that the Devil is able to represent false ideas (to speak vulgarly) to the imaginations of the confessors, what man of sense will regard the confessions, or any of the words, of these confessors?

. . . . .

In the next place, I proceed to the form of their indictments, and the Trials thereupon.

The Indictment runs for sorcery and witchcraft, acted upon the body of such an one, (say M. Warren), at such a particular time, (say April 14, '92,) and at divers other times before and after, whereby the said M. W. is wasted and consumed, pined, etc.

Now for the proof of the said sorcery and witchcraft, the prisoner at the bar pleading not guilty.

1. The afflicted persons are brought into Court; and after much patience and pains taken with them, do take their oaths, that the prisoner at the bar did afflict them: And here I think it very observable, that often, when the afflicted do mean and intend only the appearance and shape of such an one, (say G[oodwife]. Proctor) yet they positively swear that G. Proctor did afflict them; and they have beeen allowed so to do; as tho' there was no real difference between G. Proctor and the shape of G. Proctor. This, methinks, may readily prove a stumbling block to the Jury, lead them into a very fundamental error, and occasion innocent blood, yea the innocentest blood imaginable, to be in great danger. Whom it belongs unto, to be eyes unto the blind, and to remove such stumbling blocks, I know full well; and yet you, and everyone else, do know as well as I who do not [i.e., the judges].

2. The confessors do declare what they know of the said prisoner; and some of the confessors are allowed to give their oaths; a thing which I believe was never heard of in this world; that such as confess themselves to be witches, to have renounced God and Christ, and all that is sacred, should yet be allowed and ordered to swear by the name of the great God! This indeed seemeth to me to be a gross taking of God's name in vain. I know the S. G. do say, that there is hopes that the said Confessors have repented; I shall only say, that if they have repented, it is well for themselves; but if they have not, it is very ill for you know who. But then,

3. Whoever can be an evidence against the prisoner at the bar is ordered to come into Court; and here it scarce ever fails but that evidences, of one nature and another, are brought in, tho', I think, all of them altogether alien to the matter of indictment; for they none of them do respect witchcraft upon the bodies of the afflicted, which is the alone matter of charge in the indictment.

4. They are searched by a Jury; and as to some of them, the Jury brought in, that [on] such or such a place there was a preternatural excrescence. And I wonder what person there is, whether man or woman, of whom it cannot be said but that, in some part of their body or other, there is a preternatural excrescence. The term is a very general and inclusive term. . . .

. . . In short, the prisoner at the bar is indicted for sorcery and witchcraft acted upon the bodies of the afflicted. Now, for the proof of this, I reckoned that the only pertinent evidences brought in are the evidences of the said afflicted.

It is true, that over and above the evidences of the afflicted persons, there are many evidences brought in, against the prisoner at the bar; either that he was at a witch meeting, or that he performed things which could not be done by an ordinary natural power; or that she sold butter to a sailor, which proving bad at sea, and the seamen exclaiming against her, she appeared, and soon after there was a storm, or the like. But what if there were ten thousand evidences of this nature; how do they prove the matter of indictment! And if they do not reach the matter of indictment, then I think it is clear, that the prisoner at the bar is brought in guilty, and condemned, merely from the evidences of the afflicted persons.

The S. G. will by no means allow, that any are brought in guilty, and condemned, by virtue of specter Evidence, (as it is called,) *i.e.* the evidence of these afflicted persons, who are said to have spectral eyes; but whether it is not purely by virtue of these specter evidences, that these persons are found guilty, (considering what before has been said,) I leave you, and any man of sense, to judge and determine. When any man is indicted for murdering the person of A. B. and all the direct evidence be, that the said man pistolled the shadow of the said A. B. tho' there be never so many evidences that the said person murdered C. D., E. F. and ten more persons, yet all this will not amount to a legal proof, that he murdered A. B.; and upon that indictment, the person cannot be legally brought in guilty of the said indictment; it must be upon this supposition, that the evidence of a man's pistolling the shadow of A. B. is a legal evidence to prove that the said man did murder the person of A. B. Now no man will be so much out of his wits as to make this a legal evidence; and yet this seems to be our case; and how to apply it is very easy and obvious.

As to the late executions, I shall only tell you, that in the opinion of many unprejudiced, considerate and considerable spectators, some of the condemned went out of the world not only with as great protestations, but also with as good shows of innocency, as men could do.

They protested their innocency as in the presence of the great God, whom forthwith they were to appear before: they wished, and declared their wish, that their blood might be the last innocent blood shed upon that account. With great affection they entreated Mr. C[otton]. M[ather]. to pray with them: they prayed that God would discover what witchcrafts were among us; they forgave their accusers; they spoke without reflection on Jury and Judges, for bringing them in guilty, and condemning them: they prayed earnestly for pardon for all other sins, and for an interest in the precious blood of our dear Redeemer; and seemed to be very sincere, upright, and sensible of their circumstances on all accounts; especially Proctor and Willard, whose whole management of themselves, from the Jail to the Gallows, and whilst at the Gallows, was very affecting and melting to the hearts of some considerable Spectators, whom I could mention to you—but they are executed, and so I leave them.

Many things I cannot but admire and wonder at, an account of which I shall here send you.

And 1. I do admire that some particular persons, and particularly Mrs. Thatcher of Boston, should be much complained of by the afflicted persons, and yet that the Justices should never issue out their warrants to apprehend them, when as upon the same account they issue out their warrants for the apprehending and imprisoning many others.

This occasions much discourse and many hot words, and is a very great scandal and stumbling block to many good people; certainly distributive Justice should have its course, without respect to persons; and altho' the said Mrs. Thatcher be mother in law to Mr. [Jonathan] Corwin, who is one of

the Justices and Judges, yet if Justice and conscience do oblige them to apprehend others on the account of the afflicted their complaints, I cannot see
how, without injustice and violence to conscience, Mrs. Thatcher can escape,
when it is well known how much she is, and has been, complained of.

. . . . .

3. If our Justices do think that Mrs. C. Mr. E. and his wife, Mr. A.
and others, were capital offenders, and justly imprisoned on a capital account, I do admire that the said Justices should hear of their escape from
prison, and where they are gone and entertained, and yet not send forthwith to the said places, for the surrendering of them, that Justice might be
done them. In other Capitals this has been practiced; why then is it not
practiced in this case, if really judged to be so heinous as is made for?

4. I cannot but admire, that any should go with their distempered friends
and relations to the afflicted children, to know what their distempered friends
ail; whether they are not bewitched; who it is that afflicts them, and the
like. . . .

. . . . .

A person from Boston, of no small note, carried up his child to Salem,
(near 20 miles,) on purpose that he might consult the afflicted about his
child; which accordingly he did; and the afflicted told him, that his child
was afflicted by Mrs. Cary and Mrs. Obinson. The man returned to Boston,
and went forthwith to the Justices for a warrant to seize the said Obinson,
(the said Cary being out of the way); but the Boston Justices saw reason to
deny a warrant. The Rev. Mr. I[ncrease]. M[ather]. of Boston, took occasion
severely to reprove the said man; asking him whether there was not a God
in Boston, that he should go to the Devil in Salem for advice; warning him
very seriously against such naughty practices; which, I hope, proved to the
conviction and good of the said person; if not, his blood will be upon his
own head.

. . . . .

5. I cannot but admire that the Justices, whom I think to be well-mean-
ing men, should so far give ear to the Devil, as merely upon his authority
to issue out their warrants, and apprehend people. Liberty was evermore accounted the great privilege of an Englishman; but certainly, if the Devil will
be heard against us, and his testimony taken, to the seizing and apprehending of us, our liberty vanishes, and we are fools if we boast of our liberty.
Now, that the Justices have thus far given ear to the Devil, I think may be
mathematically demonstrated to any man of common sense: And for the
demonstration and proof hereof, I desire, only, that these two things may
be duly considered, *viz.*

1. That several persons have been apprehended purely upon the complaints of these afflicted, to whom the afflicted were perfect strangers, and
had not the least knowledge of imaginable, before they were apprehended.

2. That the afflicted do own and assert, and the Justices do grant, that
the Devil does inform and tell the afflicted the names of those persons that
are thus unknown unto them. Now these two things being duly considered,

I think it will appear evident to anyone, that the Devil's information is the fundamental testimony that is gone upon in the apprehending of the aforesaid people.

If I believe such or such an assertion as comes immediately from the Minister of God in the pulpit, because it is the word of the everliving God, I build my faith on God's testimony: and if I practice upon it, this my practice is properly built on the word of God: even so in the case before us,

If I believe the afflicted persons as informed by the Devil, and act thereupon, this my act may properly be said to be grounded upon the testimony or information of the Devil. And now, if things are thus, I think it ought to be for a lamentation to you and me, and all such as would be accounted good Christians.

    . . . . .

The chief Judge is very zealous in these proceedings, and says, he is very clear as to all that hath as yet been acted by this Court, and, as far as ever I could perceive, is very impatient in hearing anything that looks another way. I very highly honor and reverence the wisdom and integrity of the said Judge, and hope that this matter shall not diminish my veneration for his honor; however, I cannot but say, my great fear is, that wisdom and counsel are withheld from his honor as to this matter, which yet I look upon not so much as a Judgment to his honor as to this poor land.

But altho' the Chief Judge, and some of the other Judges, be very zealous in these proceedings, yet this you may take for a truth, that there are several about the Bay, men for understanding, Judgment, and Piety, inferior to few, (if any) in N. E. that do utterly condemn the said proceedings, and do freely deliver their Judgment in the case to be this, *viz.* that these methods will utterly ruin and undo poor N. E. I shall nominate some of these to you, *viz.* The hon'ble Simon Bradstreet, Esq. (our late Governor); the hon'ble Thomas Danforth, Esq. (our late Deputy Governor); the Rev'd Mr. Increase Mather, and the Rev'd Mr. Samuel Willard. Major N. Saltonstall, Esq. who was one of the Judges, has left the Court, and is very much dissatisfied with the proceedings of it. Excepting Mr. Hale, Mr. Noyes, and Mr. Parris, the Rev'd Elders, almost throughout the whole Country, are very much dissatisfied. Several of the late Justices, *viz.* Thomas Graves, Esq. N. Byfield, Esq. Francis Foxcroft, Esq. are much dissatisfied; also several of the present Justices; and in particular, some of the Boston Justices, were resolved rather to throw up their commissions than be active in disturbing the liberty of their Majesties' subjects, merely on the accusations of these afflicted, possessed children.

Finally; the principal Gentlemen in Boston, and thereabout, are generally agreed that irregular and dangerous methods have been taken as to these matters.

    . . . . .

Nineteen persons have now been executed, and one pressed to death for a mute: seven more are condemned; two of which are reprieved, because they pretend their being with child; one, *viz.* Mrs. Bradbury of Salisbury, from the intercession of some friends; and two or three more, because they are confessors.

The Court is adjourned to the first Tuesday in November, then to be kept at Salem; between this and then will be [the] great assembly [the General Court], and this matter will be a peculiar matter of their agitation. I think it is matter of earnest supplication and prayer to almighty God, that he would afford his gracious presence to the said assembly, and direct them aright in this weighty matter. Our hopes are here; and if, at this Juncture, God does not graciously appear for us, I think we may conclude that N. E. is undone and undone.

I am very sensible, that it is irksome and disagreeable to go back, when a man's doing so is an implication that he has been walking in a wrong path: however, nothing is more honorable than, upon due conviction, to retract and undo, (so far as may be,) what has been amiss and irregular.

. . . . .

Many of these afflicted persons, who have scores of strange fits in a day, yet in the intervals of time are hale and hearty, robust and lusty, as tho' nothing had afflicted them. I Remember that when the chief Judge gave the first Jury their charge, he told them, that they were not to mind whether the bodies of the said afflicted were really pined and consumed, as was expressed in the indictment; but whether the said afflicted did not suffer from the accused such afflictions as naturally *tended* to their being pined and consumed, wasted, etc. This, (said he,) is a pining and consuming in the sense of the law. I add not.

Furthermore: These afflicted persons do say, and often have declared it, that they can see Specters when their eyes are shut, as well as when they are open. This one thing I evermore accounted as very observable, and that which might serve as a good key to unlock the nature of these mysterious troubles, if duly improved by us. Can they see Specters when their eyes are shut? I am sure they lie, at least speak falsely, if they say so; for the thing, in nature, is an utter impossibility. It is true, they may strongly fancy, or have things represented to their imagination, when their eyes are shut; and I think this is all which ought to be allowed to these blind, nonsensical girls; and if our officers and Courts have apprehended, imprisoned, condemned, and executed our guiltless neighbors, certainly our error is great, and we shall rue it in the conclusion. There are two or three other things that I have observed in and by these afflicted persons, which make me strongly suspect that the Devil imposes upon their brains, and deludes their fancy and imagination; and that the Devil's book (which they say has been offered them) is a mere fancy of theirs, and no reality: That the witches' meeting, the Devil's Baptism, and mock sacraments, which they oft speak of, are nothing else but the effect of their fancy, depraved and deluded by the Devil, and not a Reality to be regarded or minded by any wise man. And whereas the Confessors have owned and asserted the said meetings, the said Baptism, and mock Sacrament, (which the S. G. and some others, make much account of) I am very apt to think, that, did you know the circumstances of the said Confessors, you would not be swayed thereby, any other-wise than to be confirmed, that all is perfect Devilism, and an Hellish design to ruin and destroy this poor land: For whereas there are of the said Confessors 55 in number, some of them are known to be distracted, crazed women, something of which you may see by a petition lately offered to the chief Judge, a copy whereof I may now send you; others of them denied their guilt, and maintained their innocency for above eighteen hours, after most violent, distracting, and draggooning methods had been used with them, to make them confess. Such methods they were, that more than one of the said confessors did since tell many, with tears in their eyes, that they thought their very lives would have gone out of their bodies; and wished that they might have been cast into the lowest dungeon, rather than be tortured with such repeated buzzings and chuckings and unreasonable urgings as they were treated withal.

They soon recanted their confessions, acknowledging, with sorrow and grief, that it was an hour of great temptation with them; and I am very apt to think, that as for five or six of the said confessors, if they are not very good Christian women, it will be no easy matter to find so many good Christian women in N. E. But, finally, as to about thirty of these fifty-five Confessors, they are possessed (I reckon) with the Devil, and afflicted as the children are, and therefore not fit to be regarded as to anything they say of themselves or others. And whereas the S. G. do say that these confessors made their Confessions before they were afflicted, it is absolutely contrary to universal experience, as far as ever I could understand. It is true, that some of these have made their confession before they had their falling, tumbling fits, but yet not absolutely before they had any fits and marks of possession, for (as the S. G. know full well) when these persons were about first confessing, their mouths would be stopped, and their throats affected, as tho' there was danger of strangling, and afterward (it is true) came their tumbling fits. So that, I say, the confessions of these persons were in the beginning of their fits, and not truly before their fits, as the S. G. would make us believe. . . .

What will be the issue of these troubles, God only knows; I am afraid that ages will not wear off that reproach and those stains which these things will leave behind them upon our land. I pray God pity us, Humble us, Forgive us, and appear mercifully for us in this our mount of distress: Herewith I conclude, and subscribe myself,

Reverend Sir, your real friend and humble servant,

T. B.

LEGAL REDRESS

Reversal of Attainder,
October 17, 1711

Reprinted from Woodward, Records of Salem Witchcraft, *Vol. II, pp.* 216-21.

Province of the Massachusetts Bay: Anno Regni Anna Reginae Decimo.

An Act to reverse the attainders of George Burroughs and others for Witchcraft

Forasmuch as in the year of our Lord one Thousand six hundred ninety two several Towns within this Province were Infested with a horrible Witchcraft or possession of devils: And at a Special Court of Oyer and Terminer holden at Salem in the County of Essex in the same year 1692. *George Burroughs* of Wells, *John Proctor, George Jacobs, John Willard, Giles Cory,* and Martha his wife, *Rebecca Nurse* and *Sarah Good* all of Salem aforesaid *Elizabeth How* of Ipswich, *Mary Eastey, Sarah Wildes* and *Abigail Hobbs* all of Topsfield, *Samuel Wardwell, Mary Parker, Martha Carrier, Abigail Faulkner, Anne Foster, Rebecca Eames, Mary Post* and *Mary Lacey* all of Andover, *Mary Bradbury* of Salisbury, and *Dorcas Hoar* of Beverly Were severally Indicted convicted and attainted of Witchcraft, and some of them put to death. others lying still under the like sentence of the said Court, and liable to have the same Executed upon them.

The Influence and Energy of the Evil Spirits so great at that time acting in and upon those who were the principal accusers and Witnesses proceeding so far as to cause a Prosecution to be had of persons of known and good reputation, which caused a great dissatisfaction and a stop to be put thereunto until their Majesties' pleasure should be known therein: And upon a Representation thereof accordingly made her late Majesty Queen Mary the second of blessed memory by Her Royal Letter given at her Court at Whitehall the fifteenth of April 1693. was Graciously pleased to approve the care and Circumspection therein; and to Will and require that in all proceedings against persons accused for Witchcraft, or being possessed by the devil, the greatest Moderation and all due Circumspection be used, so far as the same may be without Impediment to the Ordinary course of Justice.

And some of the principal Accusers and Witnesses in those dark and severe prosecutions have since discovered themselves to be persons of profligate and vicious conversation.

Upon the humble Petition and suit of several of the said persons and of the children of others of them whose Parents were Executed. Be it Declared and Enacted by his Excellency the Governor Council and Representatives in General Court assembled, and by the authority of the same That the several convictions Judgments and Attainders against the said *George*

Burroughs, John Proctor, George Jacobs, John Willard, Giles Cory and *Martha Cory, Rebecca Nurse, Sarah Good, Elizabeth How, Mary Eastey, Sarah Wildes, Abigail Hobbs, Samuel Wardwell, Mary Parker, Martha Carrier, Abigail Faulkner, Anne Foster, Rebecca Eames, Mary Post, Mary Lacey, Mary Bradbury,* and *Dorcas Hoar,* and every of them Be and hereby are reversed made and declared to be null and void to all Intents, Constructions and purposes whatsoever, as if no such convictions Judgments, or Attainders had ever been had or given. And that no penalties or Forfeitures of Goods or Chattels be by the said Judgments and attainders or either of them had or Incurred. Any Law Usage or Custom to the contrary notwithstanding. And that no Sheriff, Constable Jailer or other officer shall be Liable to any prosecution in the Law for anything they then Legally did in the Execution of their respective offices.

Made and passed by the Great and General Court or Assembly of Her Majesty's Province of the Massachusetts Bay in New England held at Boston the 17th day of october. 1711.

Order of Compensation.

By his Excellency the Governor

Whereas the General Assembly in their last session accepted the report of their committee appointed to consider of the Damages sustained by Sundry persons prosecuted for witchcraft in the year 1692 viz

	£	s.	d.		£	s.	d.
To Elizabeth How	12	0	0	John Proctor and wife	150	0	0
George Jacobs	79	0	0	Sarah Wildes	14	0	0
Mary Eastey	20	0	0	Mary Bradbury	20	0	0
Mary Parker	8	0	0	Abigail Faulkner	20	0	0
George Burroughs	50	0	0	Abigail Hobbs	10	0	0
Giles Cory & wife	21	0	0	Anne Foster	6	10	0
Rebecca Nurse	25	0	0	Rebecca Eames	10	0	0
John Willard	20	0	0	Dorcas Hoar	21	17	0
Sarah Good	30	0	0	Mary Post	8	14	0
Martha Carrier	7	6	0	Mary Lacey	8	10	0
Samuel Wardwell							
& wife	36	15	0		269	11	0
					309	1	0
	309	1	0		578	12	0

The whole amounting unto Five hundred seventy eight pounds and Twelve shillings.

I do by & with the advice and consent of her Majesty's council hereby order you to pay the above sum of five hundred seventy eight pounds & twelve shillings to Stephen Sewall Esquire who together with the gentlemen of the Committee that Estimated and Reported the said damages are desired

& directed to distribute the same in proportion as above to such of the said persons as are Living and to those that legally represent them that are dead according as the law directs and for which this shall be your Warrant.

Given under my hand at Boston the 17 Day of December 1711

J Dudley

Resolve of the Massachusetts
General Court, August 28, 1957

Interest in the Salem witchcraft trials revived in the 1950's as many writers, including the dramatist Arthur Miller, sought to trace similarities between the seventeenth-century trials and the congressional investigations of communism that so often made national headlines between 1950 and 1954. A nationwide telecast dramatizing the trial of Ann Pudeator seems to have helped persuade the Massachusetts legislature to take some action.

The following resolve, Chapter 145 from the Resolves of 1957, General Court of the Commonwealth of Massachusetts, does not repeal the seventeenth-century convictions; nor does it recognize that some action to relieve the descendants of executed "witches" was taken in 1711.

RESOLVE RELATIVE TO THE INDICTMENT, TRIAL CONVICTION AND EXECUTION FOR ANN PUDEATOR AND CERTAIN OTHER PERSONS FOR 'WITCHCRAFT' IN THE YEAR SIXTEEN HUNDRED AND NINETY-TWO.

Whereas, One Ann Pudeator and certain other persons were indicted, tried, found guilty, sentenced to death and executed in the year sixteen hundred and ninety-two for 'Witchcraft'; and

Whereas, Said persons may have been illegally tried, convicted and sentenced by a possibly illegal court of oyer and terminer created by the then governor of the Province without authority under the Province Charter of Massachusetts Bay; and

Whereas, Although there was a public repentance by Judge Sewall, one of the judges of the so-called 'Witchcraft Court,' and by all the members of the 'Witchcraft' jury, and a public Fast Day proclaimed and observed in repentance for the proceedings, but no other action taken in regard to them; and

Whereas, The General Court of Massachusetts is informed that certain descendants of said Ann Pudeator and said other persons are still distressed by the record of said proceedings; therefore be it

Resolved, That in order to alleviate such distress and although the facts of such proceedings cannot be obliterated, the General Court of Massachusetts declares its belief that such proceedings, even if lawful under the Province Charter and the law of Massachusetts as it then was, were and are shocking, and the result of a wave of popular hysterical fear of the Devil in the community, and further declares that, as all the laws under which said proceedings, even if then legally conducted, have been long since abandoned and superseded by our more civilized laws no disgrace or cause for distress attaches to the said descendants or any of them by reason of said proceedings; and be it further

Resolved, That the passage of this resolve shall not bestow on the commonwealth or any of its subdivisions, or on any person any right which did not exist prior to said passage, shall not authorize any suit or other proceeding nor deprive any party to a suit or other proceeding of any defense which he hitherto had, shall not affect in any way whatever the title to, or rights in any real or personal property, nor shall it require or permit the remission of any penalty, fine or forfeiture hitherto imposed or incurred.

Approved August 28, 1957.

HISTORICAL FICTION

YOUNG GOODMAN BROWN

By Nathaniel Hawthorne

Nathaniel Hawthorne (1804-1864), a descendant of the John Hathorne who played so vigorous a part in preliminary examinations of the Salem witches, alluded to the witchcraft trials in several of his tales and romances. In "Young Goodman Brown" he used the knowledge he had gained from Cotton Mather's works to create an extremely moving allegory of agonizing doubt and secret sin. Readers familiar with the seventeenth-century documents will recognize not only the specific setting of Salem Village and actual names and charges, but also the care with which Hawthorne's devil amasses spectral evidence for the credulous goodman. The story was first published in 1835. The text below follows Hawthorne's last revision in Mosses from an Old Manse, *Ticknor and Fields, Boston, 1857.*

Young Goodman Brown came forth at sunset into the street of Salem village; but put his head back, after crossing the threshold, to exchange a parting kiss with his young wife. And Faith, as the wife was aptly named, thrust her own pretty head into the street, letting the wind play with the pink ribbons of her cap while she called to Goodman Brown.

"Dearest heart," whispered she, softly and rather sadly, when her lips were close to his ear, "prithee put off your journey until sunrise and sleep in your own bed to-night. A lone woman is troubled with such dreams and such thoughts that she's afeared of herself sometimes. Pray tarry with me this night, dear husband, of all nights in the year."

"My love and my Faith," replied young Goodman Brown, "of all nights in the year, this one night must I tarry away from thee. My journey, as thou callest it, forth and back again, must needs be done 'twixt now and sunrise. What, my sweet, pretty wife, dost thou doubt me already, and we but three months married?"

"Then God bless you!" said Faith, with the pink ribbons; "and may you find all well when you come back."

"Amen!" cried Goodman Brown. "Say thy prayers, dear Faith, and go to bed at dusk, and no harm will come to thee."

So they parted; and the young man pursued his way until, being about to turn the corner by the meeting house, he looked back and saw the head of Faith still peeping after him with a melancholy air, in spite of her pink ribbons.

"Poor little Faith!" thought he, for his heart smote him, "What a wretch am I to leave her on such an errand! She talks of dreams, too. Methought as she spoke there was trouble in her face, as if a dream had warned her what work is to be done to-night. But no, no; 'twould kill her to think it. Well, she's a blessed angel on earth; and after this one night I'll cling to her skirts and follow her to heaven."

With this excellent resolve for the future, Goodman Brown felt himself justified in making more haste on his present evil purpose. He had taken a dreary road, darkened by all the gloomiest trees of the forest, which barely stood aside to let the narrow path creep through, and closed immediately behind. It was all as lonely as could be; and there is this peculiarity in such a solitude, that the traveller knows not who may be concealed by the innumerable trunks and the thick boughs overhead; so that with lonely footsteps he may yet be passing through an unseen multitude.

"There may be a devilish Indian behind every tree," said Goodman Brown to himself; and he glanced fearfully behind him as he added, "What if the devil himself should be at my very elbow!"

His head being turned back, he passed a crook of the road, and, looking forward again, beheld the figure of a man, in grave and decent attire, seated at the foot of an old tree. He arose at Goodman Brown's approach and walked onward side by side with him.

"You are late, Goodman Brown," said he. "The clock of the Old South was striking as I came through Boston;[1] and that is full fifteen minutes agone."

"Faith kept me back a while," replied the young man, with a tremor in his voice, caused by the sudden appearance of his companion, though not wholly unexpected.

It was now deep dusk in the forest, and deepest in that part of it where these two were journeying. As nearly as could be discerned, the second traveller was about fifty years old, apparently in the same rank of life as Goodman Brown, and bearing a considerable resemblance to him, though perhaps more in expression than features. Still they might have been taken for father and son. And yet, though the elder person was as simply clad as the younger and as simple in manner too, he had an indescribable air of one who knew the world, and who would not have felt abashed at the governor's dinner table or in King William's court, were it possible that his affairs should call him thither. But the only thing about him that could be fixed upon as remarkable was his staff, which bore the likeness of a great black snake, so curiously wrought that it might almost be seen to twist and wriggle itself like a living serpent. This, of course, must have been an ocular deception, assisted by the uncertain light.

"Come, Goodman Brown," cried his fellow-traveller, "this is a dull pace for the beginning of a journey. Take my staff, if you are so soon weary."

[1] That is, from 20 to 30 miles away.

"Friend," said the other, exchanging his slow pace for a full stop, "having kept covenant by meeting thee here, it is my purpose now to return whence I came. I have scruples touching the matter thou wot'st of."

"Sayest thou so?" replied he of the serpent, smiling apart. "Let us walk on, nevertheless, reasoning as we go; and if I convince thee not thou shalt turn back. We are but a little way in the forest yet."

"Too far! too far!" exclaimed the goodman, unconsciously resuming his walk. "My father never went into the woods on such an errand, nor his father before him. We have been a race of honest men and good Christians since the days of the martyrs; and shall I be the first of the name of Brown that ever took this path and kept—"

"Such company, thou wouldst say," observed the elder person, interpreting his pause. "Well said, Goodman Brown! I have been as well acquainted with your family as with ever a one among the Puritans; and that's no trifle to say. I helped your grandfather, the constable, when he lashed the Quaker woman so smartly through the streets of Salem; and it was I that brought your father a pitch-pine knot, kindled at my own hearth, to set fire to an Indian village, in King Philip's war. They were my good friends, both; and many a pleasant walk have we had along this path, and returned merrily after midnight. I would fain be friends with you for their sake."

"If it be as thou sayest," replied Goodman Brown, "I marvel they never spoke of these matters; or, verily, I marvel not, seeing that the least rumor of the sort would have driven them from New England. We are a people of prayer, and good works to boot, and abide no such wickedness."

"Wickedness or not," said the traveller with the twisted staff, "I have a very general acquaintance here in New England. The deacons of many a church have drunk the communion wine with me; the selectmen of divers towns make me their chairman; and a majority of the Great and General Court are firm supporters of my interest. The governor and I, too— But these are state secrets."

"Can this be so?" cried Goodman Brown, with a stare of amazement at his undisturbed companion. "Howbeit, I have nothing to do with the governor and council; they have their own ways, and are no rule for a simple husbandman like me. But, were I to go on with thee, how should I meet the eye of that good old man, our minister, at Salem village? Oh, his voice would make me tremble both Sabbath day and lecture day."

Thus far the elder traveller had listened with due gravity; but now burst into a fit of irrepressible mirth, shaking himself so violently that his snake-like staff actually seemed to wriggle in sympathy.

"Ha! ha! ha!" shouted he again and again; then composing himself. "Well, go on, Goodman Brown, go on; but, prithee, don't kill me with laughing."

"Well, then, to end the matter at once," said Goodman Brown, considerably nettled, "there is my wife, Faith. It would break her dear little heart; and I'd rather break my own."

"Nay, if that be the case," answered the other, "e'en go thy ways, Goodman Brown. I would not for twenty old women like the one hobbling before us that Faith should come to any harm."

As he spoke, he pointed his staff at a female figure on the path, in whom Goodman Brown recognized a very pious and exemplary dame, who had taught him his catechism in youth, and was still his moral and spiritual adviser, jointly with the minister and Deacon Gookin.

"A marvel, truly, that Goody Cloyse should be so far in the wilderness at nightfall," said he. "But, with your leave, friend, I shall take a cut through the woods until we have left this Christian woman behind. Being a stranger to you, she might ask whom I was consorting with and whither I was going."

"Be it so," said his fellow-traveller. "Betake you to the woods, and let me keep the path."

Accordingly the young man turned aside, but took care to watch his companion, who advanced softly along the road until he had come within a staff's length of the old dame. She, meanwhile, was making the best of her way, with singular speed for so aged a woman, and mumbling some indistinct words—a prayer, doubtless—as she went. The traveller put forth his staff and touched her withered neck with what seemed the serpent's tail.

"The devil!" screamed the pious old lady.

"Then Goody Cloyse knows her old friend?" observed the traveller, confronting her and leaning on his writhing stick.

"Ah, forsooth, and is it your worship indeed?" cried the good dame. "Yea, truly is it, and in the very image of my old gossip, Goodman Brown, the grandfather of the silly fellow that now is. But—would your worship believe it?—my broomstick hath strangely disappeared, stolen, as I suspect, by that unhanged witch, Goody Cory, and that, too, when I was all anointed with the juice of smallage, and cinquefoil, and wolf's bane—"

"Mingled with fine wheat and the fat of a new-born babe," said the shape of old Goodman Brown.

"Ah, your worship knows the recipe," cried the old lady, cackling aloud. "So, as I was saying, being all ready for the meeting, and no horse to ride on, I made up my mind to foot it; for they tell me there is a nice young man to be taken into communion to-night. But now your good worship will lend me your arm, and we shall be there in a twinkling."

"That can hardly be," answered her friend. "I may not spare you my arm, Goody Cloyse; but here is my staff, if you will."

So saying, he threw it down at her feet, where, perhaps, it assumed life, being one of the rods which its owner had formerly lent to the Egyptian magi. Of this fact, however, Goodman Brown could not take cognizance. He had cast up his eyes in astonishment, and, looking down again, beheld neither Goody Cloyse nor the serpentine staff, but his fellow-traveller alone, who waited for him as calmly as if nothing had happened.

"That old woman taught me my catechism," said the young man; and there was a world of meaning in this simple comment.

They continued to walk onward, while the elder traveller exhorted his companion to make good speed and persevere in the path, discoursing so aptly that his arguments seemed rather to spring up in the bosom of his auditor than to be suggested by himself. As they went, he plucked a branch of maple to serve for a walking stick, and began to strip it of the twigs and little boughs, which were wet with evening dew. The moment his fingers touched them they became strangely withered and dried up as with a week's sunshine. Thus the pair proceeded, at a good free pace, until suddenly, in a gloomy hollow of the road, Goodman Brown sat himself down on the stump of a tree and refused to go any farther.

"Friend," said he, stubbornly, "my mind is made up. Not another step will I budge on this errand. What if a wretched old woman do choose to go to the devil when I thought she was going to heaven: is that any reason why I should quit my dear Faith and go after her?"

"You will think better of this by and by," said his acquaintance, composedly. "Sit here and rest yourself a while; and when you feel like moving again, there is my staff to help you along."

Without more words, he threw his companion the maple stick, and was as speedily out of sight as if he had vanished into the deepening gloom. The young man sat a few moments by the roadside, applauding himself greatly, and thinking with how clear a conscience he should meet the minister in his morning walk, nor shrink from the eye of good old Deacon Gookin. And what calm sleep would be his that very night, which was to have been spent so wickedly, but so purely and sweetly now, in the arms of Faith! Amidst these pleasant and praiseworthy meditations, Goodman Brown heard the tramp of horses along the road, and deemed it advisable to conceal himself within the verge of the forest, conscious of the guilty purpose that had brought him thither, though now so happily turned from it.

On came the hoof tramps and the voices of the riders, two grave old voices, conversing soberly as they drew near. These mingled sounds appeared to pass along the road, within a few yards of the young man's hiding-place; but, owing doubtless to the depth of the gloom at that particular spot, neither the travellers nor their steeds were visible. Though their figures brushed the small boughs by the wayside, it could not be seen that they intercepted, even for a moment, the faint gleam from the strip of bright sky athwart which they must have passed. Goodman Brown alternately crouched and stood on tiptoe, pulling aside the branches and thrusting forth his head as far as he durst without discerning so much as a shadow. It vexed him the more, because he could have sworn, were such a thing possible, that he recognized the voices of the minister and Deacon Gookin, jogging along quietly, as they were wont to do, when bound to some ordination or ecclesiastical council. While yet within hearing, one of the riders stopped to pluck a switch.

"Of the two, reverend sir," said the voice like the deacon's, "I had rather miss an ordination dinner than to-night's meeting. They tell me that some of our community are to be here from Falmouth and beyond, and others from Connecticut and Rhode Island, besides several of the Indian powwows, who, after their fashion, know almost as much deviltry as the best of us. Moreover, there is a goodly young woman to be taken into communion."

"Mighty well, Deacon Gookin!" replied the solemn old tones of the minister. "Spur up, or we shall be late. Nothing can be done, you know, until I get on the ground."

The hoofs clattered again; and the voices, talking so strangely in the empty air, passed on through the forest, where no church had ever been gathered or solitary Christian prayed. Whither, then, could these holy men be journeying so deep into the heathen wilderness? Young Goodman Brown caught hold of a tree for support, being ready to sink down on the ground, faint and overburdened with the heavy sickness of his heart. He looked up to the sky, doubting whether there really was a heaven above him. Yet there was the blue arch, and the stars brightening in it.

"With heaven above and Faith below, I will yet stand firm against the devil!" cried Goodman Brown.

While he still gazed upward into the deep arch of the firmament and had lifted his hands to pray, a cloud, though no wind was stirring, hurried across the zenith and hid the brightening stars. The blue sky was still visible, except directly overhead, where this black mass of cloud was sweeping swiftly northward. Aloft in the air, as if from the depths of the cloud, came a confused and doubtful sound of voices. Once the listener fancied that he could distinguish the accents of townspeople of his own, men and women, both pious and ungodly, many of whom he had met at the communion table, and had seen others rioting at the tavern. The next moment, so indistinct were the sounds, he doubted whether he had heard aught but the murmur of the old forest, whispering without a wind. Then came a stronger swell of those familiar tones, heard daily in the sunshine at Salem village, but never until now from a cloud of night. There was one voice, of a young woman, uttering lamentations, yet with an uncertain sorrow, and entreating for some favor, which, perhaps, it would grieve her to obtain; and all the unseen multitude, both saints and sinners, seemed to encourage her onward.

"Faith!" shouted Goodman Brown, in a voice of agony and desperation; and the echoes of the forest mocked him, crying, "Faith! Faith!" as if bewildered wretches were seeking her all through the wilderness.

The cry of grief, rage, and terror was yet piercing the night, when the unhappy husband held his breath for a response. There was a scream, drowned immediately in a louder murmur of voices, fading into far-off laughter, as the dark cloud swept away, leaving the clear and silent sky above Goodman Brown. But something fluttered lightly down through the air and caught on the branch of a tree. The young man seized it, and beheld a pink ribbon.

"My Faith is gone!" cried he, after one stupefied moment. "There is no good on earth; and sin is but a name. Come, devil; for to thee is this world given."

And, maddened with despair, so that he laughed loud and long, did Goodman Brown grasp his staff and set forth again, at such a rate that he seemed to fly along the forest path rather than to walk or run. The road grew wilder and drearier and more faintly traced, and vanished at length, leaving him in the heart of the dark wilderness, still rushing onward with the instinct that guides mortal man to evil. The whole forest was peopled with frightful sounds—the creaking of the trees, the howling of wild beasts, and the yell of Indians; while sometimes the wind tolled like a distant church bell, and sometimes gave a broad roar around the traveller, as if all Nature were laughing him to scorn. But he was himself the chief horror of the scene, and shrank not from its other horrors.

"Ha! ha! ha!" roared Goodman Brown when the wind laughed at him. "Let us hear which will laugh loudest. Think not to frighten me with your deviltry. Come witch, come wizard, come Indian powwow, come devil himself, and here comes Goodman Brown. You may as well fear him as he fear you."

In truth, all through the haunted forest there could be nothing more frightful than the figure of Goodman Brown. On he flew among the black pines, brandishing his staff with frenzied gestures, now giving vent to an inspiration of horrid blasphemy, and now shouting forth such laughter as set all the echoes of the forest laughing like demons around him. The fiend in his own shape is less hideous than when he rages in the breast of man. Thus sped the demoniac on his course, until, quivering among the trees, he saw a red light before him, as when the felled trunks and branches of a clearing have been set on fire, and throw up their lurid blaze against the sky, at the hour of midnight. He paused, in a lull of the tempest that had driven him onward, and heard the swell of what seemed a hymn, rolling solemnly from a distance with the weight of many voices. He knew the tune; it was a familiar one in the choir of the village meeting house. The verse died heavily away, and was lengthened by a chorus, not of human voices, but of all the sounds of the benighted wilderness pealing in awful harmony together. Goodman Brown cried out; and his cry was lost to his own ear by its unison with the cry of the desert.

In the interval of silence he stole forward until the light glared full upon his eyes. At one extremity of an open space, hemmed in by the dark wall of the forest, arose a rock, bearing some rude, natural resemblance either to an altar or a pulpit, and surrounded by four blazing pines, their tops aflame, their stems untouched, like candles at an evening meeting. The mass of foliage that had overgrown the summit of the rock was all on fire, blazing high into the night and fitfully illuminating the whole field. Each pendent twig and leafy festoon was in a blaze. As the red light arose and fell, a numerous congregation alternately shone forth, then disappeared in shadow, and again grew, as it were, out of the darkness, peopling the heart of the solitary woods at once.

"A grave and dark-clad company," quoth Goodman Brown.

In truth they were such. Among them, quivering to and fro between gloom and splendor, appeared faces that would be seen next day at the council board of the province, and others which, Sabbath after Sabbath, looked devoutly heavenward, and benignantly over the crowded pews, from the holiest pulpits in the land. Some affirm that the lady of the governor was there. At least there were high dames well known to her, and wives of honored husbands, and widows, a great multitude, and ancient maidens, all of excellent repute, and fair young girls, who trembled lest their mothers should espy them. Either the sudden gleams of light flashing over the obscure field bedazzled Goodman Brown, or he recognized a score of the church members of Salem village famous for their especial sanctity. Good old Deacon Gookin had arrived, and waited at the skirts of that venerable saint, his revered pastor. But, irreverently consorting with these grave, reputable, and pious people, these elders of the church, these chaste dames and dewy virgins, there were men of dissolute lives and women of spotted fame, wretches given over to all mean and filthy vice, and suspected even of horrid crimes. It was strange to see that the good shrank not from the wicked, nor were the sinners abashed by the saints. Scattered also among their palefaced enemies were the Indian priests, or powwows, who had often scared their native forest with more hideous incantations than any known to English witchcraft.

"But where is Faith?" thought Goodman Brown; and, as hope came into his heart, he trembled.

Another verse of the hymn arose, a slow and mournful strain, such as the pious love, but joined to words which expressed all that our nature can conceive of sin, and darkly hinted at far more. Unfathomable to mere mortals is the lore of fiends. Verse after verse was sung; and still the chorus of the desert swelled between like the deepest tone of a mighty organ; and with the final peal of that dreadful anthem there came a sound, as if the roaring wind, the rushing streams, the howling beasts, and every other voice of the unconverted wilderness were mingling and according with the voice of guilty man in homage to the prince of all. The four blazing pines threw up a loftier flame, and obscurely discovered shapes and visages of horror on the smoke wreaths above the impious assembly. At the same moment the fire on the rock shot redly forth and formed a glowing arch above its base, where now appeared a figure. With reverence be it spoken, the figure bore no slight similitude, both in garb and manner, to some grave divine of the New England churches.

"Bring forth the converts!" cried a voice that echoed through the field and rolled into the forest.

At the word, Goodman Brown stepped forth from the shadow of the trees and approached the congregation, with whom he felt a loathful brotherhood by the sympathy of all that was wicked in his heart. He could have well nigh sworn that the shape of his own dead father beckoned him to advance, looking downward from a smoke wreath, while a woman, with dim features of despair, threw out her hand to warn him back. Was it his mother? But he had no power to retreat one step, nor to resist, even in thought, when the minister and good old Deacon Gookin seized his arms and led him to the blazing rock. Thither came also the slender form of a veiled female, led between Goody Cloyse, that pious teacher of the catechism, and Martha Carrier, who had received the devil's promise to be queen of hell. A rampant hag was she. And there stood the proselytes beneath the canopy of fire.

"Welcome, my children," said the dark figure, "to the communion of your race. Ye have found thus young your nature and your destiny. My children, look behind you!"

They turned; and flashing forth, as it were, in a sheet of flame, the fiend worshippers were seen; the smile of welcome gleamed darkly on every visage.

"There," resumed the sable form, "are all whom ye have reverenced from youth. Ye deemed them holier than yourselves, and shrank from your own sin, contrasting it with their lives of righteousness and prayerful aspirations heavenward. Yet here are they all in my worshipping assembly. This night it shall be granted you to know their secret deeds; how hoary-bearded elders of the church have whispered wanton words to the young maids of their households; how many a woman, eager for widows' weeds, has given her husband a drink at bedtime and let him sleep his last sleep in her bosom; how beardless youths have made haste to inherit their fathers' wealth; and how fair damsels—blush not, sweet ones—have dug little graves in the garden, and bidden me, the sole guest, to an infant's funeral. By the sympathy of your human hearts for sin ye shall scent out all the places—whether in church, bed chamber, street, field, or forest—where crime has been committed, and shall exult to behold the whole earth one stain of guilt, one mighty blood spot. Far more than this. It shall be yours to penetrate, in every bosom, the deep mystery of sin, the fountain of all wicked arts, and which inexhaustibly supplies more evil impulses than human power—than my power at its utmost—can make manifest in deeds. And now, my children, look upon each other."

They did so; and, by the blaze of the hell-kindled torches, the wretched man beheld his Faith, and the wife her husband, trembling before that unhallowed altar.

"Lo, there ye stand, my children," said the figure, in a deep and solemn tone, almost sad with its despairing awfulness, as if his once angelic nature could yet mourn for our miserable race. "Depending upon one another's hearts, ye had still hoped that virtue were not all a dream. Now are ye undeceived. Evil is the nature of mankind. Evil must be your only happiness. Welcome again, my children, to the communion of your race."

"Welcome," repeated the fiend worshippers, in one cry of despair and triumph.

And there they stood, the only pair, as it seemed, who were yet hesitating on the verge of wickedness in this dark world. A basin was hollowed, naturally, in the rock. Did it contain water, reddened by the lurid light? or was it blood? or, perchance, a liquid flame? Herein did the shape of evil dip his hand and prepare to lay the mark of baptism upon their foreheads, that they might be partakers of the mystery of sin, more conscious of the secret guilt of others, both in deed and thought, than they could now be of their own. The husband cast one look at his pale wife, and Faith at him. What polluted wretches would the next glance show them to each other, shuddering alike at what they disclosed and what they saw!

"Faith! Faith!" cried the husband, "look up to heaven, and resist the wicked one."

Whether Faith obeyed, he knew not. Hardly had he spoken when he found himself amid calm night and solitude, listening to a roar of the wind which died heavily away through the forest. He staggered against the rock, and felt it chill and damp; while a hanging twig, that had been all on fire, besprinkled his cheek with the coldest dew.

The next morning young Goodman Brown came slowly into the street of Salem village, staring around him like a bewildered man. The good old minister was taking a walk along the graveyard to get an appetite for breakfast and meditate his sermon, and bestowed a blessing, as he passed, on Goodman Brown. He shrank from the venerable saint as if to avoid an anathema. Old Deacon Gookin was at domestic worship, and the holy words of his prayer were heard through the open window. "What God doth the wizard pray to?" quoth Goodman Brown. Goody Cloyse, that excellent old Christian, stood in the early sunshine at her own lattice, catechizing a little girl who had brought her a pint of morning's milk. Goodman Brown snatched away the child as from the grasp of the fiend himself. Turning the corner by the meeting house, he spied the head of Faith, with the pink ribbons, gazing anxiously forth, and bursting into such joy at sight of him that she skipped along the street and almost kissed her husband before the whole village. But Goodman Brown looked sternly and sadly into her face, and passed on without a greeting.

Had Goodman Brown fallen asleep in the forest and only dreamed a wild dream of a witch meeting?

Be it so, if you will; but, alas! it was a dream of evil omen for young Goodman Brown. A stern, a sad, a darkly meditative, a distrustful, if not a desperate, man did he become from the night of that fearful dream. On the Sabbath day, when the congregation were singing a holy psalm, he could not listen, because an anthem of sin rushed loudly upon his ear and drowned all the blessed strain. When the minister spoke from the pulpit, with power and fervid eloquence and with his hand on the open Bible, of the sacred truths of our religion, and of saintlike lives and triumphant deaths, and of future bliss or misery unutterable, then did Goodman Brown turn pale, dreading lest the roof should thunder down upon the gray blasphemer and his hearers. Often, awaking suddenly at midnight, he shrank from the bosom of Faith; and at morning or eventide, when the family knelt down at prayer, he scowled, and muttered to himself, and gazed sternly at his wife, and turned away. And when he had lived long, and was borne to his grave a hoary corpse, followed by Faith, an aged woman, and children and grandchildren, a goodly procession, besides neighbors not a few, they carved no hopeful verse upon his tombstone; for his dying hour was gloom.

A MIRROR
FOR WITCHES

in which
is reflected the Life, Machinations, and Death of Famous
DOLL BILBY, who, with a more than *feminine perversity*,
preferred a Demon to a Mortal Lover. Here is also told
how and why a Righteous and Most Awfull JUDGE-
MENT befell her, destroying both Corporeal Body and
Immortal Soul.

By Esther Forbes

*Esther Forbes is a distinguished historical novelist who has also won a
Pulitzer Prize in biography. In* A Mirror for Witches *(published by
Houghton Mifflin in 1928 and reissued in 1954), she created a beautiful
novel that deserves careful study as an example of historical fiction. Her
exploitation of the historical facts, her control of point of view and
language, and her characterization can be profitably studied in comparison with Hawthorne's.*

CHAPTER ONE

I

*Certain Examples to Show Doll Bilby not alone among Women in her prefer-
ence for Evil. The Cases of Ry, Goose, Leda, Danaë, etc., cited.*

It has long been known that, on occasions, devils in the shape of humanity
or in their own shapes (that is, with horns, hoofs, and tails) may fancy mortal
women. By dark arts, sly promises of power, flattery, etc., they may prevail even
upon Christian women, always to the destruction of these women's souls and
often to that of their bodies.

A Mirror for Witches by Esther Forbes. Reprinted from the second edition, Houghton
Mifflin, Boston and New York, 1954. Copyright, 1928, by Esther Forbes Hoskins. Re-
newal copyright, 1956. All rights reserved. Used by permission of the author.

For in Northumberland, Meslie Ry was burned in 1616 because she had taken a fiend to love.

A few years later, Christie Goose, a single woman upwards of forty years, suddenly flew lunatic—and that upon the Lord's Day. Then she did confess that each night and every night the Devil, wickedly assuming the shape of Mr. Oates, God's minister at Crumplehorn, Oxon., came to her through her window. This fact amazed Crumplehorn, for Goose was of all women most pious, and had sat for years in humble prayerfulness at the feet of Mr. Oates. Some were astonished that even a devil should find need for this same Goose, who was of hideous aspect.

There was a young jade, servant in an alderman's house in London, who, although she confessed nothing and remained obdurate to the end, was hanged and then burned because she bore a creature with horns on its head and a six-inch tail behind. Such a creature the just magistrates determined no mortal man might beget, although the saucy wench suggested that an alderman might. Moreover, certain children in the neighbourhood testified that they had twice or thrice seen "a burly big black man" sitting on the ridgepole.

Some assume that as the gods of antiquity were in no way gods (being seekers after evil—not after light), they should therefore be considered cacodemons or devils. The Reverend Pyam Plover, of Boston, has written learnedly on this subject, saying, in part, "For is it not possible that the Lord God of Israel, being those days but the God of *Israel,* may have permitted certain of his Fallen Angels to stray from the vitals of Hell and disport themselves through Greece and ancient Italy? Here they revealed themselves . . . in many ways to heathen people, who falsely worshipped them as *gods.* If this be true Zeus might better assume his true name of *Satan,* and let us call Apollo but *Apollyon* and recognize in Mars, Hermes, etc., Beelzebub and Belial. Then may the female 'divinities' be true descendants of Lilith." So one may learn from antiquity (consider Leda, Io, Danaë, and others) how great is the ardour felt by devils for mortal women.

As is not yet forgotten, in 1662, near threescore years ago, a woman called Greensmith, living at Hartford in New England, confessed the Devil had carnal knowledge of her. For this she was hanged.

More strangely yet, lived, for brief space of years, famous Doll Bilby, best known as "Bilby's Doll." She flourished at Cowan Corners, close by the town of Salem, but an afternoon's journey from my own parish of Sudbury. Of other women devil-ridden, be it Leda or Ry, Greensmith or Danaë, Christie Goose or La Voisin, little can be said, for but little is known. All were witches (if we accept as witches such women as traffic with fiends), but little else is known. Yet of Bilby's famous Doll, in the end all things were known. From old wives' tales, court records, and the diaries of certain men, from the sworn affidavits and depositions of others, from the demonologies of Mr. Cotton Mather, and the cipher journal of Mr. Zacharias Zelley, we may know with a nicety what this woman was and how she lived, from whence she came, how she grew to witchcraft, how she felt, thought, and at the last how she died.

2

Mr. Bilby sails far to seek out TROUBLE, *and, having found Trouble, nurtures it.*

She was born of a wicked witch-woman and begotten by one who was no better, that is, by a warlock. These two devil-worshippers and, they say, two hundred more were burned in one great holocaust at Mont Hoël in Brittany. Black smoke, screams of death, stench of flesh settled down over town and harbour, causing sickness and even vomiting.

On that same day, by evil fortune, a brig manned by Dawlish men stood in the Bouche de Saint-Hoël. These men, seeing that it was fête day, and curious because of the smoke, the screams, and the stench, went to the holocaust. There they saw a wild child, more animal or goblin than human being. This wild child would have followed her mother, who burned in the heart of the fire, if soldiers had not pushed her back. A priest bade the soldiers let her pass to death, for, being of witch-people, she would undoubtedly burn sooner or later. The Englishmen protested, and Mr. Jared Bilby, captain and owner of the brig, caught and held the wild child, who did not struggle against him as she had against the soldiers. Instead she held fast to him, for even the wicked may recognize goodness. The priest showed his yellow fangs at the Dawlish men. He hated and scorned them. "Take the child and be gone. She was born of a witch-woman and will grow to witchcraft and do much harm—but in England among the heretics. Be gone."

The child clung to Mr. Bilby and he to her. He took her in his arms, and she lay corpse-pale and glass-eyed like one about to die. This men remembered. When he put her down upon the deck of the brig, he was badly sweated as though his burden had been more than he, a strong young man, might bear. He told his men the child weighed as though a child of stone. Some thought that his heart mistook him, and that he already regretted the acceptance of so dangerous a gift.

Gathering his men about him and having prayed, he gave thanks to Jehovah, Who, although He had never given him a child of his own body, yet had seen fit to send this poor little one to him. Then he bade his men keep their tongues behind their teeth, telling no one from whence was this child (which in the future should be his child), nor the manner of her parents' death, nor the harm which the priest swore she should live to perform. This promise his men kept for years, but in the end, when they were old men, they preferred to serve Gossip and Scandal rather than a kind master, long, long dead.

For days the child lay like death, only occasionally jumping madly from her pallet, screaming "Le feu! Le feu! Le feu!" [2] then falling back, covering her face with her hands and laughing horribly. The captain coaxed and petted her, urged her to eat, and quieted her with his hands. So by love he restored her to humanity.

Because of her small size he called her "Doll," which name she well lived up to, never acquiring the height and weight of other women. No one

---

[2] "The fire! The fire! The fire!"

ever knew her real age. She may have been seven or perhaps six when she first came to England. Being unable to talk English and at first unable to serve herself, she may have seemed younger than she was. Yet, on the other hand, Fear, Grief, and Sickness often make their Hosts appear older than the fact.

Mr. Bilby believed that the shock of her parents' death (for they were burned before her eyes, her mother crying out to her most piteously from the midst of flame) had broken the reins of memory. He thought she had forgotten everything that lay back of her reawakening to life on board his brig, which was called God's Mercy. Also he comforted himself with the belief that if—as might be—she had learned any little tricks of witchery, or if she had ever been taken to Sabbat or Black Mass, or if she had looked upon the Prince of Hell, or even if (being led on by her parents) she had sworn to serve him, she would have forgotten all these things. She was born again and this time of God and to God, whom Mr. Bilby piously swore she should serve—Him and Him alone. The child had been so vehemently frightened she had forgotten all good and needful things, how to dress herself, how to eat with knife and spoon. She had forgotten the language of her birth.

But of evil she remembered everything.

3

He brings the Foundling to his own hearth and to the bosom of his Goodwife. There the goblin-child rewards Kindness and Mercy with Malediction and Evil. She overlooks the Goodwife.

Hannah, wife of Jared Bilby, would not accept her sterility with Christian fortitude. She railed against the wisdom of God, saying, "Mrs. Such-and-Such is but half so big and fine a woman as I, yet she has three sons. Goody This-and-That, the jade, can find but little favour in the eyes of her Maker, yet, to *her* He sends more children than she can feed; but I, a pious, godly, praying woman, remain barren." Which, she wickedly averred, showed the injustice of Divinity. However, by curious chance or mischance, soon after Mr. Bilby set out with his men and brig for the coasts of France and Spain, she found herself with child. Some say the Lord tired of her railing, and, to punish her, first raised up her hopes and then sent Doll to blight them for her.

Summer wore away. The nights grew chill. She was four months with child. Then Mr. Bilby, late one evening, came to Dawlish harbour. With him was his goblin-child, now grown pretty and playful. He arrived home in the black of the night and through pelting rain. The child he carried wrapped in his greatcoat to protect her from the cruel storm. He shook the shutter which he knew was by his wife's bedboard.

"Woman, woman, get up and open to me."

The woman lay for warmth with her servant wench, Susan Croker. The fury of the night shewed forth the grandeur of God. The wind howled above the beating of the rain. Croker cried to her mistress not to open the door on such a night. It could be no living man who knocked, for it is on such vexed and angry nights as these the sea gives up its dead.

Hannah was a fearless woman. She got quickly to the door, unbarred it, and, in a deluge of wind and wet, Mr. Bilby entered with his burden. Her heart mistook her. She cried out, "Jared, what have you there in that great bundle?" So he took it to the hearth and, as the women knelt, throwing kindling on the fire, he opened the bundle and out popped the goblin-child. She shuddered away from the fire (a thing she a[l]ways feared) and clutched her foster father with her little hands, gazing into his face with round black eyes. Every thread of her spikey hair was tumbled up on end. The women cried in horror that this was no child. This was an imp, a monkcy, a pug. But Jared Bilby on his knees protected the foundling, both from the fire and the women's angry glances. He soothed her with his body and kind words, "Ah, the fire would never devour her." He was here, and he would never leave her. She was his child, etc. He would always love and cherish her—and the like. The child pushed her tously head under his chin and frozc into stillness.

Susan Croker told many that, from the beginning, the child bewitched him. Nor did the affection which Bilby gave his Doll ever seem like the love which men feel to their children, but rather the darker and often unholy passion which is evoked by mature, or almost mature women—a passion which witches, when young and comely, have often engendered with ferocious intensity. As long as he lived he was forever stroking her shaggy black hair, looking lovingly into those button-round eyes, and kissing a wide hobgoblin mouth which many a Christian would fear to kiss. Hannah was a lusty, jealous woman who could not abide such mean rivalry as that of a foundling child. The woman, who had always been a gossiping wife, now, under the baleful influence of Doll, seemed like to become a shrew. She was steely set in her hatred of the child, although she fed her, gave her a corner to sleep in, and taught her some small prayers. With her the child seemed dull, indifferent, but with Mr. Bilby she was merry, playful, and loving. So the one thought her a knowing child and the other a zany.

Mr. Bilby would not tell his wife where he had found Doll, but it did trouble him that the woman so cunningly insisted that either she was the child of a witch or the begotten of the Devil. Even Susan Croker, who was kind to the foundling, had horrid suspicions of her. She could not teach Doll the noble, sonorous lines of Our Lord's Prayer, although the imp was quick to learn worthless things, such as "This Little Pig Goes to Market" or "A Cat Comes Fiddling Out of the Barn."

The child, having been in the house a month, there occurred a chance to show what she could do—that is, what evil she could do.

4

Doll covets a ship for a toy and the whole of her Foster Father's love. She nefariously gains her ends and slays a Dangerous Rival.

The midwife promised Hannah a great thumping boy handsome as his mother, strong as his father. He should either wear the bands of the clergy or walk the quarter-deck of the king's navy. Because her husband favoured the nautical life for his unborn son, he made him a rattle in the shape of a ship. In the hull were seven balls which, when the ship was shaken, rattled. Now Doll was forever leaning against his knees and watching him as he carved out this bauble. As one after another of the seven balls were liberated in the heart of the wood, she would laugh and gloat. It was not a toy for her, but for him who should (according to nature) supplant her in her foster father's love. In her evil heart she must have brooded on these things and come to hate this other child that would possess the ship and Bilby's affection. Her hands were always outstretched to the rattle and she cried, "Give, give, give."

One day as they were thus—man and child—Hannah came in from the milk-house. The woman was jealous—not only for her own sake, but for the sake of the unborn. "For," she thought, "what shall he, who gives all to a foundling, have left for his own son? Not only has this wicked girl turned him away from me, but she takes the rightful place of his own child." Then she said:

"It is not well that a woman in my condition should be exposed to contrary and evil influences. Jared, send away your 'pretty pet'; give her to the wife of your ship's cook to keep—at least until I am delivered. Many wiser than I, yes, and wiser than you . . ." Her jaw swung loose as though broke. Her teeth stuck out, her eyes bulged, for the goblin-child, through her mat of hair and out of her wild bright eyes, was staring at her. She stared and moved her lips in a whisper, then she skipped across the room, grinning in diabolical glee. Mrs. Hannah felt the curse go through her. The babe in her womb moved in its wretchedness, and was blasted. The woman felt its tiny soul flutter to her lips and escape. She knew that Doll (being of some infernal origin) could see this same soul, and she guessed, from the roving of her eyes, how it clung for a moment to its mother's lips, how it flew to the Bible upon the stand (in which its name would never be recorded), how it poised upon the window-sill, then, unborn and frustrated, it departed to whatever Paradise or Hell God prepares for such half-formed souls. Hannah began to screech and wail, then fell back upon the bed in a swoon.

The body of the unborn child shrivelled within her, and, when a male midwife was called from Dawlish, he said she had been but full of air. She never was again with child. Some said (and Captain Bilby among them) that she never had been—even on the 'bove-related most famous occasion.

But if, as the most informed and thoughtful have said, the blasting of Hannah's infant was indeed a fact, then we have to hand, and early in the life history of Doll Bilby, an actual case of witchcraft. And is it likely such monstrous power (blasting unborn life with a glance or at most a muttered curse) should be given to any one who had not already set her name to the Devil's Book, and compacted herself to Hell?

5

The New Land holds greater promise than the Old. Mr. Bilby, Ux et filia say fare-you-well to England and take up residence close to Salem and not far from Boston, in the Bay Colony. They prosper. The child grows an evil pace.

In those days England offered little peace to men (like Captain Bilby) who would worship God in their own way, and in accordance with His own holy teachings and the dictates of their own hearts—not according to teachings of bishops or priests. So Mr. Bilby often yearned towards that newer land which lay far west beyond the Atlantic. In time he sold his brig, God's Mercy, and his freehold. The agent of the Bay Colony, in his office at Maiden Lane, London, told him to get to Southampton with his wife, child, and gear. Within the month he should sail.

Mrs. Hannah protested that if the child went she would not. Then he would humour and praise her, so at last she went, although with much bad grace.

In the year 1663 the ship Elizabeth arrived, by the goodness of God, to the colony at Massachusetts Bay, and in her came an hundred souls. There were yeomen, farmers, braziers, wainers, pewterers, etc., indentured servants, apprentices, etc., and certain gentlemen scholars, etc. But in after years the most famous of all these people was Bilby's Doll, and it is she who has made the name of the ship Elizabeth remembered. There was in the hold a cargo of close to an hundred Bibles, and to this beneficent influence many attributed the quick fair passage which the Elizabeth enjoyed. No one thought it possible that the button-eyed foster child of Mr. Bilby could be a weather breeder. In fact no one thought of the child except to wonder at the foolish fondness which her "father" continually showed her. They thought of the Bibles below and thanked God for their sunny voyage. Rather should they have thought of the witch-child. For good things, such as fine weather, may spring from evil people.

Also on this ship came one Zacharias Zelley, an Oxford man and a widower. He was no longer young, nor was he an old man. In demeanour he was sad and thoughtful. After some shiftings he, too, like the Bilbys, came to settle at Cowan Corners, and there he preached the Word of God. But in time he fell from God, and of him more hereafter.

The new land prospered the Bilbys and they were well content. The plantation which Mr. Bilby was able to buy was not only of admirable size, well-set-up with house, barns, sheds, etc., but it was already reduced to good order and its fertility was proved. Yet for many years, down to this present day, Bilby's lands can produce little if anything except that coarse yellow broom which the vulgar call witches' blood.

The cellar hole of this house still stands upon the skirts of Cowan Corners, and but six miles removed from Salem. In those days there was a good road before this house leading from Salem to Newburyport. Beyond this road were salt meadows and the sea. To the north of the house lay fields of maize, English grass, corn, peel-corn, barley, oats, pumpkins, ending only at the waters of the River Inch (as it was called in those days). To the south were the adjoining lands of Deacon Thumb. But to the west, beyond the rough pastures, and too close for a wholesome peace of mind, was a forest of a size and terror such as no Englishman could conceive of unless he should actually see it. It stretched without break farther than man could imagine, and the trees of it were greater than the masts of an admiral or the piers of a cathedral. Yet was it always a green and gloomy night in this forest, and over all was silence, unbreakable.

Many thought the tawny savages who lived within were veritable devils, and that, somewhere within this vastness, Satan himself might be found. To this Mr. Zacharias Zelley, having taken up the ministry at Cowan Corners, would not listen. "For," he said, "we left the Devil behind us in England. Seek God in the heart of this majestic and awful forest—not the Devil. When I was a boy in Shropshire I knew the very niche in the rocks where old women said the Devil lived and had his kitchen. It was there he kept his wife. Every holiday I hid close by the rocks, hoping to see his children. . . . Let us leave him there in the Old England, but in the New keep our eyes pure and open against the coming of the Lord."

Atheism as the good and learned Glanvill,[3] in his "Sadducismus Triumphatus," has proved, is begun in Sadducism and those that dare not bluntly say "there is no God" (for a fair step and introduction) content themselves to deny there are spirits or witches or devils. Yet how sad to see one of the clergy first agree that the Devil could be left behind in England and soon claim there is no Devil, no witches, no spirits. For without these awful presences, who may be sure of God?

CHAPTER TWO

I

There is a small smell of WITCHCRAFT *in and about Boston. A straw doll taken to Meeting throws many into confusion.*

In the fall of 1665 two were hanged in Boston for the bedevilment of an elderly woman, her cousin Germain, and her swine.

In that same year Mr. Saul Peterham, a godly, decent man, refused some small rotten apples to an ancient and malicious hag. For this the old crone muttered at him, making an evil sign by her thumb and her nose, and took herself off in great bad humour. Mr. Peterham, on returning to his house, found that his wife—an estimable church woman—had fallen from a ladder she had put to the loft for the purpose of observing the conduct of her servant wench and the indentured male servant, the exact moment the crone had made her evil sign. The elders of the Church had at the old woman and

[3] Joseph Glanvill, *Saducismus Triumphatus* (1681).

forced her, weeping and on her knees, to forswear the Devil, his imps, and his ways, and to continue more strictly in the ways of God. It being observed that she could both weep and say the Lord's Prayer, many believed the accusation of witchcraft to be a false one, such as is often launched against disagreeable and impotent old women.

By spring there was yet another suspicion of witchcraft in the Bay Colony, and this at Cowan Corners. In a hut close by the seashore, and in great misery, lived an old pauper called Greene and his wife. He was a tinker, but there were better tinkers than he, and he got little work to do. His wife was a proud woman, born in Kent of high rank, yet, by turn of fortune, she was so reduced as to have become the wife of a tinker. Her craft in herbs got her some money and more ill fame, nor was she content to raise and sell the honest herbs of England, but she must continually associate herself with the heathen tawny savages and thus learn arts—doubtless often evil arts—from them. The Indians venerated her, calling her "White Mother" and "Moon-Woman." She went even into the great forest with more safety than any man. She was loving towards these peoples and had much traffic with them, in spite of the fact the Church elders had warned her twice, saying it is better for a woman to keep her own house than to go abroad through the woods alone and no one knew on what errand.

One Sabbath in the midst of the House of the Lord a poppet contrived of straw and maize, with a leather head and a grinning face on it, fell from below her skirts. None at the moment questioned her boldly as to what purpose she contrived this poppet, yet all thought of those dollies witches make but to destroy again, that their enemies may dwindle with the dwindling dolly.

Later in the week three deacons called upon her and demanded explanation. She was distrait, cried out upon them in anger because of their suspicions, and said she had but made a toy for Bilby's poor little Doll, who, she said, was beaten and cruelly used by that shrew Hannah. The incident was then dismissed except for a public reprimand for a woman so depraved as to put into the hand of a child a toy upon the Lord's Day and in the Lord's House. After this the Greenes lost what friends they had, and no one came commonly to their hut upon the salt marsh but Bilby's wicked Doll.

On a February night Hannah Bilby woke overcome with retching and vomiting. In the morning Mr. Kleaver, the surgeon, being called, took away two ounces of blood from the forearm; still she continued in wretched state three days. By the oppression on her chest and especially because of certain night sweatings and terrors, she became convinced she was bewitched and frankly accused Goodwife Greene. Mr. Zelley roughly bade her hold her tongue (this being but one of many times when he befriended a witch) and declared there was no reason why Greene should wish her harm. At which statement many were amazed, for they thought every one knew that Greene loved little Doll and hated the foster mother because of her cruelty. Through all the clustering villages—Salem, Ipswich, Cowan Corners, etc.—it was whispered how Doll had surrendered to Greene either parings from Mrs. Han-

nah's nails or hair from her body, and had thus given Greene the where-
withal to work magic.

Within a year all suspicion seemed to have passed away from Goody
Greene, but in a hundred ways more doubts gathered about the child and
she was whispered of. Mrs. Bilby told many, here one and there two, usually with entreaties for prayers and commands for secrecy, that the girl was
born and bred a witch. She told how her own unborn son (that thumping
boy) had been blasted. She told them to watch—was not Mr. Bilby himself
bewitched by her? So it seemed to many. There were no clothes fine enough
in Boston for his dear Doll—he needs must send to England for them. Sometimes he held her on his knee—and she a girl of thirteen or fourteen. Even
when the elders and the minister came to call on him, and Hannah, as befitted her gender, withdrew from the room, Bilby would keep his ridiculous
hobgoblin squatting at his feet. As he talked, he patted her shaggy, spikey,
hair.

The child had nothing to do with children of her own age, nor did godly
parents wish their children to play with her. For the most part she was a
silent thing, stealing about on feet as quiet as cats' paws. To her foster father
she was pretty and frolicsome. To Goodwife Greene she was loving, and
stole from the Bilby larder food for the wretched paupers. With her mouth
she said little to any one, but her eyes spoke—those round button eyes, and
they spoke secret and evil things.

2

*Monstrous facts regarding Doll's earliest youth which Mr. Zelley repeated
almost twenty years after her death. How she attended Black Sabbath, etc.
How she saw the Devil in Brittany and probably swore to serve him, etc.*

When the time came late in his life that Mr. Zelley, being old and
broken, was accused of witchcraft, he told, after long questionings, much
that he knew about Bilby's Doll. For instance, he said she never forgot one
of those wicked things which she had learned of her parents in Brittany.

It is true, the shock and horror of their death caused such mental anguish it seemed to her a black curtain (much like the smoke of the holocaust) dropped down upon her life. All that was actual in her life was before
the curtain—that is, after her parents' death; yet all that lay behind this curtain did exist for her—only infinitely small and infinitely far away. To see
(for she did not call it *remembering*) what lay behind this barrier, she had
to think and think only of blackness. Soon was her industry rewarded. Behold, the blackness disintegrated and little by little she saw strange scenes
in piercing clarity, yet all in miniature. She saw these visions as though she
were above them—say from the height of a church steeple, and she saw her
own self, a little shaggy girl, walking below.

If no one disturbed her, if Mrs. Hannah did not cuff her for idleness,
she could watch the movements of these people for hours. There were her
father and mother, other witches and warlocks, phantom beasts, fiends, imps,
goblins, fairies, and always her own self. Sometimes these people and crea-

tures grew so small they were scarcely more than shifting sands. Yet the smaller they grew, the more intense was their actuality. Mr. Zelley said that she observed that when these images, visions, or what you will, were presented to her almost as large as life, they were vapoury and hard to see, but when they were no larger than a grain of sand she could see everything— the little frown on her father's forehead, the scales on the imps' shoulders, her mother's teeth as she smiled, even the nails on the hands of her own self; yet how small must have been those hands when the whole body of an adult was no more than a grain of sand!

Mr. Zelley, an old and broken man, was commanded to tell further. What would she see—on what business would these folk be about? She would see naked men and women with goats' horns on their heads. They danced back to back. As they danced, they cried "hu hu hura hu," in the manner of witch-people. She would see the sacrifice of a black kid, and the crucifixion of the sacred wafer. Did she ever see the Devil himself? Witch-people often select one of themselves to be, as it were, high priest in their infernal synagogue. Him they call devil. Such a one she often saw. He was young and lusty and dressed in green leaves. When they danced their sara-bands, no one jumped as high as he. He was a pretty man and women loved him. It was only on Black Sabbath he had such power over men and women. At other times he was a cordwainer.

This devil that she saw was but a mock devil. Did she never see that Scriptural Devil—that Foul Fiend Lucifer? Ah, that she could never quite recall—not even with the powerful help of her strange minute images. It is true that after hours of application she would sometimes see a woman whom she knew to be her mother walking through great oak woods (mistletoe-infested) and with her, clinging to her skirts, was a child. The child was her own self. A great light pierced the green gloom of the forest and where it fell stood a man. He was an aristocrat, carried a small rapier with the hilt of which he toyed; he was dressed in green velvet, had a handsome, ruddy face, and loving blue eyes. Nor had he horns, she said, and if a tail, he kept it to himself; but his shoes she noticed were unsightly, as though contrived to accommodate clubbed foot or cloven hoof.

To him her mother knelt, and the child knelt also. The mother said she had a little servant for him, who she promised would obey him in all things. "What shall I do with so little a one?" But he caressed her with his hands. His touch was cold as ice. Even to remember that touch raised the gooseflesh upon her. It was searing as the hands of Death. She never saw this particular scene enacted before her without experiencing a physical shock —pleasant and yet repellent. Then she could see the child accept the Book the man offered her, and she always made a mark in the Book with blood drawn from her own arm. But the end of this particular and much-loved vision was always the same and always disappointing, for she saw herself and her mother sitting by the hearth. Her mother was stirring the pot and as she stirred she talked, telling the story of a little girl who had walked with her mother in a great wood, had met the Devil, and had sworn to serve him. So it was Doll Bilby never could be sure whether or not she had actually promised to serve the Foul Fiend and had made her blood-mark in his Book, or whether it was but a tale told by her mother.

At first she felt no terror of the strange phantasies which, waking and sleeping, were always before her eyes, but as she grew to young womanhood, this uncertainty as to her true status came greatly to worry her. If she had indeed signed the Book of Hell, then was she utterly damned, and there was no hope for her. If she had not, then might she, by prayer, watchfulness, etc., escape into Paradise. Thus she endured great anguish of spirit. At last the Soul, which ever turns and struggles in the heart of man, turned uneasily within her and she tried to forget all the evil which she remembered —even the voice of her mother, crying out piteously to her from the midst of flame.

Then Conscience—that gift from God to man—raised *its* head, and she lay and moaned upon her bed, listening to the holy voice of Conscience, asking her over and over, to her utter weariness, what have you done—what have you done? So she applied herself with burning intensity to the ways of religion, and it was then, said Mr. Zelley, he first came to ponder upon her, although she told him nothing of herself or of her past until some years later. But all her pious exercises were performed without that pleasure which the good Christian habitually manifests, but rather with the terror of a lost soul. Mr. Zelley kept a diary, and in that diary he wrote (Doll being at that time in her sixteenth or even possibly in her seventeenth year) a wanton suggestion, "I mark with interest the religious fructuations of Miss D. B. but fear she fruits without roots, and but let a man, perhaps, Titus Thumb, come into her life by the door, and then shall God but pass out by the window . . ." and more light and blasphemous talk, suggesting slyly that there may be some resemblance between the carnal love of body and the spirit love of soul.

3

A good young man is taken in a witch's net.

This Titus Thumb, to whom Mr. Zelley referred, was the oldest child and only son of Deacon Ephraim Thumb, whose lands lay south of and adjoining to the lands of Mr. Bilby. There had always been intimacy between the two farms, for the men of one helped the men of the other at harvesting, planting, and building. The two women were gossips. The two men were cronies. Titus had been much away because he was a scholar at the new college in Cambridge. For one year he was home again to help in the opening-up of certain new lands. He was a studious youth who hoped in time to prepare himself for the ministry of God. This, however, never came to pass, for God willed otherwise, and, on completing his studies at Cambridge, he remains there, known to hundreds of young Latinists as "Tutor Thumb."

He was a young man of special parts and handsome person. He would be a minister and his father was rich. The wenches of the village flocked to him like moths to flame, ignoring often in the exuberance of the chase (for they were unmannerly and bold to him) proper female conduct. They mocked him among themselves, saying he was his mother's darling or cosset; that he would never seek out a woman for himself. They would torment him, pulling him behind doors and kissing him, pushing their bodies against him when he could not escape them, etc., etc. For which wanton conduct they were well served, for he would have none of them, and, keeping the fifth commandment well in mind, stayed close to his parents' house.

He had two younger sisters, born at one time, for they were twins. They were sad and puny children, and many who saw them wondered that God had seen fit to cut His cloth so close—that is, it seemed to many that He had but enough material (brains, bones, spirits, hair, vitals, etc.) to make one proper child, yet out of this little He had made two. In answer to this questioning of Divine Wisdom, Mr. Zelley said no one body could have endured as many diseases and ills as the Thumb twins were heir to. Perhaps it was as well to divide up the maladies as well as the strength. Labour had a falling sickness. She would stiffen with a horrid din, foam and go into convulsions. Nor was Sorrow of much hardier stock. She was subject to nightmares and other delusions (which Mr. Kleaver insisted arose from a cold stomach). Their mother vexed herself greatly over them, and where another woman might think it well if the miserable things but made a good end and returned early to that God Who had sent them thus poorly fortified into the world, she was always calling upon Mr. Kleaver or Goody Greene to dose them, or Mr. Zelley to pray over them. They were pretty children with soft brown eyes and yellow hair, fine and finicky, but their limbs were miserably thin and their bellies somewhat swollen.

Mrs. Thumb told them not to play with Bilby's Doll. She feared the girl because her foster mother said she was a witch. Like most sickly children, they were poorly trained in obedience. They met Bilby's Doll, whenever they could, by the willow brook which separated the two farms. Of these meetings, however, they said little or nothing. The mother often heard them whispering and laughing to each other, and, because she would hear them talk of Mistress Dolly, she knew they saw her. As they were too feeble to be whipped or even shaken, she had little control over them.

She would have been vexed to know that often her husband, sitting at the Black Moon Tavern with Mr. Bilby, planned that in due time this same girl, whom Mrs. Thumb considered too dangerous even to cast an eye upon the twins, should marry the handsome Titus. On such occasions Mr. Bilby (although he would clap him on the back, and protest his friendship) always put him off—Doll was but a child, not old enough to marry. She had the immature body of a girl of twelve. Give her time and she would grow. Deacon Thumb would not be put off. Was she not sixteen at the youngest? Had not his own mother married before that?

He was most cupidous. He wanted his son to become heir to the fine estate of Bilby. He did not heed what his wife said of danger. He cared more that his son should have a great property in this world than that his soul should be saved for the next. He was not an evil man, for he was a deacon in the Church. He was a heedless man, and too easily dismissed as gossip the true stories his wife forever whispered in his ear, in regard to this same Doll.

Mrs. Bilby was anxious that the girl should marry and so be out of the house. One day she said, "What shall we ever do with your Doll? There's not a man in the town that would marry her." Mr. Bilby said that every unmarried man in the town would be glad to get her. Mrs. Bilby said, "You mean they would be glad to get a slice off your meadows." He said he would box her ears for her. She said Doll would be lucky if she got herself a vaga-bond, or a widowed man, or an old man of eighty. Mr. Bilby boxed her ears and went down to the tavern. Then he told Deacon Thumb that, although it broke his heart even to think of parting with his treasure, yet was mar-riage the one and only proper state for woman, and he would put her hap-piness even before his own. Moreover, his wife still hated the girl, even more than she had the night she first saw her, and although a good woman (and very handsome), yet she was hard. He said he had just boxed her ears and suggested that he was now willing to talk of the marriage settlement. He would do something very handsome by Doll. "For God knows," he said, "she is dear to me."

4

In spite of the Warnings of his Better Nature a young man looks covetously to Bilby's Doll.

On certain days the men of the two farms combined their labours, then Doll brought to her foster father his midday dinner. To suit his fancy she would bring food for herself also. This food she would eat quickly and with-out speaking to any one, keeping close to Mr. Bilby. On those harvest days, when the sun was bright on the stubble and heat shimmered in the air, the shade beneath the oaks was grateful. Doll Bilby, in the bright dresses her foster father bought for her, looked as fresh within this shade as one of those little summer flowers that go down before the scythes of harvesters. This Titus noticed, and he knew, although never a word had been spoken to him, that his father wished the match and his mother opposed it.

Also he noticed that the young woman, although so small, was made in a neat and most pleasing manner. She was more dainty, more finicky in her cut than the big English girls. He often thought, as he stretched himself to rest upon the earth, that to the eye of a man of rare discernment such del-icacy and small perfection might give more pleasure than more opulent charms, yet he never went so far as to say that he himself was that discern-ing man. Likewise it pleased him that she was shy before him, for he had been over-courted. When he would stretch his body along the ground close to where she sat, she would gaze unsmilingly at him out of her wild, trou-bled eyes, and something in that gaze—some necromancy—stirred his blood, so that at nights he felt desire for her, and often dreamed impossible things of her.

During all that year of harvest he had no thought for another one but only of Bilby's wicked Doll. He knew the stories of her—for his mother was forever at his elbow whispering things. He knew of her foreign birth, how she had once blasted an unborn child, how she and Goody Greene had afflicted Mrs. Bilby some years ago, making her vomit pins and fur (for to such proportions had the story of the woman's illness already grown), and he could see for himself how she bewitched her foster father out of his seven senses.

As he gazed upon her sometimes the marrow grew cold in his bones. He thought if he were a wise and Christian man, he would have none of her in spite of his own father's cupidity. In his heart he, like his mother, feared her. He could not understand the power she, without effort, had over him, for the very sight of her coming across the hot fields of noon threw him into a cold, dismal, unnatural sweat. Now was his heart set towards this marriage, but he looked with dread as well as joy to that day which should unite her to him. He believed that whatever her secret might be she should deliver it up to him on her bridal. Half he was persuaded that he would find that she, like Sara in the Book of Tobit, had a demon lover, who would strangle any bridegroom, nor had he an angel or a fish's liver, with which to protect himself.

5

A malignant black Bull leads all astray. Young Thumb fears Doll and suspects the creature is her Familiar.

The Thumbs had a young black bull, which, with other neat cattle and quick stock, they had out from England on the ship Fawnley. This bull was a wanderer, breaking stout fences, and seeking out his own pleasure among his neighbours' corn fields, cabbage plots, and herds.

On the last day of April, Ahab, the bull, loosed himself, and climbing a high hedge of stumps, which looked strong enough to hold any creature but an angel from Heaven, he set forth. Having crossed many pastures and trampled down valuable rye, he came to the banks of the River Inch, where it formed the northern boundary of the Bilby farm. The men were far away burning brush. Mrs. Bilby was at her churn in the milk-house. Doll, a shiftless wench, was loitering by the river's edge, and there she came across the bull. He was knee-deep among the cowslips. Seeing her, he threatened playfully with his short horns, and set off as fast as he could trot with a bunch of yellow flowers dangling from his blue lips.

She knew the animal to be of great value, and that she must quickly give warning of his liberty lest he escape into the forest, and, being set upon by savages or the *ferae naturae* of the place, become but meat in the stomachs of those little schooled to appreciate his worth. She ran quickly back to the house, calling that Black Ahab was loose and she had seen him head for the forest. Mrs. Hannah, rushing from the milk-house, caught the girl by the arm, shook her angrily because the cows were up and ready for milking, and she was late to her work. She would not let her run to the upland fields where the men burned brush, nor to the Thumbs' farm so that the creature might be caught. She flung her milking-stool and her pail at her feet, and told her to be about her own business, for if she had done as she should have done—that is, if she had made cheese all the afternoon, instead of loitering about the pastures—she never would have seen Ahab or known that he had escaped. Doll sat upon her stool and bent herself silently to her work.

On his return in the evening, Mr. Bilby was angry to find that no word had been sent to his neighbour in regard to the loss of his creature. Nor did Doll tell him that it was his wife's and not her fault. Partly because she was ashamed that he thought her responsible for the loss, and partly because she was a wild girl who loved to run about, she joined the searching party, made up of the men of the two households.

They searched the pastures and the ploughed lands, the fields, the meadows. There was no place else to search but the forest, for Ahab was utterly gone. They searched the forest until it was black night, following the snappings of twigs, blowings, stampings. Not once did they see the body of the black bull. Doll kept to her foster father's heels. Her dress and hands were torn. Her feet soaked with wet. She often called, and in a lovely voice, "Ahab . . . Ahab." As often as she cried, Titus knew her whereabouts, and took himself to her side. For on that black night it was she and not the mischievous bull that he was pursuing. He thought how heavy was the night, how awful in their majesty the woods, and how wild and small the dark goblin-child. So he prayed at the same moment that God might deliver his soul from her soul, and her body unto his.

Weary and disheartened at last, all turned towards home. But Doll had lost Mr. Bilby, who had started back with Deacon Thumb. Titus, amazed and delighted to find her alone, walked by her side. Doll bitterly reproached herself that she had not given warning in time. To comfort her Titus said it was only his and his father's fault because they could not keep the beast in bonds. To his amazement he found that it was not with their loss she was concerned, but only with the fortunes or misfortunes of the wretched bull. He thought, has this woman a familiar, and is it that accursed Ahab? So his marrow froze in his bones.

Thinking that she was indeed no bigger than one of those little goblins that live by the hob and bring good fortune to those who are kind to them, and also how there was much about her shape to please a man of rare discernment, he would have touched her with his hands (witch or no witch) and supported her weariness through the rough dark pasture lands. If she would accept this much from him, it was possible (for the night was May night when all young men for hundreds of years have been allowed special license from their sweethearts) she would permit more and more, so that the day's vexations might end joyously. Many times had he felt a vital spark pass from her to him, and he could not but believe that she was conscious of it as well as he. Doll seemed not to realize his intent. As in the dark he approached his hands to her, she floated from him. Before her home was reached he came to fancy she had no body, or that by some charm (strong as that charm she had worked to bind him to her) she now had made a barrier about herself which he had not the physical strength to break.

He thought of Sara and her loving demon, Asmodeus, and wondered if such a fiend might not now be protecting her. And he wished he had never heard that holy story, for Sara, according to Sacred Writ, had seven husbands and each young man in turn had been strangled upon his marriage bed by the fiend Asmodeus, who loved her.

6

A young Christian witnesses an Awful Metamorphosis and shoots a bullet, but not a silver bullet.

The young man's bodily fatigue was great, and his soul tormented. It grieved him to think that when at last he had gotten Doll Bilby by herself (and that upon a May night) it had profited him nothing. That night he could not sleep, but lay hot and lustful upon his bed. When he believed day about to dawn, he got himself into breeches, jerkin, hose, and shoes, and, having drunk a jorgen of ale, he went again to the search of Ahab.

Because there might be danger in the forest, he took with him his bastard musket. He came out of the house. It was not yet day. There was some light from the east, but it was a specious and unreal light, and the mists and fog from up over the sea were heavy and blue. He misliked the day.

First he looked about his own cow-pens and then about the cow-pens of his neighbour, for he knew the creature loved the company of his own kind and if alive would be like to return to them. There was neither bull, nor sign of bull. With his musket upon his shoulder, he took a path through Mr. Bilby's meadows and came down to the smooth waters of the River Inch. He thought, "This Ahab is a greedy drinker. As soon as the sun is up he will get to the river and gorge himself with water." The fogs lay heaviest over the river, and they lay flat and white like piled counterpanes. Steadily the watery light grew from the east. He thought he would sit upon a boulder under a willow tree. The sun would soon shine out and drink up the fogs and dews of night. He kept his bastard musket on his knees, partly because the strangeness of the twilight vexed him, and partly because he knew that not far from him—no farther than he could shoot with his gun—was a path from out of the woods down which wild animals often came early to drink from the river. It was down this path he hoped to see Ahab, and in the meantime he might get venison for his mother's larder. He sat quietly, and a doe stepped out, followed by twin fawns. But these he would not shoot, for their grace and smallness reminded him of Doll. Everything reminded him of Doll—the birds that sang, the flowers in the grasses, even the mystery and silence of the dawn. Yet these things should not have reminded him of a woman, but of her Maker.

In time he heard a crashing and breaking of twigs, and laughed to himself that he had read the bull's thoughts so well, for nothing that lived in the forest would make such a commotion; only a domestic barnyard animal would carry himself so noisily. Nor was he disappointed, for out of the fogs and through the brush came the young bull, looking vast and large in the unreal light of dawn. He thought to let the creature settle himself to his drinking and then to steal up from behind him and catch his halter. So he sat quietly until he saw with astonishment that what he believed to be an Indian was astride him, and, having rigged reins to the halter, was endeavouring to turn him from the water.

To see a rider on Ahab did not surprise him, for he knew the bull had often carried even his little sisters, the puny Labour and Sorrow. It did astonish and anger him to see a savage in possession of his father's property. So he called out roughly and forbade the man to turn the creature away from him. What next happened he never truly knew, for he was sure that the tawny (which at the instant seemed a large and ferocious brave) jumped from the bull's back and made at him with his tomahawk. Titus knelt upon one knee and fired. In spite of the fogs and bushes that partly confused his sight, he took his aim most accurately against a bit of beadwork above the heart of his enemy. Now he saw this boy or man most clearly, the deerskin fringe to his jerkin, the feathers, the dark, angry face, the tomahawk, the patterns made by beads, and he knew that his aim was accurate and good; yet, even as the bullet sped to its mark, the Indian was there no more, and instead stood Doll Bilby with her hands clasped to her heart.

He knew the bullet went through her. When he first saw her, she was still staggering from the impact, but, when he reached her side and pulled away her hands (crying out and lamenting that he had killed her), there was no mark of blood upon her grey gown, and she assured him in a weak and frightened voice that she was unhurt. This gown Doll had on that day was made of strong fustian, and, as Mrs. Hannah always said, it had not a hole nor tear in it. Yet the next time Doll wore it there was discovered above the heart a minute and perfect patch, put on, evidently, to cover a hole no larger than a sixpence.

So great and so unreasonable was Titus's love for Doll, he at first hardly considered the awful metamorphosis he had witnessed. Instead he was sick to think how close she had been to death.

As this story (which has just been set down in its true form) spread through the village, it grew incredibly larger in the mouths of certain people, and yet in the mouths of others it dwindled down into nothing. For the former of these insisted that Doll did not come alone, but was escorted by a vast troop of infernals, witches, etc., and that Ahab spoke to his master, making sundry infantile observations, such as might occur to the intelligence of a beast. Those who would make nothing of the story (and among these was Mr. Zelley) said Titus was no solid rock upon which to build the truth, and that his fancy had ridden him. There never had been an Indian upon the bull's back, only Doll. He never had seen the beads, fringes, tomahawk. When he shot, his aim was confused and he had gone wide the mark.

Mr. Zelley, in his diary, quotes Scripture in regard to this curious incident, saying in part that Our Lord warns us against the putting of new wine into old bottles, lest the new wine prove too strong and burst the bottles. "So a torrent of feeling—especially when arising from the passions—is of the greatest danger to a weak container, and young Mr. Thumb is that weak container."

At that moment, however, Titus had but one thought, and that was that at last the wench was in his arms, for she was so weakened by fear (or perhaps from the actual shock of the bullet) she could hardly stand. He comforted her, stroking her hair, kissing her, and saying over and over that he would have died rather than hurt a hair of her head. Concerning the fact that, but a second before, she had been in other shape and enjoying a different gender, he said nothing, for he thought that she might wish to remain mute concerning the matter, and then he thought: "It was because of kindness, at least if not towards me, towards the bull, that made this modest young female assume another shape. How could she, as a white girl, have ventured to the forest and found Ahab?" So he said nothing. Now that at last his arms were about her, he felt none of the fire and anguish he had endured the night before; rather, it seemed to him, that he was caressing and comforting one of his own sisters. So he set her sideways on the bull, and took her to her own house.

By the time he had reached his father's farm, he was once more swept by such inordinate and passionate desire he could not believe that earlier in the same morning he had kissed and comforted her, thinking her only a child —not even a witch and much less a woman.

CHAPTER THREE

I

Young Thumb dwindles. The witch torments him and her foster father discerns that she is not nor ever can be a Christian woman.

From the day on which Ahab was lost and recovered, Titus began a secret courting of Doll. Witch or no witch he would have no other. On the one side of him was his father, winking at him and pointing out the richness of Mr. Bilby's fields, the weight of his cattle, the size of his barns. On the other side of him was his fond mother, whispering and whispering, "The girl's a witch, she'll come to no good end, she'll hang yet, the girl's a witch . . . witch . . . witch." Of all these matrimonial plans Mrs. Hannah knew nothing. She saw that Titus was much about the house, but, being very proud of her beauty (which was remarkable in a woman of her years), she believed in her own heart that she was the reason for the young man's constant presence. She could not believe so handsome and sought-after a young man could see anything to desire in the ridiculous hobgoblin-child. Doll Bilby flouted him at every turn, yet was he always after her, hungry as a cat for fish.

Many noticed, even by June and still more by July, that young Mr. Thumb was suffering from some malady that sapped strength from body, colour from face, and dulled the eye. He was a listless worker in the fields, leaning upon his scythe, scanning the horizon, sighing, and weakly returning to his work. He ate little and slept less, so that his flesh fell away enormously, and, where four months before had stood a hale young man, now stood a haggard. He would mutter to himself, sit out in night vapours to consider the moon as it shone on the distant roof of Bilby's house.

Thus things went from bad to worse. His mother noticed his condition and guessed its cause. She brooded over the young man, and this made him vexatious and bilious. When his little sisters had met (as they sometimes did, in spite of their mother) "Mistress Dolly" by the willow brook, he would beg them to tell him everything the young woman said to them. How did they play? Did they build a little house of pebbles? Had they made dolls from stones? They would never tell him, but ran quickly away. The truth came out later. Doll amused them with stories of salamanders, elves, fairies, etc. They feared their mother would be angry if she knew—for she often had said that all the *good* stories were in the Bible, and if a story could not be found there it was proof that it was not good. So the twins ran away and told nothing of their visits with Doll. They often talked to each other, however, after they were in bed, and went on making up wicked things like those she had told them.

All her life Mrs. Thumb swore she knew her son's distress was from no ordinary cause. If that were true, people asked her, how did she come to give consent to her son's marriage with this same Doll? When she was an ancient lady, living in her son's house at Cambridge, she once said: "I saw my son like to die, and he swore there was but one cure for him—that is, marriage with this young woman whom our magistrates later judged to be a witch. Therefore I said little to oppose the marriage. Then, too, at that time I placed much confidence in the wisdom of Mr. Zelley. He stood at my right hand, saying, 'The girl is innocent. It will be a fine match.' Titus would cry out in his sleep for this witch-girl. How could I deny him when I thought it the only way to save his life?"

Hannah raged when she learned that the marriage was arranged (although nothing yet had been said to Doll). Bilby could not fathom her anger, for he thought she would be pleased to get the girl out of the house. He did not know that his wife believed herself the reason for Titus's mopings and pinings. Indeed she had ordered for herself a new red riding-hood from Mr. Silas Gore, of Boston, so that she might have finery with which to fascinate the young man.

At last Doll knew she was to marry the good young man, for her foster father told her so. He told her roughly, for his heart broke to think of losing her to another. Sorrow made his tongue unkind. She would not listen to him, but, laughing, clung about his waist, saying she would never leave him, that he was the only man she could ever love. He wanted to keep her with him forever, but he knew that she was a strange girl, not like others, and he believed that if she were married she would become less secret and, having a house and children of her own, she would be happier.

Then, too, he knew that his wife was cruel to her, and he thought that it would be better for her to live under a roof where there was only love. It was in vain that he told her that she was now a woman grown, and it was time that she went about the business of women—that is, the bearing and raising of children. Did she have a deep aversion for her handsome and godly young neighbour? Would she not be proud some day to be a minister's wife? No, no, never, never—she only wanted to be his dear foster child. He hardened his heart against her, and unwound her arms from about his waist. He told her to marry young Thumb, or to think up better reasons why she should not. He would not have such an ungrateful, stubborn woman about his house. If she did not wish to do as he wished, she could find another place to live. He never meant such hard words. He acted for her own best good. He pushed her from him, and made off to the fields.

She overtook him in a field of flax where the flowers were even bluer than the rare summer sky. The air was heavy with the murmur of bees. She flung herself on her knees and caught him by the long blue smock he wore.

"Father," she cried, "wait, wait, I beg of you." She put her hands over her face and wept. He could have wept himself to see her thus. He hardened his heart and would have pushed by. She cried out she had something to tell him, so he waited silently, but without looking at her, for he was afraid that at the sight of her his heart would melt. She seized him by the hem of his smock and began to talk in a hoarse voice and a roaring voice like nothing he had ever heard out of her before. She had something to tell him, she said. There were reasons why she could not marry, especially not a young man who wished to be a minister. She feared she was not a Christian woman. She looked up at him from the ground, and he looked down upon her. Their eyes met, and in one horrid instant Mr. Bilby realized what it was she meant, why she feared she might not be a Christian woman. Of Evil she remembered everything, and at that moment he knew it.

He did not dare question her. He did not dare know what she knew. He essayed to comfort her and said he did not care who her parents really were. It mattered no more to him than who might be the sire of the cat that caught the mice in his barn. He also said what was not true, for he assured her that what one may have done or promised at a very tender age had no importance in the eyes of God. So he talked vaguely, and made off to his labours.

She left him and went to a secret spot she had among the birch trees on the hillside. She was not comforted, and her heart was hard set against the thought of marriage.

Those things which Doll told Mr. Bilby frightened him. He went straight to his neighbours that same afternoon and said the time had come when Titus, with his own tongue and in his own body, should do a little courting. Titus said how could he when Doll was never a flea-hop from her foster father's heels? Thus it was arranged. Doll, that very night, should be left alone in her father's house—Bilby and wife should go to Thumb's. Titus would come to her, court her, and persuade her to marriage. After a sufficient time, all would return to Bilby's and celebrate the happy betrothal with sack-posset, hymns, psalms, prayers, etc.

To this Titus and all agreed. Even Doll had nothing to say, but at her foster father's bidding she put on her most wanton dress—a giddy dress of scarlet tiffany such as no pious woman would wish to possess.

2

A woman is seized by a Frenzy. And how a man may court without profit.

Now, when she found herself alone, she ran back and forth, back and forth, through the house. She locked and barred everything. She locked the cupboards and the doors and shuttered the windows. She went to the attic and locked the trunks, the boxes, the cribs, and the cases. She went to the cellar and bolted the door. Doors she could neither bolt nor bar, she barricaded. Even when this was done, she could not stop her strange running round and round the house, sometimes turning in small circles like a dog gone mad. She said over and over to herself, "I must be a witch, for I can feel myself weaving a charm." So she ran fast through the house, but here was nothing more to lock.

It was not yet seven o'clock and the evening was still light. Yet so closely had she barred and shuttered everything, the house inside was dark as midnight. Then she got old blankets, and in the end, in her desperation, new blankets, and tried to stuff the gaping chimney hole in the fire-room so that the whole house should be utterly barred and tight. But all the time (as she afterwards told Mr. Zelley) she would ask herself, "Why, why do I do these things?" In the midst of her most desperate work with the chimney hole, she would stop and begin to run through the house—unable to stop herself. She thought to herself that she was working some charm or rather some charm worked within her. She was powerless before her great need to run back and forth, back and forth, through the locked and barred house.

Titus Thumb, dressed as though for a bridal and carrying a nosegay of lad's-love and a turkey-leather psalm book for gifts, came proudly to the house, knocking to be let in. Doll heard him, for she was crouched upon the cold hearth of the fire-room, striving to stuff the chimney hole. She thought, "I will let him in, and then he can do this thing better than I."

Titus was astonished to find the house dark and his lady's hair a ragged black mat on her shoulders, her gay scarlet gown disordered and torn open at the throat, as though she had but recently wrestled with an enemy. And her face astonished him, for her cheeks were bright red. Fuller and more beautiful than ever before, her eyes glittered indeed like a goblin's and her wide mouth was pulled up at the corners in a wicked but most provocative smile. She, in the dark house, seemed more like imp or puck than human woman. All that was human in him—that is, intelligence, conscience, reason, and so forth—was afraid and bade him turn back; yet all that was animal in him—that is, the hunger and desire of his body—urged him to enter. So he entered.

Already that awful necessity that had made her run so madly through the house was gone. She explained the blankets by the cold hearth, saying that they were damp, and that she had planned to build a fire and dry them out. So he built a fire. She explained her dishevelled condition. She had heard a rat in the cellar and had taken a poker and hunted for him. Could he not at that moment hear the rat scampering in the cellar? So he took a light and a poker and went to the cellar, and Doll, a little ashamed and fright-ened, quickly ordered her clothes and hair, and unlocked everything she could before he returned. Yes, he said, he found a rat and he had killed it. This surprised her, for she had really heard no rat, and the thought came to her that perhaps the Devil had sent that rat to excuse her conduct.

The young man sat on the settle with his head in his hands and prayed God to deliver his soul from the woman's soul, and her body unto his. At last he spoke to her, his face turned away from her. He told her that she knew why he was come. He wished to marry her, and that he would be to her a true and loving husband. No, she said, she could not marry him. He was surprised, for Mr. Bilby had told no one of the young woman's aversion to marriage. He had understood that he had only to ask and she would assent. He told her that it was all settled—the very spot on which their house should be built. How could she now so coldly say no? She only said again that she could not marry him—nor any other. "If that is so," he said, "I'll take my hat and go." But why, if she had no idea of marrying him, had she so kept him at her heels? She had not kept him at her heels. She was always trying to rid herself of him. She knew that was not true. The very way she drew back from him was the surest encouragement a man could have. She said she thought he was talking nonsense. Her eyes glittered at him, round and bright in the firelight, like a cat's.

He was afraid. He got up. He said again that he would take his hat and go. "I wish you would," said Doll. They could not find his hat. It seems that, while Doll was straightening herself and ordering the house (Titus at the moment ratting in the cellar), she had by chance picked up his hat, with many other things, such as the sooty blankets, and had stuck them un-der her own bed. So now they could not find his hat.

The young fellow was afraid, and now, as never before, he believed she was a witch. His blood pumped through him as though about to burst the veins; he knew that she wished this hat to work further charms upon him. But if she were so set upon charming him, making him her slave, why would she now have none of him? Why should she torture him, making him love her past all human endurance, and yet now so coldly dismiss him?

Doll said she was very sorry about the hat. "Oh, it is not the hat," he cried in despair, his head again in his two hands, "but, my dear Doll, why will you so torture me? Have I ever been anything but kind and respectful to you? Look what you have done. A year ago I was twice the man I now am. You have done it. You've sucked the strength and manhood out of my veins." Then he talked strangely so that she could not at first understand him. At last she understood him well. He believed that she had cast a witch spell on him, and had thus made him love her so beyond all reason. For, as he frankly told her, she really was not so wonderful nor half so beau-tiful, etc., as he had come to think her. He said he could remember back three years ago when he thought her a scrawny, rather ugly, little thing with too big a mouth.

All this made her very angry. She jumped up and down in her rage— more like an imp than ever—and screamed at him to be gone. She ran into her own room and came back with his hat—for she had guessed where it really was, but had not found an opportunity to get it for him. She jumped up and clapped the hat onto his head, pulling it down so sharply over his ears that she bent them, and continued to scream, "Go! Go! Go!" He grabbed her roughly by the arm, called her witch, hellcat, succubus. She turned and bit his wrist, so that it was marked for days. He pulled her off him, shook her with great fury, and flung her from him so that her head struck against the settle and she moaned in pain. Her plight touched his heart infinitely, and he knew that, witch or no witch, she was his dear, his own girl.

So the parents and foster parents, returning, found them. The man, a valiant officer in the militia, a scholar, and the heir to a fine estate, was convulsed with weeping and sobbing. The girl lay terror-stricken in the corner, as harmless as a trapped rabbit. Mr. Bilby had no idea that Titus had flung her into this corner. She was a strange child, and he thought she had picked it out for herself. He pitied the terrible (if somewhat unmanly) grief of the young man, and swore that, in spite of Doll's ridiculous and, he felt, unnatural objections, the marriage must go ahead.

Mrs. Thumb took her son home, and Mr. Bilby took Doll to bed, and he comforted her with that more than female solicitude that a man often shows towards children or women in distress.

Mrs. Hannah was in a rage when she found her fine blankets blackened with dirty soot. Nor would Doll offer an explanation to her foster mother, although afterwards she told Mr. Zelley everything.

3

The voice of Hell is heard in the House of the Lord.

Mrs. Thumb went everywhere whispering: "Look to my son. Is he not bewitched? Look at my boy—so gentle he would not kick a cat, yet you all know that once he shot at this Doll Bilby, and but a few nights ago he struck her and flung her upon the ground. Then he cried for hours. I took him home. Is it according to God and Nature for a man to love thus? Hating her, loving her, loving her, hating her. Would God the wench were dead, but she is not, and he will marry her."

Every one thought the girl a witch. She went her own way quietly, working as she always did, a little shiftlessly, her mind on other things.

The harvest was late that year and heavy. One year Nature would starve her stepchildren (for so the colonists felt in the new land) with too little, and the next year break their backs with too much. Mr. Bilby, harassed with many things, did a wrong thing. He went to Mr. Zelley and begged him on the next Sabbath to publish the banns for his foster child and young Thumb, and he led Mr. Zelley to believe that Doll had assented to these plans.

It may well be that Doll, in some secret way common to witches (that is, through some imp or familiar used as spy), really did know that upon a certain Sunday the banns were to be read. If she did know, she said nothing of this thing to any one, keeping her own dark counsel, and working her secret spells. On a Friday Mr. Bilby sickened slightly, and upon Saturday he could not touch his proper food, only a cheat-loaf she baked with her own hands for him, and a barley gruel. Mrs. Hannah always believed—and doubtless with reason—that the young woman was at the bottom of this sickening and was endeavouring to keep him from the Meeting-House, for when she heard he was set upon going she begged him not to go, saying he was too ill, etc., and must be ruled by her, etc., and sit at home in idleness.

But he would not be persuaded, and he went to church as always. She rode with him upon the pillion. Mrs. Hannah rode the fat plough horse.

By the windows and doors of the Meeting-House were nailed the grim and grinning heads of wolves, freshly slain. In the stocks before the Meeting-House were two Quaker women, the one in an extremity of despair and cold (for there was some ice upon the ground) and the other brazen, screaming out profanities and laughing in her disgrace. Upon the roof-walk paced back and forth Captain Buzzey, of the train-band troop, beating his drum in great long rolls, summoning all to come and worship.

Inside the Church Mrs. Hannah and Doll sat together on the women's side, and Mr. Bilby, as befitted his station in the community, sat close to the minister. After certain psalms, prayers, etc., Mr. Zelley held forth from the Book of Judith for the space of two hours. There were announcements by the clerk, etc., and then Mr. Zelley again ascended the scaffold. Couched in proper form, he read how Titus, son of Deacon Ephraim Thumb, and Doll, foster child of Jared Bilby, engaged themselves for holy wedlock and desired the pronouncement of these banns.

His voice was drowned by a sharp and most piteous lamentation. At first none knew from where this infernal sound had come. Deacon looked to deacon, wife to wife. Mr. Cuppy, the tithing-man, ran up and down among the wretched small boys. Mr. Zelley stopped in astonishment, looking first up, as if he thought the sound had come from the corn crib in the loft of the Church—or from Heaven—and then down, as though seeking its source from Hell. Doll Bilby was on her feet, her arms outstretched, addressing her foster father. Her voice rose and died out. None there could ever repeat what it was she said. That noon, in the noon-house, between the two services, men and women got together whispering, wondering, and asking each what it was that Bilby's saucy jade had—to her own unending shame and to the great indignity of the sacred service—dared to pipe forth.

Mr. Zelley—the least disturbed of all—saw to it that Bilby and his beloved Doll be got to horse and to home, without waiting for the second service. He was perplexed and harassed by the occurrence, and refused to discuss with his deacons what would be a fitting punishment for the young woman, although most were agreed that it would be the stocks or the pillory. Instead of listening to the discussions in the noon-house, he went out of doors and stood before the evil women in the stocks, exhorting them in the name of Christ Jesus to repent and to be forgiven. Theodate Gookin, a stout child, mocked them and pelted them with small apples. This action of the child enraged Mr. Zelley more than had the foul blasphemies of the Quakers. He roughly ordered Theodate to lay off his own warm overcoat. This he spread kindly upon the back of the most insufferable of the blasphemers. By which act of charity, he stilled her lying tongue, and reproved the levity of the child who would sport about and enjoy himself on the Lord's Day.

4

Evil cursing bears bitter fruit. Mr. Bilby, though struck down, swears to the innocency of his Destroyer and makes a Pious End.

Bilby went stiffly to his horse, his mouth drawn, his face grey. His wife got on the pillion behind him and soon left Doll (on the fat work animal) far behind. When the girl got to the house, she did not seem to understand why her foster mother shook her fist, spat, and made at her with a warming-pan. She did not seem to know that she had cursed the man—that kind man, whom she loved.

Mr. Bilby suffered from a cruel congestion of the lights.[4] Mr. Kleaver said from the first there was little chance to save him. For on one day came the surgeon, with his saddle-bags stuffed with motherwort and goldenrod, and on the next came the minister with his big Bible, and on the third day they were like to send for Goody Goochey, the woman who had the laying-out of the dead—so sick was he.

But he delayed his passage into eternity, fighting death with hardly Christian resignation; for to your true Christian the years spent on this world must seem but as the nine months which the child spends in the womb. His death-day is in fact his birthday into the kingdom of God. Should he fight against death any more than the infant should fight against birth?

There were gathered in his sick-chamber night and day rarely less than ten or twelve people, praying for the departure of this fell disease, or, if this were impossible, they prayed in the hope of giving the shrinking soul a heavenward lift.

Mr. Bilby bade them save their breath, and, although his face was settling into lines of death and he breathed horribly and with an animal roaring, he still begged, as he had from the first, for a sight of his child Doll. The room was then cleared of the pious exhorters, who returned to the Thumb farm and there prayed and drank rumbullion. Only Mr. Kleaver, Mr. Zelley, and the wife remained. Mr. Zelley commanded Hannah to find the child, and Hannah, frowning, went away, but she came back soon and said she was not about. The truth is the woman had struck and cursed the girl so savagely that now, when she heard her name called, she did not dare to come.

The doors of the death-chamber were shut and sealed. Camphor was burned on the hearth; then the wife stood by her husband's side, and, in the presence of Mr. Zelley and the surgeon, asked him three times and in a loud voice whether or not he believed he died of a curse pronounced upon him by his foster child. Mr. Bilby rallied his wits, and, in spite of the agony of his breathing, he stoutly denied the charge. But some (among them Han-

---

[4] I.e., lungs.

nah) believe that he was already dead when he seemed to speak, and that an evil spirit had succoured Doll by leaping into the head of the corpse and thus making answer. For he spoke up in a loud, clear voice, and yet one in no way like his own, and the next moment he was not only dead, but looked as though he had been dead for a half-hour or hour at the least.

5

Doll forswears the God of our Deliverance and embraces Beelzebub who prepares (for her instruction) a PROCESSION.

The four days Bilby was dying, Doll spent in the hayloft—night and day. She had overheard the farm servants talking, and she knew of what she was accused and why it was Hannah would not let her into the house. She remembered that strange time when she had run and run through the house, working, she knew, a spell, or rather feeling a spell work through her, and she was sick to think that perhaps she had some power she did not understand, and had really put a charm upon her dear foster father when she had not intended. Perhaps it was also true that unknown to herself she had bewitched Titus Thumb. None went to her or knew where she lay but the youngest of the indentured servants, a good and gentle lad. This boy brought her food and water. When it was night he went to his poor lodgings in the cow-shed and took a blanket from his bed and gave it to her.

From the loft Doll stared down at the house and yard, and could guess, by the close attendance of the surgeon and the clergyman and by the multitudes gathered to pray, how sick he was. Every morning she saw Hannah go early to the dunghill and catch a fowl. This bird Doll knew would be laid for warmth at the sick man's feet, for under the dark covers the creature lay quietly and gave off a good and healing warmth, yet was no bird imprisoned longer than twenty-four hours lest its heat be translated into the chill of death.

On the fourth day—that is, the day on which Mr. Bilby died—Doll determined to leave the loft and if possible to find Goody Greene, who would at least tell her how her father did. Perhaps Greene might stay his sickness, for Doll had more confidence in her and her herbs than in Mr. Kleaver and his bleeding-cups. At this time of year the woman often went to the Bilby river meadows after an herb called "Love-lies-bleeding," so Doll, finding the opportunity to slip out unseen by any, got from the loft and decided first to hunt for her Sister-in-Evil along the river-banks. She dared not pass through the town.

She sat by the river until sundown, crying long and bitterly. She remembered that time Titus had found her there, and cried afresh—for even those had been happier days.

Wherever she went she found the flower stems were broke off close to the ground, and she saw the print of a small Indian moccasin in the mud. She knew that Goody Greene (being a pauper) wore these moccasins and that her feet were small, so she followed this trail, and this led her to the great forest. Here she paused, for she feared it. But she feared the cruel suspicions of her foster mother more, so she took a farewell look about her at the pastures and fields, and, finding a small path (still seeing here and there a moccasin print), she entered boldly.

It would seem, then, that another of those fits of senseless weaving back and forth overtook her. She knew the danger of being lost in this great wood, and she had not for a long time seen a footprint. Suddenly she began to run through the woods on those little paths beaten out by animals, hunters, and Indians. She could not pause either to consider her direction or to determine what it was she really sought, for she had almost forgotten the idea of finding Greene. The sun had set and the November night was coming down fast. The gloom and overwhelming silence weighed her down. She began to think that she smelt smoke or saw the glimmer of a fire. Wherever she looked she could see light smouldering in the underbrush. Sometimes she thought there were hundreds of tiny Indian encampments, with teepees but a few inches high, and, because she knew of Goody Greene's fondness for Indians, she tried to come to these miniature encampments. She also knew that she was lost (although this knowledge did not horrify her as it would a reasonable person), and not only did she wish the goodwife's company, but she needed the warmth even of the smallest fire, for the night was frosty cold.

At last, after much running, sniffing, and circling, she came to a small cleared spot, where she always maintained she found a fire burning, and over this fire was a great pall of black smoke. So she gathered more twigs and fagots, and built up the fire—not knowing that she only made a heap of rubbish upon the cold wet ground. At least her "fire" seemed to warm and comfort her. She lay back upon the moss and fell quickly into deep sleep.

After some time, she waked, startled, for she heard her name called. "Bilby's Doll!" cried the voice, "Bilby's Doll!"

"Yes," she answered, springing up from her unhappy bed. There was no answer to her "yes." Whatever it was, she considered her "fire" was almost out. "Who calls?" she cried, and her voice echoed and the awful silence of night mocked at her in solitude.

Then at last, being wide awake, she realized with terror and dismay that the voice that called her was none other than that of her dear foster father. Yet would he never have called her thus, saying "Bilby's Doll," but "Doll" only.

Then she knew that he was dead, and that she would never see him again. It was his lonely spirit, fresh torn from the earthly body, that had stopped this moment on its heavenly flight to cry out to her thus sadly. She flung herself, moaning, upon the ground, unable to shed a tear. Witches, she knew, have no tears, and she realized with horror that her tears had dried up. She began to pray to "Dear God in Heaven. . . ." She heard a rustle in the forest, and then low and malicious laughter. She stopped her prayer. After a moment of writhing and moaning, she prayed again—"Infinite Master, Lord God of Israel . . . I never meant to hurt him. He was the only person I have ever loved. I never meant to kill him . . ." "Why, then, did you curse him?" asked a voice, and she again heard malicious laughter. She would have found relief for her remorse in tears, but there were no tears, nor did they ever come to her again.

She felt the presence of a large and probably dangerous animal about, so she flung more wood on her "fire." She listened to its padded feet, and told herself it was lynx or wolf, yet in her heart she hoped and feared that it might be at last a messenger from that infernal King to whom she now was convinced her parents had promised her. For, between the moment that she heard a voice call "Bilby's Doll" and that moment in which she had felt a corporeal presence in the wood, she had become fully convinced that she was a witch with all the powers that belong to such an evil estate.

Slyly she made one last appeal to Jehovah, for she thought that He might even for so evil a one as her own self make His awful majesty manifest. "O God, who seest all things, who rulest above, O Great God of Israel, give me a sign, give me a sign. . . ." Then in her impudence she lifted up her impious voice and commanded God, "Put back the soul of Jared Bilby, for it is not yet gone far and his body is yet warm. Do this and I will serve You. Desert me now, and I wash my hands of You and Your cruel ways!" The rustling and the commotion crept nearer. No angel this thing which approached her on its belly. She stared, expecting to see horned head and grinning demon face. She saw nothing. She cried once more to God. The solitude echoed her voice with laughter. Then she cried to the powers of Hell below and to the Prince of Lies, "Great King of Hell, if I serve you, you must serve me" (for she knew this was a stipulation in a witch's contract). "I will do anything, sign any book, if you will but give me back the soul of Jared Bilby." But this poor soul was now in the keeping of angel hosts. Not Lucifer himself could snatch it from such guardians. As she thought thus, a windy voice cried, "Too late, too late." "Satan, you shall give me a sign," she cried. And there close to the ground were two great cat's eyes, larger than saucers. They glared at her with a green hellish light that transpierced the darkness and her very soul.

She cried out desperately to those eyes, "Whoever you are, step forth. I will do anything, sign any book. Tell me now, in Satan's name, is there no way back to life for Jared Bilby? For it was I, I, I, who slew him—with a witch's look. Oh, kind spirit, if you are old, I will be your daughter; if you are young, I will be your bride—stand forth now to me."

The yellow eyes turned from her as she struggled with her unhallowed thoughts, and the thing was gone. Far away, mile after mile, a voice no bigger than a sparrow's cried sadly to her, and in great agony of spirit, "Bilby's Doll. . . ." She thought to run after the voice, to catch the naked soul in her hands. Of what avail? Gone already a thousand miles. In the littlest voice, no larger than voice of flea or worm, she heard once more her foster father cry to her, "Bilby's Doll. . . ."

She knew that, as there are certain forms and incantations for the destruction of life, so must there be others for the rekindling of it. What had Our Lord said before the tomb of Lazarus? Could she but remember the words she herself had said in church—perhaps by repeating them backwards she could countermand the curse.

She fell to the ground in an ague, and lay sobbing dryly, exhorting the powers of Hell. Twigs snapped in blackness about her. Feet padded in silence.

The cold of the night, the terror of her soul, the dearth of food, the sorrow of her heart struck her into a stupor from which she could not move. Through this stupor, in steady procession, and with much pomp and circumstance, a long parade of figures, fiends, witches, warlocks, imps, beasts, familiars, satyrs, and even the beautiful chaste Diana herself, moved in fleshly form: a wicked, most fantastic procession. Goblins were there with faces of cats and owls, salamanders but lately crawled from fire. Basilisks were there, serpents, vampires with bats' wings and horrid mouths swollen with blood. The pretty pink bodies of innocent babes were there, who had died unbaptized, and therefore must stand as servants in the halls of Hell, and with them were pucks and pugs.

After them rolled through the forest a great orange cloud—like an old and tarnished fire—no longer heat-giving. At first her eye could make nothing of it. Then she saw projecting through the dun vapours were naked legs and arms, bits of bodies, and drawn and skull-like heads with tortured eyes. These were they the French burned at Mont Hoël in Brittany. Although she might not know them, her parents were among them. A group came slowly after these, shrouded and shuffling through the woods. In the midst of these she saw Goody Greene. This woman, alone of all the passers-by, turned and looked towards Doll. But her eyes were blind.

Last of all came Ahab shaking his black head, a cowslip hanging from his blue lips. She would sleep and wake, but the procession would still be passing by, and every so often Ahab would pass by. The woods were humming-full with an infinity of unearthly things. There was continuous lovely singing—or rather a rhythmic humming that rose and fell and rose again.

6

With daylight the tides of Hell recede. Doll wakes but to a more determined Evil.

At last she awoke to see, not the procession of Hell, but bright day. The humming, however, still continued in her head, rising and falling, but not going away. She was frozen cold to her marrow. Now the loss of her foster father had become a tiny thing infinitely far away and long, long ago. All her previous existence seemed removed from her as if again a barrier had come down upon her, shutting one part of her life from the next. So, although she thought sadly of the kind man's death, it already seemed one with the destruction of her parents—that is, a thing which has happened long back in childhood.

She recalled to herself the story of a girl who had slept in a fairy-wood for a hundred years, and she looked fearfully at her hands, expecting them to be gnarled with a century. But they were as they always had been. Her hair about her shoulders was black. She thought that it was possible (and at that time it even seemed most probable) that, although her body might have retained its youthful form, a great flight of time had passed. She would go back to Cowan Corners to find the dark forest had swallowed it. There would be cellar holes lost in thickets, where Boston, Salem, Cowan Corners, Ipswich, etc., had stood. She felt herself alone upon a whole continent. Her body had grown so light and so unreal, she scarce could stand, nor was she wholly convinced of her own reality until she observed she still could cast a shadow.

Doll Bilby had always longed for the comforts of religion, so it was natural that she, having as she believed just witnessed a manifestation of her "god," should now reverently stand and give thanks. She called upon her Father in Hell, thanking him that he had made manifest to her visible proof of his greatness. She called upon her father and mother, blessed them in the great name of Hell, and promised to serve them. She called upon all that vast host of evil things, blessed them, and promised to serve them.

So she floated lightly forth, intent to see the place where Cowan Corners once had stood. Voices called her through the wood, and these she knew were true voices of men, not the eerie cries of ghosts or demons. She answered, "Here am I."

Four men came to her, nor was one of them a minute older than he had seemed last Sabbath at Meeting. Mr. Zelley cried out in pity, for her five days of despair, suffering, and even the astounding pleasures of the night before, had marked the face of Doll Bilby, altering its pretty childish shape.

"My child," he said, "you need not have run away. There is no reason to believe Mr. Bilby's death due to anything but nature. Such a congestion of the lights is not uncommon and often results in death. Doll, as he lay dying, we questioned him if he was worked upon by any witchcraft, and he cried in a loud voice, 'I die spirit free.' "

Doll wept with her hands over her face. None saw that she shed no tears. But she knew that the springs of her tears had dried in the night. Mr. Zelley kissed her gently upon the forehead, and with that kiss he entered into pact with her, for after that he cherished her and became at last her confidant in all things, even in all evil things. And he had once been a minister of God.

Mr. Zelley walked by her side. The three other men looked at her doubtfully, thinking each to himself, "This young woman is a murderess and a witch." They soon outdistanced the minister and the woman, so it was he alone who took her back to her own home.

He told her that from now on, for a little space of time, life would be hard for her. She must live peaceably in the house with Hannah (there was no other place for her to go). She must, by a godly, upright, and virtuous life, and by the goodness of her conversation and dignity of her demeanour, give the lie (he said) to all those who would with tedious rustic simplicity believe her a witch. Both he and Mr. Kleaver knew Mr. Bilby died by nature and not by art. She was, moreover, in all things to trust him. He would clear her name (he said). He had power among these people (he hoped). She was to be of good heart, and the Lord God would be with her. Also he promised to come to her often, praying with her, and strengthening her.

So he took her to her door. In the yard they saw the two indentured servants nailing together a wooden coffin. A group of serious men stood, watching them, and discussed the mutabilities of life, etc. Now and again one helped himself at the barrel of cider that had been rolled out to accommodate their thirst (for thirst is like to rise from serious discourse and ponderous thought).

Mr. Zelley took her within the house. The ovens were fired and pots boiled on the hearth. There was the leg of a great ox on a spit over the coals. The little turnspit dog, which ordinarily served at the tavern, had been brought over to serve for the sad yet pleasing occasion. He turned the spit, as he had been trained to do. His eyes were red and rheumy. The hair was burned away from his hind quarters, and they were red and scorched. Doll remembered how often her foster father at the tavern had given scraps of food to this same miserable small dog, and how he called it "Old Father Time" even when it was a pup, for it had always seemed bent, wizen, and full of many cares. She turned away her head.

The house was full of neighbour women who had come to help prepare the funeral meats. Doll entered. All found reason they must go to the milkhouse, the cellar, the barn, the pantry, or to the best room where the corpse lay and the widow sat in black. Doll and Mr. Zelley were left alone except for a squat and horrid form, who stood its own and feared no woman nor man nor witch. This was the form of Goochey, she who had the laying-out of the dead. She had a face and voice like a man's. Indeed many believed that she was a man who, perhaps having committed offence in the Old World, had fled, thus disguised, to the New. She came from the Welsh borders, and would never touch a corpse unless she had first set upon her hands ten iron rings—one to each finger; for she feared that, without this protection, the spirit of the corpse might enter her veins and thus havoc her body.

When Doll saw this dwarfish man-woman standing in the fire-room, fitting iron rings to her fingers, she shrank from her in horror. Goody Goochey muttered at her, and Mr. Zelley was distressed because he believed she was calling the distrait young woman a witch. However, such was the hoarseness of Goochey's voice and such was the coarseness of her nature, he could not be sure. She might have been calling her another, no more flattering, but surely less dangerous, epithet. Mr. Zelley sincerely hoped so, for he was far more concerned with the reputation of Doll than he was with the good or bad language of Goochey.

CHAPTER FOUR

I

Two Women sleep in the House of Hate. Doll Bilby, having ruined the fortunes of a Student of Divinity, now turns her powers upon a DIVINE.

As soon as the harvest was in and the grave of Jared Bilby was filled, winter came raging in with unwonted ferocity. It came in foot after foot of dazzling snow, at first snowing only in the night, the sun sparkling out brightly in the daytime. But by the New Year (the snow already standing

up to the window-sills and over the fences) the winter grew black. There
was no sun, and such storms blew from out the north and northeast as none
had ever seen or heard of before. There was no ceasing of wind, snow, and
black days. The sea roared continuously, like a thousand lions seeking food
from a false god.

The dead could not be buried. The cattle froze. The wolves went to the
barnyards killing sheep, pigs, cattle, horses. A woman found a lynx among
her ducks. The deer came out of the forest, joining the dairy herds, seeming
to ask food of man and shelter in his barns. Such was the cruel winter that
settled down on the dead man's house, where lived his widow and adopted
child.

These two women lived alone, shut off together from the world in solitude. They lived almost without speaking and in hate. The two farm servants slept in the cow-sheds, and often afterwards said they dreaded even to
enter that gloomy house, where the two women sat watching each other,
hating and being hated.

As was his duty, Mr. Zelley came often to see them. The snows were
so deep he could not travel by horse, so he came on snowshoes with his
Bible under his arm. Each woman he saw separately, praying with her and
trying to comfort her. What he said to Mrs. Hannah all heard as soon as
the roads were broken out and she was out among her gossips, but what
he said to Doll no one knew, although in after years much that she said to
him was known. Mrs. Bilby said that once he came out of Doll's chamber
like a soul spewed out of Hell. He looked roundabout him wildly as if he
had seen a most frightful sight or heard most frightful things. Without as
much as a word for the woman (who hoped he would pause and elucidate
for her certain problems she had found in Leviticus), he seized upon a bottle of rumbullion, swallowed half of that, and made out of the house as
though the devils were after him. The truth is on that day Doll had confessed to him that she was a witch.

Up to this time he had always praised the Christian fortitude, the piety,
the humbleness, and sobriety of Bilby's Doll. But after that he came to be
much agitated at the mere mention of her name, shaking his head, exclaiming, "Dear me," or mentioning the fact that we are all miserable sinners.
He was about the Bilby house more than ever, seeing Doll always alone and
in her own chamber.

When it was said that Doll was a witch, he would reprove the speaker,
sadly bidding him keep such light thoughts on serious matters to himself.
Of course the Bible proves to us that there were witches in the days of
Leviticus and Kings—but today . . . now, he was not sure such things exist.

"Then you do not believe that Jonet Greene . . . ?"

"There does not live a more excellent Christian. Fools call her a witch
because she begins to lean upon her staff and she has a wandering eye.
Many do so and have such."

"Nor yet in the justice done upon the bodies of certain witches in Boston?"

"I will not judge of Boston. I speak only of Cowan Corners."

By these beliefs he gained some friends and lost others. If one does not believe in witches, how can one believe in devils, and if not in devils, how then in Hell?—and Hell is, as all know, the fundamental principle on which good conduct and Christian faith are built.

The women in the Bilby house rarely spoke. Each knew her own duty and did it. The indentured servants kept to the barn, so there was no noise but the swish of the women's skirts or brooms, the rattle of cooking ware, the slam of a door. Even the house dog, grown old and deaf, never barked. The cats, five in all, partook of the silence. They slipped from room to room, eyeing the women suspiciously, but without half the suspicion with which Hannah eyed them.

On a cold night, Gideon, a big malty tom, being chill, sought animal warmth. He jumped upon Widow Bilby's bed. She woke gagged with fear. She seized Gideon and, in spite of the clawing that shredded her arms, strangled him.

The next day with an axe she killed every cat in the house. This brutal slaughter of innocent and pretty pets dismayed Doll almost beyond endurance. She had loved and fed every one, and they often slept upon her bed at night. Filled with abomination towards the woman, she thought at least to give her a headache, or in some way work her a small harm. She looked about for nail paring or wisp of hair with which she might fortify a poppet and work magic against the woman. She found to her astonishment that Hannah evidently suspected her, for any combing from her hair was instantly burned, and she never pared her nails except over a dark cloth which she shook out into the fire. While she did these things, she would look slyly at Doll, as if to say she understood her game, and would take every precaution against her. So she had done ever since her husband died, but Doll did not notice this precaution until February.

Much of the time Doll lay in her own room upon her own narrow bed, and prayed to the Prince of Hell that he send some instructor or messenger to her . . . but thus far only Mr. Zelley came to instruct her. She looked forward to the spring with longing, and because of a dream she had three times concerning a young man asleep in a bed of violets (yet the man she knew, even as she gazed at him, was infernal), she came to believe that in spring, when the violets blossom, a messenger would come.

By February, the roads being broken, Widow Bilby was again about, but Doll in her discontent walked solitary. She saw no one except perhaps once in a long time Goody Greene, and once a week Mr. Zelley (whom she filled full of the phantasies of her childhood). She did not go to Church, and this shocked and angered the whole community, although Mr. Zelley himself insisted that she was too weak and sick to take the hard trip on horseback. Of her neighbours, the Thumbs, she saw nothing. Titus (because of the stories which Widow Bilby told his mother, and she, in turn, told him) went in daily terror of his life. He believed Doll had a poppet of him. If his head ached, it was because she pinched or pricked the head of the poppet. Were it his stomach, lights, bowels, that hurt him, he thought she was rubbing poison on the belly and body of this same poppet. When a black sow he had raised up by hand suddenly jumped into the air and fell dead, he thought she had in passing glanced at it.

Of all things, however, Titus most feared Ahab, the black bull, who had, from the day Doll found him in the forest, changed his gentle nature to one most ferocious and perverse. He urged his father to butcher the animal before it took human life. The deacon said it would be gluttonous to put into the stomach such costly steaks, roasts, etc., and any man who did so deserved to have his bowels rot.

2

Showing that the Sun will always shine again, no matter how black the Winter.

The winter had come early, but (contrary to country superstition) it remained late. For April was full of the racketing of wind, and May was drenched and all but drowned in rain. Not until the end of that month did the earth rally from adversity, and there come still and sunny days. The skies were of heavenly blueness, crossed only by herds of fleecy clouds, as sweet and innocent as wandering lambs. The grass grew green and was prettily pied with multitudes of little flowers. The fruit trees glanced but once at sun and sky, then burst into rapturous blooming. The beauty of these trees is not idle and barren. Their deeds (that is, their fructuation) is as good as their promise (or blossoming). Man may enjoy the loveliness of these flowers, knowing that their loveliness is one of accomplishment.

Special lectures were held at the Meeting-House, giving thanks (where thanks were due) for the beneficent weather, the fertility of all things, the abundance of fish, game, wild foods, and good health of the community. In his praying Mr. Zelley (so it was observed) twice asked with particular passion that the old hatreds, the old jealousies, and the old cruel superstitions might be left behind, and that, in the new land, the spirit of man might break forth as a chick breaks the egg.

The widow's house had stood fast-shuttered for six months. Now it was open to sun and gentle breeze. Doll had been pale, sad, all winter; now she felt the gladness of the earth singing about her in the sweetest voice, calling her to set aside the dark mantle of the soul to take on joy, hope, and even pleasure. She felt frolicsome (as she had often felt with her foster father) and played with the calves and colts, secretly met the Thumb twins by the boundary brook, and filled them full of devilish lies.

She went again to the Meeting-House, and even wantonly enjoyed herself during service, for she found that (such were her latent powers for harm), by merely twisting her fingers together and staring hard at Deacon Pentwhistle as he led the psalm singing, she could twist his throat so that he broke off into a coughing fit. Once, on seeing Titus enter the pasture where Ahab grazed, she slyly and only by thought ordered the creature to have at the young man. Behold! She had the inimitable pleasure of seeing Ahab make at him, and Titus barely reached a tree in time to save his limbs. If Ahab had gained too much on this swift and willing runner, she would have crossed her legs and this would have stopped the bull, for she wanted her old lover frightened, but neither maimed nor slain.

Mr. Zelley continued to wrestle with her in prayer, begging her to believe that she could not be a witch because he (being little better than an atheist) thought such things could not exist. He always claimed that he strove to save her soul. She rewarded him by destroying his. She went often to his house and read in his library, especially of all such books as the "Malleus Maleficarum" and "Sadducismus Triumphatus," etc., which treat of witches and witchcraft, for she was unskilled and wished to learn proper charms and methods for working evil. She also questioned Goodwife Greene. Still she never could learn (except by accident) how to do any of the things she wished. She could not even summon the Devil, who, when he came, came as pleased him—not to her order.

3

An Intimation comes to Doll that some Infernal is about. She believes that he whom she (in wicked abomination) worships will soon send sign to her.

On a morning she awoke, knowing she must go to Greene's house. "I must see Goody Greene," she thought. "I must talk to Goody Greene." She left the pots unwashed, the room unswept. She put on neither coat nor hat, but went as she was, for the day was warm. Now the new year seemed to promise great things, and she felt confident these things she would find. There was every happiness close to her, hiding, waiting to be found. Through these pleasant and cheerful thoughts came racketing the clangour of a brass bell and the terrible blasting of a fish horn, and the voice of man (in this case the voice of the town crier) tolled out to her and to all the world those things that were lost.

Mr. Minchon, the crier, put the fish horn under his arm and took the brass bell by the clapper.

"Gone away!" he cried. "Gone away! Gone away! Four pirates from the Boston Jail, one day before their trial. Calico Jack and Black Pig Murch, Ben Bottle and the Bloody Shad. Likewise, from the pasture of Deacon Thumb, one priceless bull known to you all, the young bull Ahab." (Ding-dong! Ding-dong!)

"Lost or stole, lost or stole, a wallet and the money in it of Captain Tom Buzzey, for he put it on the tavern step, turned, and it was gone. Lost or stole, the wallet of Tom Buzzey—a wallet with the money in it." (Ding-dong!) Mr. Minchon, blowing again upon his fish horn, took himself and his sad news of things lost or things stolen to the next street corner; there, having gathered a crowd about him, he proclaimed again. He moved again and yet again. Knowing the matter of which he spoke, Doll could even at a long way recognize the names of the four pirates, for he always began with full lungs, so she heard four times the crying out of these names, Calico Jack and Black Pig Murch, Ben Bottle and the Bloody Shad, but of Captain Buzzey's loss she heard but once, for Mr. Minchon arrived at it with spent ardour and small voice. Doll continued on her way to Greene's hut.

Between the house of Mr. Zelley and the House of God, she met seven Indians who walked the one after the other, with feet silent as panther paws. They were dressed in the paint and regalia affected by their chief men, in the hope of giving to their persons, by external and childish methods, that true dignity which never can come from without but arises only from the soul. The Indians passed (as they always do) without so much as glancing at the white woman, but she gazed hard upon them, thinking that perhaps they really were devils—as many ignorant people then believed—and that the sign or messenger which she had come to look for constantly would be from them. As she watched, a feather floated or rather seemed to be lifted from the headgear of one of these, and, after wavering a second, it came to rest at her feet. This was a scarlet feather with a yellow tip to it. She stooped to it, and hid it in her bosom, looking longingly after the seven chief men, thinking that having vouchsafed her this favour they might sign her to follow them. They did not.

She went her way, but she went exulting, with red cheeks and smiling mouth. The young men she passed at the tavern drew back that she might not cast a roving eye upon them and desire them, for they all knew of the bewitchment by which she had afflicted Thumb. They guessed, by the unaccustomed red of her cheek and the sparkle of her eye, that (spring having come again) she was wandering about looking for a new young man to devour. The young men stood back; Doll went her way.

She came to the waste marshes by the sea on which sat the tinker's hut. She rapped on the door and cried out her own name. The woman did not call "Come in," as was usual, and Doll heard rustlings, whisperings, tramplings, within. She thought how this woman, like herself, was a witch. Her heart beat quicker with the (to her) delightful thought that perhaps at that very moment she had discovered Greene in confab with some fiend spirit or familiar, and that was why the door was not opened to her, that was why there were rustlings from within. Then Goody Greene opened the door and with her usual affection drew the girl into her miserable house, kissed her, and put out the stool, a joint-stool, for her to sit on. Greene went on with her own business which was concerned with sorting out into heaps dried toadstools and mushrooms.

Doll stared at her and saw how hard the pulse throbbed in the old woman's neck, how her hands shook at her work, how again and again she swallowed as if choked by an oppressive secret. But the girl could not tell the woman she thought her a witch and say, "I would like to see the familiar I know must be close by," for the moment she stopped upon the threshold she was aware that she and the goodwife were not alone. She could feel the air tremble about her; she could almost hear it, all but see it. It was there, close in the one room of the hut, with them. It had not flown at her coming; it had hid itself. She saw that the hangings upon the bed were drawn. "It is yonder," she thought; "the fiend hides in the bed behind drawn curtains." She was sick with fear, but her hopes rode high. She took from her bosom the feather the Indian had dropped. What did Goody Greene think of the feather? Greene said it was a bright and pretty feather, and proved the Indians to be more skillful than we in dyeing. But did it mean nothing more to her than that? No, nothing more. She put it back into her bosom. What would Goody do with so many fungi? She would mix them with snake fat and cure rheumatics. She said she did not know snakes had any fat. Greene said that any distillation from flesh was called "fat." Then they sat for a long time without speaking.

Doll helped with the sorting.

Doll thought to herself, "Be my friend, Goody Greene; confess you are a witch, show me your familiar, and we will work magic together, for I cannot bear to be so lonely." The woman set a pot on the fire to make a gruel for dinner. She put three handfuls of maize into the pot. Doll asked her, "Does the goodman come back for dinner?" "No," said Greene, "I put in the extra handful by mistake." This was very strange, thought Doll, but in her mind made note of the fact that a familiar will condescend to eat maize gruel like a poor man. It distressed Doll that the woman would not trust her and produce her familiar.

The woman squatted before the pot, Doll knelt beside her, and, because she was sick with bitter loneliness, she pressed her face against the woman's sleeve and said, "You are the only mother I have ever had since I was a tiny child, and I, Goody Greene, I am the only child you ever had." The woman let the wooden spoon slip from her fingers so that it was lost in the gruel, and Doll, who jumped up to fetch her another one, saw from the corner of her eye that she glanced at the bed. "Ah," thought Doll, "perhaps she has made herself a popinjay from broom or rags or scarecrow, and calls this thing 'son.' Perhaps that is what she has about her in this room—and in the bed most likely."

As they ate their dinner (of which there was far too much for the two women), Doll asked Greene to tell her again some of those old stories by which she had enchanted her as a child. Greene told her of the unfortunate earl's daughter, who consented to a boat ride with a handsome stranger-man. (The masts were of gold, but did not bend before the wind. The sails were of taffety, and did not fill with the breeze.) They sailed three leagues and then she spied his cloven hoof and wept most bitterly, knowing it was no man but a devil with whom she must cope.

Greene told her other ungodly stories from an ungodly antiquity. Doll questioned her at every turn. She must know how each magic trick was worked; she must hear how it was Fair Jennifer of Bageley Wood called her demon to her. Greene told her the true story of how a lycanthropic man, believing himself to be a wolf, killed fifteen in the Midlands before the soldiers got him. She told her of Queen Mab and her tiny tinsel court. At last Doll got to her feet to go. She heard the bed creak, and saw a moving lump bulge out the drawn curtains. But the familiar did not make itself manifest. As Greene stared at the hearth, Doll slyly drew the red and yellow feather from her bosom and, brushing by the bed, she slipped the feather within. Calling a hasty good-bye, she left abruptly, and began to run, for she (in spite of hopes) half feared a great, scaly, black fiend would leap from the bed and on the instant shoulder her, and march off down to Hell.

4

Doll finds an Imp in a cellar. It proves unfriendly to her.

On the next day Doll returned to the marsh hut. Again she found Goody Greene seemingly alone, yet the one room was mysteriously filled with a Presence. That day Greene was making teas, infusions, etc. She had four pots on the coals, and was much confined, in her thoughts and in her words, by watching them.

Beside the hut was a cold-cellar dug into the ground, and in this Greene stored her herbs, her drugs, fats, oils, bottles, pans—all the matter for her trade. She wanted organy, dittany, and galingale root. Doll ran quickly to the cellar. She knew where these things were laid.

She opened the door, which was in the shape of a bulkhead, and ran down the short flight of stairs. Here she had played in childhood, and the strong odours of herbs, roots, and meat oils were fragrant to her. So she paused a moment, sniffing about. There was a rattle on a dark shelf behind a clay crock, and a snake skin shook. She thought she had left the familiar behind her in the good woman's bed, yet she cried out in her horror, calling by mistake to the *true* God—not to the Satan she had sworn to serve; for there, peeking about the clay crock, was a ball of tawny fur and from out the fur glared a little man's face. His features were like an Ethiop's, and his head no bigger than an orange. She noticed, even in the brief moment she paused to look at him, that hands and even nails were perfect. Behind dangled a long ringed tail—a pretty tail of black and dun.

This imp was much offended by her, for it scolded her in strange languages, and its eyes were red with hate. So in terror she, who thought herself brave enough to stand up before Lucifer, fled from the littlest of his servants. This servant she saw again, and the next time without fear.

She ran to Goody Greene, crying she had seen a terrible thing.

"Hush," said Greene; "you saw a skull or two, or a snake skin . . ."

"No, no, no, it was alive. It was a little imp."

"You dreamed it—or it may have been a cat. Cats get into my cellar for the sake of the fats."

"It was not a cat."

But Greene knew it was not an imp.

At the end Doll was cast down because Greene trusted her so little she would not confess the truth, even when she had seen the actual fact of the imp's body, had heard it chatter. She was distressed, picked up her bonnet and put it on her head. There was much work to do, she said. Mrs. Hannah was plucking geese, and she must be back in time to rub ointment on them where they bled.

"Doll," said Greene, "I heard you cry out to God for help when you saw the cat in the cellar."

"I forgot myself," murmured Doll, and was ashamed that in her extremity she had called upon God and not upon the Foul Fiend she had sworn to worship. She guessed this was the reason both for the imp's rage and Greene's mistrust. "I will not forget again," she said.

Goody Greene assumed an attitude which seemed indeed to the girl one of mock piety. She rolled her eyes and said, "Always give thanks where thanks are due."

Doll thought she was reproving her. "I will next time," she promised. Then she went away.

CHAPTER FIVE

I

The night crackles with Fire. Hell laughs and a Witch meets that which she long has sought.

Still in the month of May, catastrophe came to Cowan Corners. On three nights, consecutively, great fires broke out. The first took the noon-house of the Church. The second the rope-walk of Deacon Pentwhistle. The third took the barns, sheds, outhouses of Deacon Ephraim Thumb. This last fire was upon the thirty-first day of May and the morrow would be June.

The farm servants of Widow Bilby came up from the cow-sheds. They called to the window in the attic where Hannah slept (for since the nights were warm she preferred the desolation of an attic to the proximity of her detested companion), "Widow Bilby, Widow Bilby, there's a great fire at our neighbour's. Shall we not go to help?" The widow told them to go and do their best, and God go with them. She, too, would follow soon. She got into her clothes, and Doll heard her stamping down the stairs and out of the house. Doll looked from her window and the sky was orange. She clutched her throat, for fire terrified her (because of her parents' death), yet it fascinated her (because of her unnatural yearning for Hell).

Will she, nill she, the young woman dressed and, much perturbed, she reached the outskirts of the onlookers. With them she could not mingle, for they feared her, and she dreaded this same fear. She withdrew to a big straw stack, and beneath its overhanging top (for the cattle had rubbed against it) she found herself a hiding-place.

Every able man in the village was there, and half of the women. She saw Titus passing buckets and getting out gear, nor could she have looked at him without some slight regret, for he was a goodly, comely man and a young witch has an amorous eye. She heard the shouting, the running about, the snap and rustle of the flames. Sometimes other idle watchers came close to where she hid, and from their talk she learned that these three fires had all been started by a cat breathing fire. Widow Bilby had said that this same cat could be no other than her old tom, Gideon, now dead a three-month, thus maliciously returned from Hell. Doll heard her own name spoken and saw heads shaken. She also heard that Ahab was still within the vehemently burning barn. Because of his ferocity as well as because of his wanderings, he had lately been closely penned. So far no one had been able to loose him, although several had essayed to do so. The horses, savage with fear, had been moved far from the fire lest they, with the fondness of their kind, return to their accustomed stalls and perish. The cattle were running about the barn-yard, where they interfered with the work, upsetting buckets, etc. Such swine as the Thumbs possessed burned to their deaths, their stench polluting the air. Doll sickened at the smell, for she never could forget the holocaust of Mont Hoël. Until the fire burst the ridgepole, the doves flew constantly from their cotes under the eaves. Some were so singed they fell to the muck of the yard and, trampled under foot, perished.

Just before the fall of the barn floor, Ahab was loosed. With sparks upon his coat, his eyes rolling most horribly, he came out of danger at a gallop. Seeing the crowd, he charged furiously, passing over the bodies of three, yet not staying to gore them, so intent was he on the men who ran. Wherever he went, the crowd melted and the shouting rose. Many believed it was this wicked bull, and not the Hell cat, that had set these fires, for now he seemed intent on guarding the fire and would let no one near it. Doll thought the creature was her friend—perhaps sometime he would become her familiar; but when she saw him coming for her on a brisk and determined trot she ran up the short ladder leaning against the straw stack, not relying unduly on either charms or friendship.

The same moment the roof fell and sparks flew up, rising into the night air an hundred feet and more, until the sky seemed filled with departing souls flying up and up to the Throne of God.

Doll, panting from her vexatious exercise upon the ladder and sweating from her recent fear, found herself upon the top of the straw stack. She was sprawled upon hands and knees. In the fury of the orange light (which with the fall of the roof suddenly was most horrible) she gazed about her. Then she saw she was not alone, for with her was a luggard fiend who stretched his length upon the straw. His eyes were red as though filled with blood. He wore (she said) a costume like a seaman's, except that, where a seaman's clothes are coarse, his were fine and dainty. For instance, the hoops in his ears were not of brass but jewels. She said he had a silk kerchief tied about his head. Upon his breast he bare—as if in mockery of that virgin whose worship the Catholics prefer to the worship of God—the very imp, the little servant, whom she had seen in Greene's cold-cellar. She guessed he was her god, or a messenger from her god, so, crying out, "Master, master, you have come for me," she further prostrated herself before him. Now she was no more alone, for this fiend had come for her.

At first the demon made no response; then, after a little and with a few high but kindly words, he permitted her to approach. She said she could scarce believe that, after such long waiting and such unanswered prayers, he had at last come. "Oh, I have been lonely, lonely; I have had no one," and she sobbed (no tears came).

"Why do you sob, Bilby's Doll?"

"Because I am happy at last."

He reproved her gently because she had ever doubted his advent, which he said he had announced to her by the lighting of these three great fires.

It was his will that turned her steps to the ladder and, as she became too intent upon the fire to notice the summons of his will, he loosed a fierce black bull who urged her up the humble ladder and into his presence.

"And you really are from . . ."

"From Hell," he said, and showed her his teeth that were white and strong as an animal's. She shrank a little from him. He told her not to fear to approach and touch him, for he was in human guise. There was no sulphur on his person, no blasting fire in his hands. To prove his wholesome humanity he touched her wrist, and she experienced a shock of joy such as she had formerly experienced when her mother had led her to Satan in the heart of the oak wood. This joy she accounted a religious joy—such (so she explained to Mr. Zelley) as a Christian would experience at receiving the visitations of an angel.

Now was she no longer alone in this sad world, for her god (that is, Satan) had come to succour her, or had at least sent her a messenger. She asked him which he was, Satan or lesser demon. At the mention of Satan's name, he bowed his head reverently. He admitted that he was but one of many fallen angels who had left Paradise with the Awful Prince. At first she was cast down, for she had hoped to hear that it was the Prince himself. But she looked again, and marked how handsome a man he was and of what a fine ruddy complexion. She saw how strong were his shoulders, and how arched and strong his chest. She was thankful then that Satan had not seen fit to send her merely some ancient hag or talking cat, ram, or little green bird, but this stalwart demon. She thought, "He can protect me even from the hate of Mrs. Hannah." She thought, in her utter and damnable folly, "He can protect me from the Wrath of God."

The whole barn fell into the cellar hole. As she looked towards this glowing pit, she thought of that vaster and crueller bonfire in which her soul would burn forever. She thought well to ask him a little concerning those pains which she later must suffer. He laughed at her. There would be, he said, no pain. Those who served Satan faithfully in this world were never burned in Hell. Was not Satan King of Hell? Why should he burn those who loved and obeyed him? She was stuffed full of lunatic theology. The only souls that suffered in Hell were such of God's subjects as had angered Him and yet had made no pact of service with Satan. These the devils burned—even as God ordered. It gave them a thing to do. He pointed out there were no angels in Hell watching out that God's orders be fulfilled, so naturally the devils did not carry out the cruel sentences God meted out to true subjects of Satan. Again he said, "Why should they?"

She asked him of news concerning her father and mother—good witches whom the French had burned in Brittany. These he assured her roamed happily and at free will, finding cooling breezes even in Hell. When it pleased them, they sat and conversed with antiquity or with the greatest kings, princes, etc., who had ever lived in this world. But her mother was a kindly woman and got more pleasure out of good deeds than from idle conversation. Therefore Satan permitted her to go about among those who burn and give them water or fan away the smoke. Doll was convinced that the messenger had indeed seen her mother, whom she always remembered as a gentle and loving woman.

Was this kind mother aware of her daughter's sufferings? Was it she who had thought to send him to comfort her? No, no. A mortal who is dead cannot see back into life. It was Satan himself who had pitied her and ordered him to her side. Him he bade her worship, "Truth in and humbly." At first she could not understand this reversal of many sacred phrases. Later she came to know this blasphemous jargon well. For every night she said Our Lord's most holy prayer backwards—thereby addressing herself to Satan; but what came to her as punishment for this wicked practice we shall see.

He had about him a bottle of grog, and from this he baptized her, "Ghost holy and son, Father of name the in." Now he said she was no longer Bilby's Doll. Now she was the Devil's Doll. And he kissed her reverently upon the forehead. His pretty imp peeked out from within his blue blouse where he kept it. He bade her stroke it. This she did. She said it was a warm and gentle imp, with tired and thoughtful (but not malicious, as she had at first thought) eyes. It was well furred and, if it were not for its wise, sad face and minute black hands, she might have thought it indeed but an animal. She came to love this imp, playing with it and petting it. Its name, he said, was Bloody Shad. "Why," she said, "that is the name of one of the pirates that escaped." The fiend said he knew that fine fellow well. He had taken his nickname from the imp the young woman now held in her pretty little hands.

The fire was laid and the dawn gave more light than the embers. Birds shook the thin, watery air with their calling. A few men still stood about the fire. The one called to the other that Ahab was in a village garden devouring new-set cabbage plants and terrifying women. Doll leaned towards these men, listening to their news. As she turned back to inquire of her instructor the true status of Ahab in the community and in the Hierarchy of Hell, she found to her great sorrow that he was gone.

At the same time one of the barnyard fowls who the night before had suffered bitterly, being as he was a cock, struck a gallant attitude upon a heap of dung, and, lifting his head, greeted the coming day with a triumphant cock-a-doodle-doo. She heard the cocks on her own farm answer this challenge with distant fairy cries.

This was a new day, and with it came great hopes.

Later she was asked if she did not know that cocks crow at an earlier hour—for they generally begin before the light. Yes, this she knew. But her demon must have had the power to stay the crowing of the cocks, for he never remained later than the first cry from such a bird, yet often he stayed until the day was almost light—for instance, on that first meeting. It was light when he left, and yet no cock cried until he was gone.

Where did he go to?

He went back to Hell.

2

How Doll became a Servant to the Servant of Hell.

This fiend—this caco-demon—came to her again and yet again. But after his first visit there was a pause and it seemed likely that he might not come again. She thought daily to get his summons, either to Black Sabbath or to class of more instruction. Would he bid her mount a broom and fly to him? Against this emergency she went to Dame Cosset's, a broom-maker, and paid sixpence ha'penny for a new red broom that she might appear handsomely mounted before her lord. This broom she hid in her chamber. Likewise she hid rushes and clay for the devising of poppets, and glass, knives, pins, and needles, for the working of her master's will.

On the eighth night from the time of the Thumb fire, she heard close by the house the hooting of an owl—which she knew was no owl. And Hannah, too, recognized the falsity of that cry, for she started up, saying that Indians were about. That was at eight o'clock. At nine they heard again the crying of an owl, and the dog at the barn began to howl dismally. Hannah swore that it was the bonded boys playing tricks. By ten again the hooting of the owl, but Hannah slept. Doll Bilby got to her room, and, taking clothes and a pillow, made a dummy of herself which she thrust into the bed, thus to deceive Hannah if the woman should look about for her. Grasping her red broom, but not essaying to mount it, she ran joyously from the house, anxious to meet her god or the accredited messenger of that god.

She came out of the house and found the moon to be rising and the night to be of a dainty, delicate, springtime beauty. Birches twinkled in the moonlight; their slender trunks seemed to be the white limbs of nymphs. The grasses that her broom brushed were sweet with flowers. She ran up and down the pastures, along the fences, over the fields. She ran until she was like to drop, and then found him where hereafter she always was to find him—in an opening in birch woods, enthroned upon a tussock. In the flowery pasture land this spot which he had selected for himself was a darling fairy bower. The exact spot is known to this day, for Doll, on seeing the fiend, threw her red broom into the birch trees, thus marking the spot, for she never took it back with her. Five years later boys found it and, on being taken to Dame Cosset, the woman said yes, it was one of her own brooms, and indeed the very one she had once sold to wicked Bilby for sixpence ha'penny. It is noticeable to this day that cattle will not graze there, and that dogs coursing for rabbits will stop frozen at this place and howl; yet so inferior is the good sense and righteousness of man to that of beasts, it has become a common tryst for lovers, who, in each other's arms, repeat with foolish laughter (and yet, it may be hoped, with some sensible fear) the story of how Bilby's wicked Doll there met and loved a demon. Then they will go by moonlight to the cellar hole of the Bilby house, and pick a little of the yellow broom which country people call witch's blood.

The demon Prince permitted the witch to kneel to him and let her kiss his feet (which were not cloven). She noticed how cold to touch he was—

like the fiends and devils in old tales. But the big hands he put upon her head (she reverently kneeling) were warm as any man's, and this heartened her. So he welcomed her "Fellowship Christian in." Then he seated himself and permitted her to sit. At first the talk was of great dignity, but soon it was much like that of one gossip to another. He told her how his work had prospered him in Salem, in Boston, and how in Hartford. And how another fiend (but this one in shape of woman) worked in New York among the silly Dutch, as far north as Albany, and yet another (this fiend in the shape of a great tawny dog) in Virginia and the Carolinas. "Ah," cried Doll, "how thankful I, or rather all of us witches roundabout the Bay Colony should be that you have deigned to appear to us in the shape of a true proper man." The fiend laughed horribly, saying there had been much complaining among the wizards and the warlocks because he was but a man—not a wild free wanton wench like her of the Dutch country.

Then he asked her if she could come with ease to him on such nights as he should call her, and she answered yes, she could come to him, but she must always wait her foster mother's sleeping and then leave secretly by her own window. She begged him to cry no more as hooting owl, for this aroused suspicion—the woman guessing it to be a man's voice. At this he seemed angry, and said the cries she had heard were in truth no man's cries, for he had bade an owl to go about the house and hoot. He explained to her that, as man may not laugh convincingly upon command, neither may owl hoot. Still, for such clumsiness the owl must die. So they argued for a while, Doll pleading with him to spare the unfortunate owl, and in the end, going back on her early statements, she said the cry had not sounded like a man, but exactly like an owl, and that the creature had hooted amazing well. He agreed, therefore, to spare the owl and to send him often to call her out.

She was rejoiced and humbled to think that he, so great and busy a fiend, would find time to send for her again and again, and she confessed to him the unendurable loneliness, desolation, and despair of her life—especially since her foster father had died; how even Titus, who had once professed to love her, now fled in terror from her glance, fearing her witchcraft; how Mrs. Hannah dreaded her so she would not leave a combing of hair nor a paring of nail about the house, and also how this woman had butchered Gideon and her other creatures.

As she talked the fiend came close to her, soothing her with his hands upon her body. Then she suddenly stopped her rehearsal of sorrow, and for a moment she went in deathly fear, for she guessed what the fiend intended. Still, such was her wickedness, she also felt uplifted and glorified, and in the end, it were these feelings that conquered in her, for she entirely forgot or set aside Christian fears and Christian modesty. The fiend kissed her and told her to be of good heart, for of all the many witches he had met in his recent travels through New England, it was she he most fancied and she should be his paramour. So she consented, and thus came to be the servant of the servant of Hell.

3

A thought for a Wise Man. Is Beauty of Flesh a good or evil thing? And
the opinions of pagan Antiquity as contrasted to our own THEOLOGY.

There is one quality in this world which men call goodness. This is the
beauty of the spirit, and is from God and of God. There is another quality,
which is beauty of the body, and from whence comes it?

The heathen Greeks, whom the Reverend Pyam Plover has suggested
were but devil worshippers, believed these two things to be identical; that
is, what is good is beautiful, what is ugly is evil. Yet need the thoughtful
Christian but read history, or look about him today, to see that rather than
identical these two beauties should be considered noncongruent or mutually
antagonistic. All must have observed how often the most virtuous women
have been of no great bodily beauty, and yet certain famous wantons have
been blessed (or cursed) with bounteous fleshly charms. One should but consider the lives of Cleopatra, that Helen known as Helen of Troy, Dido, etc.

Beauty of the body, in that it excites to lust and evil thoughts, is wicked,
but the sick, ugly, maimed body, in that it excites the sweet and gentle
passion of pity, is from God. From this reason modesty in the young, blooming, comely female is of greater necessity than in the sick and ancient.

But it is not alone in a consideration of the needful and (in its proper
place) decent female body that one may observe how often Evil has wormed
its way into the hearts of humanity under specious guise of Beauty. For when
the Devil would steal the soul of Bilby's Doll, he showed her lavishly and
in wanton profusion such sights of pagan beauty no Christian, godly woman
may ever expect to see.

For her this seemly ordered earth, on which we set our houses, in which
we humbly plough and delve—this quiet earth for her broke open into a
rare flowering. She saw the satyrs (close by the salt marshes) gambolling
upon mud flats. In the morning she saw the goatprints of their hooves. She
heard nymphs sing all night in trees. She saw birch trees in the moonlight
spun out of solid silver, and those common flowers, which by day (and in
the sight of God) are but buttercups, turned into glittering jewels which
by their very brilliance frightened her. Even that fiend the Devil sent to her
was handsomer far than any mortal man might be. He was lovely to the
eye, and his touch was as the touch of fire. The strength of his arms was
beyond that of mortal men (who are born but to praise God and die). So
was every moment that she spent with him a moment of ecstasy. How can
mortal man contend with fiends in the love of woman? Have they such unholy power to arouse passion?

It is well known that no woman who has ever accepted an infernal lover
may content herself with the ruck of men—such seeming, after the love of
Hell, but pale, unsubstantial shadows. And the same may be said the other
way over, for men, it is said, who have known nymphs, elves, or succubi,
will long for them all their lives, eschewing the feeble impuissant arms of
women.

So it is an established fact that Beauty that delights the eye is more often a curse from Lucifer than a blessing from God. Let the reasonable and righteous man content himself with that which is plain and seemly—whether it is a church or wife or horse or land that he considers. Let him not yield to the delights of the eye, but rather to the beauty of goodness, piety, etc., which burns from within.

4

Some remarkable Wonders of an Invisible Kingdom.

For fairy women came to her by night, whispering . . . "Get up . . . get up . . . get up . . ."

Strange hands plucked at her bedclothes, pinched or patted her.

Although her window was fast shut, once a great scaled and hairy arm came in by that same window, and she trembled. Now the arm grew to three times, four times, the length of human arm. She saw it sweep the room with a blind and scythe-like motion. It searched for her. She remained still. Then it was gone as miraculously as it had come.

There was a vast animal that rubbed nightly against the house, sniffing and blowing.

A monster (she thought it a demon) treaded the roof-tree by night.

Such was her appreciation of these awful and yet to her (coming from him she chose to accept as God) pleasing sights, she scarcely slept, being more awake by night than day, for at night she could hardly lie upon her bed nor close her eyes. She was forever staring and listening, listening and staring. With the crowing of the cock these disturbing visions retreated to that same Hell in which they had their geneses.

Sometimes she floated forth without volition, as on a certain night when she cried out, "Master, command me and I will come." Then far away and from the midst of the moonlight, she heard fairy women cry, "Get up . . . get up . . . get up . . ."

"Then I will," she said. Of a sudden her body was filled with lightness and (at first maintaining her horizontal position) she was elevated from off her bed. Thrice around the room she floated and, looking down, she saw her own vacant body as it lay still and flat as any corpse. "If I am going out to walk wet fields," she thought, "I should put on slippers." Then the red slippers Mr. Bilby once had bought her in Boston appeared upon her feet. She floated through the window, but once this was cleared she was set in vertical position. However, she felt no contact with the grass, and she took no steps. She floated on.

The moon was big upon the hills. The night air shook ravishing perfumes from the flowers and new leaves. The air was full of birds' songs (although it was dead of night), of voices, strange music, laughter. She floated on. The silver birches twinkled and bowed to her. Her name was called by a thousand little voices. A million gleaming eyes watched her. At last she was thus conveyed to the fiend, who was seated upon a hillock, as on a throne. He raised her up when she would prostrate herself to him. He bade her have no fear, for, although in Hell he was indeed a great prince, upon earth he was as mortal man and her true love.

In the morning, when she awoke in her own bed, she believed that the adventure of the night had been but another dream. She drew her body from between the sheets, and set her feet upon the floor. Upon her feet were the red slippers, and they were wet. Upon the sheets were green stains from the grass crushed beneath her feet.

How could she know truth from dreams and dreams from truth?

5

We are informed that there is no marriage nor giving in marriage in Heaven, but in Hell it well may be otherwise.

She never saw her fiend by day. He came at dead of night. He went by cock crow (yet, as already pointed out, sometimes delaying this same crowing). He ruled by love and not by terror. She gave him soul and body, both as act of impious homage, and of true love. So a month wore away— the month of June.

At every turn and in every way he comforted and charmed her. She confessed to him how greatly she dreaded that day, which he said must now soon come, when he would be summoned back to Hell. She begged him to take her with him—for without him she had no use for this dull earth. She begged him to slay her now, and thus, her spirit released, she would take her way with him to Hell, and there live with him, once more with her parents—whom the French burned in Brittany. So she fitted his hands to her throat. He would not. He only promised her again and again that when she lay dying he himself would come to her once more, and stand at her bed's head. He promised her a short life, and life everlasting.

So this young woman, who had often shown a need for true religion, found great comfort in a false one. It was a fiend that fed, it would seem, her soul's hunger. By him and by the hopes of Hell she was comforted, as the true Christian is by his Lord and the hopes of Paradise. She became reconciled to life, to death, to adversity, loneliness, and despair.

There was no problem that he could not answer for her, no doubt he 'did not lay. For instance, she was distressed to think that when her true life should begin (that is, when she died and entered Hell) she would not see the kind foster father, but would undoubtedly encounter his disagreeable wife. No, explained the demon, she was wrong, for he knew that Jared Bilby was already there, well and at peace. He had committed mortal sin by saving her when a child, for she was already a witch, and it is mortal sin to save a witch. "But at the time he did not know I was a witch. I do not think he ever believed it." The demon said that made no difference. Mortal sin was mortal sin, but Satan, grateful to him for saving the life of Doll, had never carried out the cruel sentence which had been meted out to him at the Awful Judgement Seat. Doll wanted to know what this sentence was. He said it

was of so revolting a nature he could not tell her. His words made her hate
Jehovah, and she felt Satan was a kinder "god."

The demon went on to assure her that Mrs. Hannah would undoubtedly be given place in Heaven. She was a pious woman, always at meeting,
lecture, and prayer. There were already millions of just such vixens singing
miserable psalms, badly out of tune, about the golden streets. If she did in
some way get sent down to Hell, he promised they would all get together
and make it hot for her. They couldn't endure such ugly scolds in Hell. Doll
was surprised. "She is not ugly. She is remarkably handsome." The devil was
surprised. He said he had supposed from what he heard that she must be
very ugly.

There was now only one thing with which she could vex herself, for
her demon comforted her at every turn. Sometimes as he held her in his
arms she moaned a little and pulled away. He begged her to tell him. He
was her true love. Let her tell him and he would help. Then she told him
that she knew that upon occasions fiends do actually marry mortal women.
He laughed at her, and tried to turn her fancy from such homely thoughts.
She would not be turned. He said witches and women talked alike, and yet
he did not refuse to marry her.

With the commendable and proper thought of marriage in her head, she
sought out Goody Greene (whom she had seen but little of late). She walked
with her through the woods, helping her gather that bitter flower which the
Indians call the jug-woman's-baby. The old woman was tired and the two
sat upon a stone. From where they sat Doll could see the birch woods, the
rough pastures, where by night she met her devil.

"Dear Goody, tell me as you used to tell the story of the goblin or infernal who came to a maid's window on a May eve and wed her in a respectful and seemly manner. Why cannot devils always do so? It is sad to
think that a loving wench—betrayed by love—may become but the doxy of
the devil." She was near tears—although now she never had tears to shed.

The old woman told the story of Fair Jennifer of Bageley Wood. She
had a demon lover—a black and scaly fellow, cold to touch as serpent or any
ice or iron. He came to her window three times, calling her to get up and
come to him. She lay disobedient upon her bed. Then on the third occasion
he entered her chamber by the chimney hole, bearing in his hands green
branches, and he was dressed in green leaves. Jennifer and the demon walked
around and around the bed. He promised to be her loving husband until
death, to avenge her of her enemies, and she promised to be his obedient
wife until death and after death, and to deny God and Christ Jesus. Then
upon the hearth she made him a cake, and in the cake they put blood drawn
from the veins of both their arms. They ate this cake and were man and
wife. His name was Karlycuke. But Fair Jennifer of Bageley Wood has been
dead three hundred years. Such a thing cannot happen today. Doll thought
otherwise, but kept her own counsel. Nor was she wrong.

On the way back to the hut on the waste land, Doll asked her how it
was she could always remember these old stories. The woman said she had
told them many, many times. "To other children, as once you told them to

me?" "Yes," she said, "to other children." Then she set down her basket and
put her arms about Doll. She said once she had a son, but she would say
no more of him and Doll guessed he was a long time dead.

One night, a night of full moon, Doll woke and found the fiend there
in the room beside her bed. He signed her to silence, but Doll, who had
many times by night stolen out of the house, knew that Hannah in her attic
room slept soundly. All that the black and scaly fiend did for Jennifer, he
now did for his love, and more. He set his imp upon the bedpost for a witness, and on the whole nothing could have been more seemly. There was
no hearth in Doll's chamber. They could bake no cake. He pricked his wrist
and her wrist, and each drank a little from the other's veins. This slight cut
upon her wrist never healed, as would a normal cut. It was red and angry
to the day she died. Thus does Nature (which usually essays to heal) shrink
from the lips of Hell.

It was the last of June, and the summer solstice (for on that day he
married her) was passed. The leaves broadened into summer and the night
air no longer held the rhapsody of spring. Now Doll had always known that
he must leave her, but it hurt her to find that he could go without farewell.
She comforted herself with the memory of his sweet love and her hopes for
the future.

6

The Quenching of three Evil Firebrands.

There were hanged upon a spit of mud in the tidal waters of the Charles
at Boston, on the tenth day of July, 1671, three pirates, long wanted for their
unparalleled offences. These three, Black Pig Murch, Ben Bottle, and the
Bloody Shad, had been taken into custody some two months earlier, but,
having escaped their guardians, separated each to his own hiding. By agreement they came together again upon the second of July, thinking the hunt
to be up and that they could get a pinnace and sail south to safety. So all
three were taken together, but the fourth, Calico Jack, was never taken. Being duly indicted and tried, these fine rogues were found guilty of many
homicides, robberies, and cruel acts of mayhem upon the high seas, so were
condemned to hang.

Justice was done upon their bodies, and in due time (after the corpses
had hung in chains some weeks, serving as due warning to others, especially
to seamen) these bodies were buried in mud, close to the place where they
had died.

Sic transeunt maleficii mundi! [5]

[5] Thus pass the malefactors of the world.

CHAPTER SIX

I

A Trap is set for two Tender Souls.

Doll never thought the demon would wait until her death-bed to come to her. Every moonlight night and every sunny day she looked for him and thought, "Perhaps this day or this night he will come to me." She always wore even quite commonly her prettiest, most worldly clothes, and she kept her shaggy black hair as neat as she was able. She thought, "He sees me always, everything I do, everything I wear," and she kept herself comely for him. She guessed he even knew her thoughts, and so she dedicated them to him.

In her own chamber she daily worshipped and prayed to Satan, as the fiend had taught her; that is, by foul blasphemies, such as the reversal of the Lord's Prayer, etc. She even wrote little hymns to Satan and entuned them for him. She felt that she should be about some harm, such, for instance, as the bewitchment of the godly, but she received no command, so she did, for some time at least, no devilment. She was happy and grew sleek.

The widow was already courted by three men, all reputable widowers and church members. Now that the windows were opened and Doll sang as she worked, and her own mind was taken up with her suitors, she did not fear her so much. Each went her own way.

Doll had always shown a dawdling and trifling attitude towards honest labour. And in this offence Bilby had encouraged her. For he had had her out in the woods and the fields (where there was nothing a young female could do) with himself, instead of leaving her at home to serve Hannah, as would have been more proper.

Now that he was gone, Doll still continued in her childish and frivolous wanderings. She often sat herself on the stone fence by the willow brook which divided the lands of the Bilbys and the Thumbs. The bonded boys upon the farm said they often saw her sitting upon the stone fence and feeding small rotten apples to Ahab (whose ferocity now had grown hideous). Yet this girl patted him freely, talking to him, laying her face against his cheek, and all these attentions Ahab accepted of. She wished him for her familiar, but the creature (so she told Mr. Zelley) would never do one of the things she asked of him, except to pursue and render ridiculous young Thumb.

Mrs. Thumb heard that her black bull was often down on the boundary with Bilby's Doll. She asked that he be penned, for she guessed that Doll was at the bottom of Ahab's remarkable dissatisfaction in Titus. She wished the bull withdrawn from the young woman's influence. By so doing and thus making these fields by the willow brook safe to cross, she did great harm to her own household, for now it was Labour and Sorrow who came daily (if they could) to see Doll. Undoubtedly she had been waiting for the twins to come and play with her. She must have seen in these weak and disobe-

dient little girls fit matter for her to work upon to the further enlargement
of the Kingdom of Hell. For she lay in wait there, and finally they came
to her. They came slyly. No one at first knew they came, and they played
at ungodly games, furtively, where no one of either house could know. Thus
passed September, and October, and the half of November.

2

*The Horrible Example of the Thumb Twins, or to what a Pass Disobedience
may bring a Child.*

Doubtless some who read these words will recall how in childhood they
were brought to obedience and wholesome respect for authority by hearing
a mother, or grannie, or aunt, or servant tell them the awful story of the
Thumb twins, and to what their disobedience brought them. It is true that
these children had never been well, and for them to fall from health to point
of death was not a long fall. Nor when one considers what good use has
been made of their example, and how many other children have learned decent docility from their story, can one wholly regret the incident which occurred as follows.

On the twentieth day of November (the day had been a mellow, warm,
yellow day) the disobedient Labour and Sorrow went to the willow brook,
and there found, as they hoped to find, the witch-woman awaiting them.
She was all in fine scarlet as her fancy was. The children said they dared
not stay and play—their mother had sent them to Goody Greene's to buy
mints. She would wonder if they did not return within the hour. They said
(a long time later) that Doll smiled at them in a terrible fashion and suggested to them that what their mother wanted was of no importance. But
the twins for once were mindful of their good mother's wishes. They said
again they could not stay. They had only come to tell her that they could
not stay. "Well, take that then," said the witch, and angrily tossed across the
brook and to their feet two dolls that she had contrived out of corn husks
and pumpkin seeds. So she went away, and the twins went to Greene's.

They came home again and they were late as usual, or rather as always,
for they were dawdling, mischievous children. Their mother was angry with
them. She could not whip nor even shake them. She dared not, they were
too feeble. She put them to bed without their dinner and there they lay to
supper-time, talking and whispering, laughing to each other. She bade them
get up for supper. They would not, but lay in their bed. No one thought
further of them until morning. The truth is that, having no dinner and no
supper, they grew hungry and so they ate the dollies, which were made mostly
of pumpkin seeds. The pumpkin in all its parts, even the seeds of it, is wholesome food. It could not be this that sickened the children, yet from that day
they sickened.

For forty-eight hours they were afflicted in their stomachs. This passing
a little, an even more grievous malady seized their bowels, which seemed to
rot away. Their very bones gave out from within them, refusing to support
their weight, etc. They pined, would not eat because of the pain they were

in. First it was "My belly, mamma, oh, my belly!" and the next, "My throat, mamma!" or "My head, mamma, my miserable bowels! My vitals are decaying within me." These frightful pains were the result of their disobedience, for if they had done as bidden—that is, if they had eschewed the young woman and received no presents from her—they never would have so suffered.

They had thus sickened and suffered for a week, and then Mrs. Thumb, putting fresh linen upon their bed, found, between bed and wall, all that remained of the pumpkin-seed poppets. It was plain that these two poppets were intended to represent the twins. They were all but identical, yet was the one (Sorrow) plumper than the other (Labour). They had dark eyes, made from little buttons, and light hair fashioned from corn silk. In this respect they simulated the brown eyes and yellow hair of the twins. The one was tied about the waist with a red rag, and the other with a blue, and it was thus in these two colours Mrs. Thumb habitually dressed them.

The twins gaped at their mother as she found these things, and their eyes were guilty eyes. She asked them from whence came these dollies. They swore they did not know. Perhaps a cat had brought them in. They were sure a cat had brought them in. Their mother told them they were lying and they said nothing. She said she would shake them, and they said that they were far too sick, and Labour offered to fall into a spasm. Well, if they would not tell from whence these things were, would they tell who it was that had eaten out the pumpkin seeds that had made their vitals. The twins responded heartily, yes, it was they themselves who had eaten up the vitals. The woman cried out in anguish, "My children, oh, my poor children, it is your own vitals that you have eaten, God help us all!" And she rushed from the sickroom, weeping, wringing her hands, screaming to her husband, her son.

For three days the twins would not say from whence were these poppets. Their mother fancied it was old Goody Greene had given them, because she knew that the girls had been to her evil hut on the very day they sickened. Now Greene, as well as Mr. Kleaver, had been called in every few days to advise in the care of the twins. Mrs. Thumb was enraged to think that she had thus allowed the woman access to her darlings. But Widow Bilby told her to look to Doll, for she knew that she had in her own room pumpkin seeds with red and blue rags, and corn silk. She warned her, "Look to Doll."

In her heart the woman was convinced that her little ones suffered from witchcraft. Mr. Zelley, who showed at that time a most stubborn disbelief in such infernal manifestations, or perhaps wishing to protect the wicked, pooh-poohed the idea. Mr. Kleaver also said that such wasting fevers were indeed far from rare. By the New Year he promised the twins would be well or in their coffins. He himself had seen no signs of demoniacal possession.

The woman asked the children—for who should know as well as they? At first they stoutly denied the idea and then weakened, admitting that it was possible. When their mother pressed them further, they put their heads under the bedclothing and remained mute. The mother decided to spy upon them to see if between themselves they might not prove more honest.

She told them she was going abroad. And she left the door of the chamber open into the fire-room. Having bid them farewell and slammed the front door, she returned on tiptoe to the stool she had set herself behind the chamber door. There she listened. They talked little and but casually. And then at last Labour said, "I wish we had not eaten the pretty poppets Mistress Dolly made us. I wish we had them to play with." So she knew that in truth the poppets were from Doll. Nothing more of consequence was said.

That very night, however, they woke up the whole house, screaming that a great tawny cat had come down the chimney and had sat upon their chests, kneading its paws and purring most hideous. Father, mother, and brother flew to them. They saw no cat, but there were two red fresh scratches on the face of Labour. Their father reproved them for their fancies, reminding his wife how since early childhood they had been subject to night fears. The children were ashamed. They put their heads under the bedclothing. From then on, however (when their father was not present), they often spoke of this cat, and suggested even more horrible visions that came to torment them. Every day their plight was more piteous.

Almost in the middle of December, close to the shortest day of the year, the woman sat by her hearth, pondering these things. She was determined to find the truth for herself. Husband, doctor, and minister were all wilfully blind.

The children lay sick in the next room, and often seemed like to die. The one said to the other, "She will come again tonight." At the word "she" the woman pricked her ears. It was only of the cat they had spoken before, and this cat they called "he." The child said, "She will bring her baby and let us play with it." The other said, "Oh, I hope she will not come. Although she seems kind to us, I am afraid that it is she who hurts us, for God knows we are bewitched." (She vomited a little.)

The woman went to the door, saying, "Pretty pets, who comes to you, and of whom is this baby?" She spoke quietly. They hid their heads and would not answer. The woman went again to the fireplace and listened. "I think," said one, "it is her cat that comes to hurt us," and the children whispered together. The woman trembled with excitement. She did not go immediately to the children; instead she sat close by the fire and listened. Sorrow said, "And the little black man with the little black hat . . ." She could hear no more. But later Sorrow was saying, "Little people came, no bigger than my finger. They ate a little feast of honey and suet, served out to them in acorn cups—like those Mistress Dolly makes for us . . ." And later, "There was a tiny queen. She looked just like Mistress Dolly, only smaller, a Mistress Dolly you could put away in a teacup, and her baby was no bigger than a thumb nail . . ." The mother now felt she had proof. She hurried to her children, begging them to tell her all. Could Mistress Dolly, then, shrink no bigger than a poppet? And who was the little black man? At first the children would not speak, but, as was usual, stubbornly hid their heads.

She wept and prayed over them, begging them to be frank with her, for, if it were only known who bewitched them and how, they might be cured. As it was they would grow sicker and weaker, and finally languish and die. They protested they did not want to die, and began to weep and cast themselves about. And at last they confessed to everything (but in the midst, Labour was thrown into a grievous fit). They told how it was Bilby's Doll had given them the poppets; how she came to them every night—not cruelly using them, but amusing and diverting them. "And she had with her a book . . ." said Sorrow. "My children, my poor miserable children . . . was it a black book, and have you signed?" Yes, it was a black book. No, they had not signed.

Then the pious woman got out the Bible, and she made them kiss it and swear that no matter how ill-used they were, or how delicately they were tempted by the witch, they would remain fast-sealed to God and not sign away their souls to Hell—no matter if devils did come and pull their vitals up by the roots and run needles through their eyeballs and brain-pans. The children, lamenting, shrieking, and yet for once obedient, promised and swore as they were bid.

3

A Hideous Malady and a Bridle for it.

From the day mentioned above Doll made no further pretence at kindness, for she began to come to these twins in hideous and cruel aspect. The deacons of the Church, the elders, the constables, the neighbours, took turn and turn about, in praying with them. These good words would often frighten away the witch, with her black book and infernal troop, and the little ones would rest a little or even sleep.

At last was the godly father of the haunted children convinced that this was witchcraft. He or his son Titus sat night and day with a bastard musket in the hand and a silver bullet in it.

At last was Mr. Kleaver convinced, and the doctor from Salem was convinced, and Mr. Increase Mather from Boston was convinced, that here at Cowan Corners was being enacted the most heinous and wicked witchcraft ever practised by any one in the New World. Here was indeed a witchcraft. Where was the witch?

Doll Bilby claimed that at this time she knew the children to be sick, but because week in and week out no one spoke to her (she went no more to Meeting) she had not guessed they were bewitched nor that she was talked about. She said she was sorry for what she mockingly called "her little friends." So she made a junket, and a fowl being killed she made a broth and put expensive cloves and nutmegs in this broth. She laid these things in a basket and asked the youngest of the farm servants to go present this basket to the Thumb twins, but not to say from whom it was.

When the mother saw the basket she cried out. Upon the handle of the basket in pretty Indian fashion were strung blue beads, identical with those the poor little wretches had but lately spewed forth. The children set up a great clamour at the sight of this food, for, although so hard to tempt, this particular food they would eat. She consulted Mr. Zelley (it was the last time she ever consulted him). He said it was good food and let the children eat. So they ate and quickly fell to sleep. That night they woke in horrid writhing fits, and almost died. Not only did they see Doll Bilby as she floated about over their bed, but Deacon Pentwhistle saw her and three others. Also Mr. Minchon, on going to the horse barn to get out his horse and ride home (for it was late), was bitten mysteriously in the arm. Lot Charty, a poor boy, that same night saw a fiery rat, and he said to this same rat, "Who are you?" The rat said, "I am who I am." And he said, "Whom serve you?" And the creature replied, "I serve Hell and the will of Bilby's Doll." Then with a clap like thunder he was up the fire hole.

A woman by the Ipswich Road that selfsame night sat nursing a feeble babe. She said the room grew light and there before her stood an awful female form. She never had set an eye upon Bilby's Doll, but by description she knew that this was she or her apparition. The child in her arms gave a great screech and the female form made off. Then (although it was midwinter) to the mother's apprehension, lightning came and struck the babe, squeezing it flat as a plank so it died.

Doubtless there were many devils abroad. The blessed God permitted their escapement from Hell that they might give bodily confutation to all atheists who should say "there is no God." So must ever the Prince of Lies and his servants serve the will of God. Because of the powers of an invisible Kingdom manifested in the years 1671-72, the churches were gorged with the pious and the entire community awoke to an awful realization of the potency of God.

Non est religio ubi omnia patent. (Which might be translated, Where there is no mystery there is no religion.)

All in all there seemed no proof lacking that Cowan Corners and more particularly the Thumb twins were suffering from a cruel demoniacal tormentation. Mr. Kleaver and the Salem doctor, the deacons, the elders, Captain Buzzey, the marshal, and others gave affidavit in writing to the magistrates that the woman Bilby was a witch of provable perversity and that she should be set in jail. Mr. Zelley alone among all the men of standing had nothing to do with the signing and drawing-up of this paper. In fact, such was his strange, distrait, and heretical attitude, no one asked him to assist. Already it was bruited abroad that he was a man to be looked at, for, after all, have not some of the most potent wizards done their blasphemies under a cloak of piety?

So Captain Tom Buzzey, of the Train-Band troop (and he was also sheriff), taking two constables with him, rode to the house of Widow Bilby and there served warrant upon the young woman. She showed neither surprise nor terror, but looked up at her captors fearlessly. She wanted to know of what she was accused. She was primarily accused of afflicting the Thumb twins. Why, then she was as innocent as a babe unborn.[6] She would have explained to the sheriff that she had been the friend of these little ones ever

[6] Compare the testimony of Bridget Bishop, p. 22.

since they could toddle. The sheriff told her that all were agreed that they were bewitched. If not she, who was it? Then she became confused and in the end said, "It was the work of *another witch*," thereby denying all and confessing all.

Captain Buzzey, as he had been instructed, searched her chamber and the house. He did not find the pumpkin seeds, corn husks, etc., etc., that Widow Bilby said the girl kept under her bed to work evil out of. It is likely the young woman really did know that her name was talked about and had rid herself of them.

She rode upon a pillion back of Captain Buzzey. A great jeering crowd had gathered to see her off to Salem jail. Widow Bilby laughed loudly from where she stood in the crowd between two of her suitors, "You've got it now, you jade, you jade!" she cried.

Captain Buzzey said the girl bowed her head and he heard her whisper, "He has not abandoned me. My god, my god, protect me and save me." Thinking that she was referring to our Lord Jesus Christ and to the true God, he, in his heart, pitied her. She begged Captain Buzzey to hurry. "Oh, for pity's sake take me out of this crowd." He clapped spurs to his stallion, and the young horse, in spite of his double load, put off at a gallop. The day was a winter day, crisp and cold, and the snow was fresh and spotless under the horses' hooves. So at a tremendous pace the cavalcade of armed men and the one prisoner passed through dark woods and by a winter sea. They rode for six miles and came to Salem, where again they encountered angry faces, hoots, gibes, and threats of instant death.

That night she lay upon straw and without a mattress. The dungeon was so cold the water froze in the jug. She could not sleep for cold, but spent hours upon her knees in prayer (as the jailor later reported), yet now it is known it was to her demon or to Satan that she prayed. At last a heavenly quiet descended upon her and she slept.

Concurrent to her jailing, the Thumb twins were a little eased in their misery. It would seem that the witch had been put to fright at the fear of bodily incarceration and pain, and that she had diminished the force and malignancy of her spells.

CHAPTER SEVEN

I

JUSTICE *arrives. She will not be stayed nor thrown from her scent, although the morning wears slowly and some fear* JUSTICE *will be balked.*

On the twenty-seventh day of December, 1672, Judge Lollimour and Judge Bride, of the Court of Assistants, Boston, entered with pomp into Salem. They were escorted by the Boston marshal, by constables, aides, etc., in full regalia. This pretty cavalcade drew rein by the horse block of the Black Moon, where ordinarily preliminary hearings were conducted.

Judge Bride (this was the great Judge Bride) said to Judge Lollimour, his colleague, "Sir, what will we do with this great crowd gathered here-about, waiting to hear the findings of Justice?"

"Sir," said Judge Lollimour, "the tap-room of the Black Moon could not accommodate one fifth of this great multitude. Let us move on to the Meet-ing-House."

After them straggled the populace of some five villages—yes, and learned men, elders, doctors, jurists, etc., out from Boston. The crowd was black with the gowns of the clergy.

Every seat in the Meeting-House was quickly taken. The aisles were filled. Body pressed close to body, rendering breathing difficult. In this way a stale heat was engendered, and a fear, and an expectation. One said to another it was a fatal day. Some would have left if it had been allowed them, but the room being filled the Judges ordered the constables to permit neither egress nor entry. They feared a milling about and a turmoil that would be a detriment to the dignity of the Court.

The magistrates were set in great chairs before the pulpit. At their feet were pallets whereon the sick children should be laid when their time came to testify. The constables pulled a table (a heavy oak table) close to the mag-istrates. Upon this the accused should stand in the sight of all men—yes, and in the sight of God.

Certain men cried out, "Make way! Make way!" and in came Captain Buzzey and the prisoner. She looked most wild and shaggy and of a touch-ingly small size. Captain Buzzey lifted her to the table set for her, and then, addressing the Court, showed true warrant for her arrest and swore that as commanded he had diligently searched the house for poppets, images, etc.; having found what he found, he now produced these things in the bundle which he laid at their honours' feet.

Judge Bride, looking about him at the many black-robed clergy, said, "Gentlemen of the ministry, who among you officiating in these parts is senior?" He was told Mr. Zelley was senior in these parts, but that the fa-mous Mr. Increase Mather was present. "Sir," said Judge Bride, "will you, Mr. Zelley, offer up a prayer?" Mr. Zelley prayed, begging God to discover evil where there was evil and innocency where there was innocency. He prayed that the prisoner confess if she might be guilty, but if she were in-nocent, God strengthen her not to confess merely to save her life. To this prayer the magistrates gave fervent amen.

Judge Lollimour thus addressed the prisoner at the bar: "You under-stand, Doll Bilby, whereof you are now charged, that is, to be guilty of sundry acts of witchcraft, more specifically the wasting and afflicting of twin sisters, Labour and Sorrow Thumb. What say you to it?"

"I am as innocent as the babe unborn."

"You are now in the hands of authority and, God helping, you shall have justice, and the afflicted shall have justice. May God help us all."

Then Judge Lollimour called on many witnesses. He called on Mr. Kleaver the surgeon, and the older doctor from Salem whose name was Bunion. He called upon the Thumbs and upon Widow Bilby. This latter woman showed such spite and malice in her testimony that Judge Bride frowned upon her and reproved her. Thus, instead of hurting the accused, she helped her, for the Judges felt some pity for the tousled, wild child (she seemed but a child) perched upon the table in the sight of all men—yes, and in the sight of God.

Mr. Zelley was called. He was a bony man of fifty years, and his hair was white. In contrast to the big fine presence of Mr. Mather and many another clergyman then present, he seemed a poor thing; that is, uncertain, ill at ease. He spoke in a low voice, saying how good had been this young woman as a child. How in earliest womanhood she had shown a most exemplary piety. How she was often at her prayers, and came to him for religious comfort, etc. As he spoke, he twisted his hands in his sleeves as a boy might. Then he said in a defiant voice that the girl had since childhood endured the most cruel abuse from her foster mother—that is, from this same Widow Bilby, who had but lately been heard. This last statement had much weight with the Judges, who thereafter did not permit Widow Bilby to testify, or, if they did, they took her words with knowing glance. By this dismissal of Hannah they also dismissed the earlier tales of Doll's witchcraft. Although they heard how the green fruit of Hannah's womb was blasted, how she had suffered a wretched and unaccountable illness, it was evident they were not impressed—rather were they bored. To the death of Mr. Bilby they listened with more attention, questioning a number (especially Mr. Kleaver and Mr. Zelley) with some pains. When they heard that the dying man with his last breath denied any witchcraft, they would not permit Hannah to explain how it may be that an evil spirit enter a corpse and then cry out.

At noon, while they ate their bloaters and drank their rum punch at the Black Moon, the barmaid heard Judge Bride say to Judge Lollimour that it was easy to see through the whole miserable affair. *In primo:* This rustic town was so tedious they had to patch up an excitement—he would begin seeing devils himself if he lived there. *Secundo:* This jealous, scolding widow was at the bottom of it. *Tertio:* The wench indeed looked like a goblin, and, no matter how pious a life she might lead, village gossips would always speak ill of her—especially, as in her own ungodly way she was a pretty mouse. *Quarto:* They would both of them be back in Boston within the three-day, the case being dismissed and the local people reproved for their gullibility. Said Judge Lollimour, "Sir, we have not as yet seen these afflicted children." Judge Bride said, "Blah," draining the last of his rum punch.

2

From Noon to Sundown rages a famous battle, with Righteousness and Justice on the one hand and Witchcraft and Evil upon the other.

On the afternoon of the same day, Doll Bilby was set again upon the table. The crowd within the Meeting-House was even greater than it had been in the morning. Many had not even gone out for dinner, so ravenous was their hunger to hear the findings of Justice and to observe the conduct of a witch.

Judge Bride: Once again are we assembled in the eyes of all men and in
the eyes of God to administer justice as well as mortal man (a puny,
weak, and miserable creation) is able. Mr. Mather, of Boston, sir, we
beg your blessing and your prayers.

Then Mr. Mather prayed most decently, and as if in sight of God's most
awful throne. To this prayer the Judges gave amen and bade the sheriff go
and fetch the bodies of the Thumb twins, who should next be questioned.
Out of the mouths of babes and sucklings wise men may be instructed, and
an innocent child may speak with greater knowledge than is given to the
cloudy heart of maturity. Mrs. Thumb was asked to tell all she might concerning the health and humour of these twins since birth. These things she told.
She told of the past-nature love her son Titus bore this woman now accused,
and at the moment the sheriff entered and the cry "Make way!" went up.
After him was Deacon Thumb, and he bore Sorrow Thumb, and after him
was Titus. He bore Labour Thumb. It was explained that the children were
taken in fits at the threshold of the courtroom. They lay in a swoon as though
dead, their faces green with pallor, their eyes closed. The bearers laid them
on the pallets.

Judge Bride: Titus Thumb, stand up and answer me. You see this woman
who stands thus before and above you all. Now is she charged with
crimes which, if proven, shall cost her her life, yet a year and a little
more and she was your dear heart and you were about to wed with
her. You have heard your mother say that this Bilby won you by
wicked spells, that once she assumed the shape of Indian and you
shot her through the heart—yet she did not suffer for it. That again
she perversely set upon you, tempting and staying you beyond the
puny endurance of our sex, and you struck her a blow that would have
killed an ox, yet *she* rose up unharmed. We have listened to some
length of how violent and beyond the usual wants of nature was
your desire for her. Your flesh fell away, etc. What do you now say?
Are these things true?

Thumb: Sir, as God hears me, these things are true.

Judge Bride: There has been no enlargement upon fact?

Thumb: None.

Judge Bride: It does not seem to you that you mistook for enchantment
what another would call lust? Possibly you are a young man of gross
sensual nature, who might strike what he loved?

Thumb: God knows I am the least sensual of all men. I have never sought
out women. Ask any here.

At that a girl was possessed and now a demon began manifestly to speak
in her. The demon belched forth most horrid and nefarious blasphemies. The
constable took her out. A dozen cried to the Judges, begging to vouch for the
young man's purity. All were silenced.

Judge Bride: Thumb, I see your eyes avoid to look towards this young
woman. Perhaps your heart regrets that you give testimony most like
to lead her in the halter. Look upon her now. Is she not your enemy?
Tell her she is a witch and that you wish her hanged for it.

Thumb (after a most tedious pause, looked to her feet): You are a witch.

Judge Bride: Better than that, louder and firmer. Come, you shall look upon her face. You shall not mock this Court.

Thumb: Sir, I cannot.

Judge Bride: What, are you still bewitched, or is it that you still love her and will not harm her?

Thumb: I love her. (He put his arm across his eyes. He wept.)

Judge Bride: Get to your chair again. How can you who love her give good and valid testimony? Get to your chair again. Your mother, she is made of sterner stuff. I see the children stir. They are about to be recovered to consciousness. Sheriff, cover the face and body of the accused so that they may not see her until the time comes.

Captain Buzzey took off his scarlet cape. It was a good new cape that had cost him two pounds. Within the month it rotted mysteriously, and the Assistants bought him another one. With this scarlet cape he now covered Bilby's Doll from head to foot.

Labour: Oh, for Christ's dear sake, sister, where are we now? Oh, for God's sake . . .

Sorrow: Oh, my back, oh, my bowels!

The children aroused themselves a little, sat up, and gazed about the court. Now it is noticeable that Judge Lollimour took to himself the questioning of the children. The reason is he had seven such at home, while the great Judge Bride had none.

Judge Lollimour: Children, do not be afraid, for is there none among us but wish you well. You are only to speak the truth as your good mother has taught you—the whole truth, and nothing but the truth.

Sorrow (in loud, bold voice): There is one here who does not wish us well. I can feel her presence.

The Judge gave no heed, although many were amazed that the child had not seen Doll, yet knew there was one there who did not wish her well.

Judge Lollimour: You have been strangely sick, and I see you are not well. What, think you, caused this sickness?

Sorrow: Oh, sir, have you not heard? We are bewitched. She gave us our own vitals to eat, and she comes at night and torments us.

Judge Lollimour: You say "she," yet half the world are "she." To whom do you refer?

Sorrow: I can't say her name, oh-oh-oh . . .

She gagged and went purple in the face, she clawed at her windpipe.

Labour: Oh, don't you see, don't you see, the witch has her by the throat? She won't let her answer. Oh, sir, she'll die. (The puny child struck the air above her sister's head.) Go away, you wicked witch, go away!

Judge Lollimour: Now that you are restored, I shall name some to you, and when you reach the name of her whom you think torments you, you shall make a sign. Abigail Stone, Sarah Black, Obedience Lovejoy, Alice May, Delilah Broadbent, Doll Bilby . . .

Then the afflicted did cry out, and fell back weak and dumb.

Judge Lollimour: So you accuse Doll Bilby, that she bewitches you, caus-ing your sickness? What else does she do to you?

Sorrow: She will have us sign in the Black Book.

Judge Lollimour: Come, you contrive a fancy. I do not believe she comes with a black book. Tell me how.

Sorrow: She comes with devils and imps and hideous animals, and they torment us, pressing out our lives, sticking pins and knives into us, and while they torment us she presses close to us, bidding us sign her book. But we will none of her, and God helps us and will save us.

Judge Lollimour: You claim that this woman comes to you by night, bringing such with her as prick and torment you. How does she come, in her own proper form?

Sorrow: At first she would come as a great tawny cat, and then again as a pig, or as a mouse, and once I remember she came as a black dog. And she brings fiends with her, hairy little black men, and these tor-ment us. Of late I think she comes only in her own proper form. Sometimes it is hard to tell, for she can at will assume any shape. And sometimes a hand puts into the bed amongst us and pulls at our vitals.

Judge Lollimour: When this woman came to you and offered you a book to sign (as you claim), what would she say?

Sorrow: She would say, "Sign."

Judge Lollimour: And no other word?

Sorrow: Sometimes she would say, "Sign, or I'll squeeze your vitals for you."

Judge Lollimour: But you, being good and Christian girls, would not sign?

Labour: Oh, sir, once a most awful and majestic voice spoke out, and I do believe it was the voice of God, and He bade us not to sign. Then the fiend flew away in a clap and did not return for a three-day.

Their mother said, yes, this was true. She herself heard the clap and it was three days before the affliction again commenced.

Judge Lollimour: And if you sign, what does she promise you?

Sorrow: Prettiest things to play with—little goats, no larger than a cat and a cat as small as a kit, and brooms to ride on through the sky— and her own pretty babe to play with.

Judge Lollimour: And when you refuse to sign?

Sorrow: Oh, she pinches and torments us, or lets her fiends and familiars torment us. They but do her bidding and I do not think are as wicked as she. Once she set my father's great black bull Ahab upon us. He tramples us like to break our bones.

The mother interrupted to say, yes, this was true. The bull was a witch's familiar beyond good doubt, and they but waited the finding of the Court before they butchered him.

Sorrow: Sometimes the witch shakes us cruelly.

Thumb: Sir, it is true. Those small and puny girls were so shaken two strong men could not hold them in their beds.

Judge Bride: What, young Thumb, is this girl, even though proved a
    witch, so strong, she can best two strong men—how think you?
Thumb: Sir, I think the Devil helps her and he gives her strength.
Judge Bride: You who were once her lover—you should know her strength.
    Was she then so brawny-strong those times you bundled her?
Titus was confused. He believed the Court to be against him. The con-
gregation was angry, for bundling is a pleasantry for yokels, and no more
likely to occur in Salem than in Boston, nor in the Thumb house than in the
house of Bride or Lollimour. It was felt the Judge intended an insult. Some
feared the magistrates might dismiss the whole case but from caprice. But
Judge Bride was a godly man, who would not lift his nose from a scent until
Justice herself was satisfied, although those who knew him best said he often
seemed to pause and idly bay the moon.
Thumb: I never got such favour from her.
Judge Bride: One more thing you shall tell us, although you are not a
    likely witness. Is it true, as your mother has said, that you shot silver
    bullets up the fire hole, and that upon occasion you think you struck
    the accused?
Thumb: It is true, sir, but I shot only three silver bullets—these were
    buttons from my coat. My sisters cried, "There she goes up the flue."
    I fired where they pointed and they exclaimed that I had struck her
    on the wrist. Some here will tell you that there was indeed the next
    day a bullet-gouge on her wrist, nor has it yet healed—to this day. I
    saw it when you bade me look at her. You may see this mark your-
    self. Her apparition came commonly to afflict my sisters in an old black
    riding-hood.
Captain Buzzey said he had the very one with him in the bundle at their
honours' feet. He took it out, and Labour and Sorrow both said, yes, it was
the very one. Captain Buzzey held it up before the magistrates. It was riddled
with bullet holes.
Captain Buzzey: Widow Bilby gave me this coat. See, it is burnt with
    fire, shot full of holes as a sieve, and still smells of soot from the
    Thumb chimney, and gunpowder from Thumb's musket.
A boy (crying out from the back of the court): I know that coat, sir, well.
Judge Bride: And who may you be?
The boy: Jake Tulley, bonded man to Widow Bilby, and I know that coat
    for the one our scarecrow has worn these three years, and but yester-
    day I saw the coat gone and the scarecrow naked. Mate and I (that
    is the other farmhand) often shot at it for practice. Why, it means
    nothing that it is full of holes.
Judge Bride: And are you and Mate such miserable poor shots you must
    press your pieces into the very belly of the scarecrow to be assured of
    your aim? Look, how the powder has burned the cloth.
The Judges took the coat up between them and discussed in low voices.
Jake sat down in confusion.
Judge Bride: Mr. Kleaver, you have already given generously of your

knowledge. You have told us in what way the maladies arising from witchcraft differ from those arising from the proper body—in other words, what are the differences between diseases inflicted by the Devil for wicked ends, and those by Jehovah for our own good. And you have told us how you came to recognize the case in hand as one provoked by art. Will you tell us further?

Mr. Kleaver: Invisible hands often clutched the twins by the throat. I have seen them.

Judge Bride: The invisible hands?

Mr. Kleaver: No. I have seen the throats. And I have also taken the needles, pins, and such from their flesh. These children have vomited strange things—fur, insects, glass, long hanks of hair—blue beads. . . . (He stooped to the bundle at their honours' feet.) Sirs, here is the basket in which the young woman sent poisoned or possessed food to the afflicted—mark the blue beads on the handle. Three days earlier, the one of them spewed forth these blue beads I now take from my pocket—mark, gentlemen—they are identical.

Mrs. Thumb: There was never a bead like that before in my house.

She wept. The children screamed out in gibberish at sight of the beads, and fell back upon their pallets.

Judge Bride: Mark the children, Mr. Kleaver, are they now, in your opinion, possessed?

Mr. Kleaver: Not exactly possessed. (He whispered to the magistrates.) They are conscious of a malignant presence. They know the witch is in the room.

The twins: Oh, oh, oh, God help us, oh, oh, oh!

Judge Bride: Sheriff, uncover to us the accused. Now, children, stand up, if able, and look there at the table above you.

The room was filled with their piercing din. Labour fell in a fit, foaming, rolling her eyes. She was stretched out stark and dead. Sorrow flung herself in hideous terror upon the feet of the Judges, crying out piteously that they save her. Then she fell back stark and dumb. Judge Lollimour was touched by her plight, her fear, and the appeal she made to him. He raised her up, felt of her hands and face. They were dank with a cold sweat which both Judges knew no art could imitate. Her pulse scarce moved. Her tongue was tied in her throat. She could not speak. She looked up out of tortured eyes.

Mr. Mather: Here, sir, if ever, is demoniacal possession.

Judge Bride: Here is witchcraft—now to find the witch.

Mr. Mather: It has been proved an hundred times in English courts that a spell cast by a witch's eye must return to the witch's body—if the witch touch the afflicted.[7]

Judge Bride: Sheriff, carry the body of this Labour Thumb to the prisoner. She shall touch her. We shall see. Observe. The child is utterly lifeless now.

Captain Buzzey: She has no pulse, sir.

Mrs. Thumb: Sir, sir, you have let her slay my child before my eyes. Oh, God, oh, God! . . .

[7] Compare Increase Mather's statements, pp. 122-23.

Judge Bride: No one can say that this child knows who touches her. Sheriff, take her, alive or dead, to the prisoner.

Captain Buzzey took her up. The witch readily assented. She reached down and touched the child. The colour returned to the child's face. Captain Buzzey felt her pulse leap in her wrist. He felt her heart stir under her hand. The child turned in his arms, smiling prettily, as though in sleep. With a smile she woke. She glanced to the Judges, noted her sister (still in semi-trance). She smiled at her mother. Her eyes went up, and there on the table beside and above her was the awful vision of Bilby's Doll. With a wail of terror no art could simulate, she clung to Captain Buzzey. At that moment all in the courtroom realized how hideous had been her weeks of anguish. No one could so fear a person who had never done her harm.

Judge Bride: Lay the child upon her pallet—and you, Sorrow, go you now and lie upon your pallet.

Sorrow (her tongue still tied): Gar, gar, gah, gah, gah.

Judge Bride: Labour and Sorrow, as you fell into these fits, tell me what occurred. Did a fiend or familiar come to torment you? Did the accused send her apparition to you, there before your very eyes—leaving her body, as it were, vacant upon the table? Tell us.

Now was Labour also taken with dumbness. All saw how the lower lips of the afflicted were sucked in, and the teeth were clamped down upon them. Mr. Kleaver essayed to break the lock on their teeth. He could not.

Widow Bilby: Look to the witch, look, look!

It was seen the witch bit her lip—thus locking the jaws of the children. Captain Buzzey struck her slightly, and bade her loose her lip. Then the children were released. They said it was her own devil came to them.

Judge Bride: Doll Bilby, I have asked several the meaning of the manifestation of evil, so recent among us. Mr. Kleaver and Mr. Mather have both explained it to the satisfaction of many—is it to your satisfaction?

Doll Bilby: I am an ignorant woman. I cannot explain.

Judge Bride: Now you are to talk freely, deny the truth of the statements which you have heard made, explain and elucidate for us—or, if you wish, you may confess.

She was silent.

Judge Bride: At least you can concur with the judgement of those wiser than yourself. At least say this, Was it or was it not a devil who tied the children's tongues for them?

Doll Bilby: That I do know—it was not.

Judge Bride: How do you know? No one else can claim to be so wise.

Doll Bilby: If it were a demon, I would have seen him.

Judge Bride: You have, then, so nice a sight you can see devils?

Mr. Zelley: May I speak?

Judge Bride: Speak.

Mr. Zelley: If this young woman could command a devil to serve her, would he then be so unmindful of her safety as to come into this court and work tricks so likely to hurt her cause?

Mr. Mather: Cannot God as well as this wretched girl or Satan command devils? Has it not been proved often and often that it sometimes pleases Him to suffer them to do such things in this world as shall stop the mouths of gainsayers and exhort a Christian confession from those who will believe only the most obvious of His truths?

Judge Bride: Bilby, give us your thoughts on the matter. These Divines have spoken wisely.

Doll Bilby: I think it was perhaps an angel—come to do me a mischief.

Judge Bride: Do angels come to do mischief to good and baptized women?

The defendant saw she was in difficulty. She twisted her hands in the folds of her gown. Then were the children afflicted.

Judge Bride: Bilby, if these are indeed your tricks, keep them for more seemly time. Constable, seize her hands. And if, as you suggest, these manifestations are the actions of angels, I pray God to spare us His angels until the Court is adjourned.

A woman was taken in a fit. She fell down laughing and sobbing, and was passed out through a window.

Judge Bride: Do you think those who are afflicted suffer voluntarily or involuntarily?

Doll Bilby: I cannot tell.

Judge Bride: That is strange; every one may judge for himself.

Doll Bilby: I must be silent.

Judge Bride: You have heard this morning two learned medici explain in what way witchcraft is like to resemble natural ailment, and in what ways it differs. Keep this counsel in your mind, and tell me what you would say of the illness of these children.

Doll Bilby: It would seem they suffer from witchcraft.

Judge Bride: So it would seem to many here. And where there is a witchcraft there must be a witch.

Doll Bilby: Yes.

Judge Bride: Where is that witch?

Doll Bilby: God knows I do not know. God knows I never hurt a child. I know of no witch that would afflict these children.

Captain Buzzey stood up. He said that when he and his men came to arrest this woman, now standing trial for witchcraft, he and his men heard her deny clearly the afflicting of the Thumb twins, and yet she had said—most meaningly—"'Tis the work of *another witch.*"

Judge Bride: You shall explain this for us, Bilby.

Doll Bilby: How shall I explain?

Judge Bride: Confess now, as you did then, that you are a witch.

She was silent.

Judge Bride: Confess now, and your life shall be spared.

She was silent.

Judge Bride: Confess now and turn against these other witches—for it is possible that many are about—and I swear to you your life will be spared.

She was silent.

Judge Lollimour: Will the prisoner at the bar recite the Lord's Prayer?

Doll began readily enough. As she spoke the Holy Words, Mr. Zelley covered his face in his hands, and made them with his lips as though he would help her. She went on without chance or mishap till she came to the last sentence, which begins, "Lead us not into temptation." She got no further. Mr. Zelley clenched his hands until his knuckles went white. He turned up his eyes to God. Then quickly she began and said, to the horror and consternation of all, "Ever for, glory the and, power the, kingdom the, is thine for, evil from us deliver, but temptation into not us lead—Amen." She did not know what she had done. She looked about with assurance. There was an incessant and horrid silence in the court. The Judges looked to each other. Clergyman looked to clergyman, then turned eyes to God. So was she utterly undone, but the Court was not yet satisfied.

Judge Bride: You have responded to my colleague's request to the satisfaction of all, but there are some small matters yet to clear. Be of good heart, soon we will let you go. I see you are pale and distrait. Constable, see to it that she does not fall from the table. What did you mean when you said the bewitchment of the Thumb twins was "the work of another witch"?

Doll Bilby: Sir, how can I explain?

Judge Bride: There is nothing you cannot either confess to, or explain.

Doll Bilby: Sir, I am confused and amazed.

Judge Bride: Answer but a few minutes with frankness, and you shall go to your own cell—we are not your enemies—open your heart to us.

She was mute.

Judge Bride: Be stubborn, and you shall stand there all night—yes, and the next day. Come, have you ever seen a devil?

She nodded her head.

Judge Bride: Ah, then you have seen a devil. Do not feel ashamed of that. Did not Christ Himself see Satan? Was not Luther often tormented by his presence? Some of the best of men have been the most foully pursued. Feel no shame, Doll Bilby. Speak out freely. When was it first?

Doll Bilby: I was a child in Brittany; my mother took me to see him in a great wood.

Judge Bride: An instructive and remarkable experience—and have you seen him since?

Doll Bilby: Last spring I saw him—he came to me again.

Judge Bride: In proper human form?

Doll Bilby: He came to me by night. Yes, he came in form of proper man. He wore seaman's clothes and with him was an imp—a black-faced imp with a long ringed tail. He wore this imp upon his bosom.

There was a commotion at the back of the hall.

Judge Bride: When did he come last spring to you?

Doll Bilby: The last night in May—the night the Thumbs' barn burned. Oh, sir, I am sick, let me go to my cell.

Captain Buzzey held her up.

A high, wild voice from the midst of the confusion: I will speak, sirs, you shall hear me.

Judge Bride: Who cries out?

Voice: I am Jonet Greene, the tinker's wife. There are things I know . . .

Judge Bride: Stand back, all, from the woman. Dame Greene, deliver yourself of these things.

The crowd drew back. Goody Greene, an old woman and of great dignity, was revealed to the Judges. Mr. Kleaver whispered to the Judges that she was an evil woman.

Goody Greene: This girl never saw a devil. She saw my own son Shadrach. He was wanted for piracy—Heaven help me, I hid him by day, but he prowled by night. He had a monkey, he wore seaman's clothes. He saw in my house the girl and lusted after her. I speak . . .

A man from back: Her husband says she lies—she never had no son.

Goody Greene: Believe me, for Christ's dear sake, believe me. I had a son and I hid him . . . but they found him just the same . . . God found out his sin. They hanged him; he was called the Bloody Shad.

The man: The woman's husband, sir, says she never had no son. Time has broken her memory.

Goody Greene: Husband, you are afraid. You coward, who will not confess to the son of your own loins, lest you come to shame—now is Doll indeed undone . . .

Judge Lollimour: The woman is lunatic. See how she rolls her eyes.

Judge Bride: Could you have had a son of which your husband knew nothing—why did you never speak of him to your neighbours? How can we believe your fables? You are lunatic.

Goody Greene: God help me! God help me. . . . May God help Doll!

Judge Bride: Constable, throw out this ancient—let her learn to be a sager hag—and her husband after her.

A confusion and clamour of tongues rose from all parts of the courtroom. Some wished to say what they knew of the Greenes; others had stories to tell of lunacy, devils, etc. And there was laughing and crying among women, and children wailed and would be taken home. Judge Bride stood up in a noble wrath.

Judge Bride: Clear the court! Clear the court! What, shall Justice find her house in Bedlam? Constables, pick up and carry out—if they are too weak to walk—the Thumb twins, and you, madame, who are their mother, go with them. Every one shall now be turned out into the snow except those who are the witnesses and proper officers of the law, and the six that I shall name. Mr. Increase Mather, Mr. Seth Dinsmore, Dr. Zerubbabel Endicott, Mr. Zacharias Zelley, Mr. John Wilson, and you, sir, also, Colonel Place Peabody. Gentlemen, the case shall be continued *in camera.*[8] I beg of you few, however, to stay to the end.

---

[8] I.e., privately.

3

From Sundown to black Night the battle continues. The Witch is thrown to confusion. Justitia triumphans. Deus regnat.

Now was the courtroom, empty and vast, silent as the grave. Only twenty remained in the room where a minute before had been many hundreds. The day had worn to sunset and the room was dark. Flares were lighted and candles were set where there was need. But the light of flare and candle made the far reaches of the room and the dark corners behind the scaffold even blacker. Such humanity as was present were huddled about the platform and the great chairs of the Judges. By candlelight Judge Bride glanced over the notes that he had taken, and by candlelight Titus Thumb looked to the witch upon the table. She stood there ghastly pale and like to swoon. Her eyes were round and struck terror to all. She did not look again to Titus, only to Judge Bride, whom she in her simplicity thought to be her friend.

Judge Bride bade the sheriff fetch a chair—a good chair with a back to it, for he said he saw that the accused was tired past human strength. Captain Buzzey got a chair. It was a great chair similar to those in which the Judges sat. Judge Bride had it placed on the platform between himself and Judge Lollimour. The three sat thus for a moment in silence, a judge, and next a witch, and then a judge. So they sat in great chairs and upon crimson damask cushions. The witch's feet could not reach the floor. Judge Bride gave her wine to drink from the silver goblet set out for his own use. She drank the wine and was grateful to him.

Little by little—tenderly—he questioned her. And little by little she told him all. Of the Thumb twins he asked no word, he asked her only of her own self, and of that demon who had but so recently gone from her. She told in so low a voice those but a few yards away could not hear, and Mr. Mather several times cried out, "Louder—an it please the wench." She told of her father and mother in Brittany, and the night that Mr. Bilby died. She told of the long winter, and the expectations of the spring and the fulfilment of these expectations—for the messenger had come, a most vigorous and comely fiend. Sometimes she reddened and turned away as might a modest Christian woman. Sometimes she sighed, and once or twice she smiled a small and secret smile. And three times she said she loved and did not fear the demon, and that he had been kind and pitiful to her.

Judge Bride: You say this devil was your lover and that he conducted himself as has many a shameless mortal man to many a woman, for he loved you, and when he had stayed himself of you he went away, whistling, we may presume, and shrugging his shoulders—ah, gentlemen, how shocking is the conduct of the male, be he demon or tomcat! And now, Doll Bilby, we are almost to the end. Do not fear to weary us with the length and detail of your history. Come, tell us more. The ears of Justice must ever be long and patient ears.

She told more. There was nothing left untold, and where she would have turned aside, Judge Bride encouraged and helped her. Mr. Zelley moaned and cried out, and his head was in his hands. Titus went ghostly white and, trembling, staggered from the room.

Judge Bride: But did not your conscience hurt? Did you not know that you lived with this strange lover of yours in sin?

Doll Bilby: I begged him to marry me. So he did.

Judge Bride: A most virtuous and homely fiend. And did you find clerk or magistrate to register your vows?

Doll Bilby: No, we married ourselves.

Judge Bride: Ah, the Governor of Connecticut but recently gave you example.

And he pointed out to Judge Lollimour with much leisure how evil is bad example in high places. He questioned Doll further. She told him all there was to tell about the marriage, and it humiliated her to tell that she had accepted this fiend before marriage.

Judge Bride: Come, come, is it then so sorry a sin for two young people to be too hot and previous in their love? Surely honest marriage may be considered salve to such misconduct.

He glanced through his notes. There was not a sound in the room, not the scamper of a mouse, not the taking of breath, no sound except the fiery rustle of the flares and the crackle of the paper.

Judge Bride: Doll Bilby, I notice that the children spoke often of a pretty babe—which they called yours. Now to what do they refer?

Doll Bilby: Sir, I cannot be sure.

Judge Bride: You may guess, perhaps?

Doll Bilby: Oh, sir, sir . . .

Her eyes sought Mr. Zelley, but his face was in his hands.

Judge Bride: Speak freely.

Doll Bilby: I think it was to my own babe they referred.

Judge Bride: And where now is this child?

Doll Bilby: It is not yet born.

Judge Bride: And to whom the honour of its paternity?

Doll Bilby: Who else would it be but the fiend who came to comfort me?

Judge Bride: Do not hang your head, young Bilby, for to conceive is natural to woman. Rather should you redden and look down if after such expenditure of infernal ardour you had proved sterile. Conception is the glory of woman.

He stood up and dismissed the hearing. Then Captain Buzzey in a great sweat of fear took the witch back to her cell, and all others went home. That night the Boston Judges lay at the Black Moon. The barmaid heard Judge Lollimour say to Judge Bride, as these two sat by the hearth and drank their sack-posset: "Sir, this hearing is done as quickly as ever you prophesied. We will be back to Boston on the third day. I warrant the finding is more than any expected. There is enough against the wench to hang her three times over—but that is yet for the magistrates of the Superior Court to decide. We, at least, shall hold her without bail or bond." Then he said in wonder, "To think that God has vouchsafed to our eyes the sight of a woman who has embraced a demon . . ." The Judges whispered. The barmaid would not repeat what they said.

These learned men called for ink-horn, sand, and pens. By ten o'clock they had written thus:

> Doll Bilby of Cowan Corners (Essex County), being this day brought before us upon suspicion of witchcraft and upon the specific charge of afflicting Labour and Sorrow Thumb, twin daughters of Deacon Ephraim Thumb, we heard the aforesaid, and seeing what we did see, together with hearing charges of the persons then present, we committed this same Doll Bilby (she denying the matter of fact, yet confessing herself a witch, also confessing having had carnal knowledge of a fiend, also to being at this time pregnant by him, also to being married to him by the ceremony of Max Pax Fax) unto their majesties' jail at Salem, as per mittimus then given out in order to further examination.
>
> ADAM BRIDE   } *Magistrates*
> RALPH LOLLIMOUR

By eleven they slept upon their beds.

4

Doll, having cooked her goose, now must sit to eat it. And one who later proves a warlock comes to sit by her side.

Next day Doll rose early, thinking she would be called again before the magistrates. Judge Bride had talked kindly to her and at the end nothing had been said about the Thumb twins. She had not guessed his mind to be made up against her.

She rose early, an hour before dawn, and by a rushlight prepared herself for court. The jailor, John Ackes, could watch her through a chink in the masonry. He saw her put on hat and cloak and set out wooden pattens. He ran in fear to the Black Moon where Mr. Zelley that night lay, and begged him—if he dared—to come a-running, for he believed the witch was about to fly through the roof. She was all dressed and set to go.

Mr. Zelley went to the dungeon and found her waiting to be taken before the magistrates. He sat upon her straw bed by her side, and he took her hands. He said, "Poor child, lay by your hat and riding-gear, for 'tis all done."

Done? She had thought they were but started. The matter of the Thumb twins was not yet proven—Judge Bride himself had confessed as much. Mr. Zelley said that now there was another warrant for her and another *mittimus.*[9] But Mr. Zelley must have heard Judge Bride say there was no offence in having seen a devil—had not even Christ talked with Lucifer? And obviously the magistrates had approved her marriage and had even forgiven her that she had been too pliant to her lover's desires. How, therefore, could the Court be done with her—unless they were about to set her free?

"You are to be held for a jury—a jury, my poor Doll, of your own angry

[9] Warrant or writ for imprisonment.

neighbours, and for the February sessions of the Superior Court of Judicature."
He explained that Judges Bride and Lollimour could only examine her and
hold her over to a higher court. It is true they could have dismissed her as
innocent—if it had pleased them; but they could not give sentence of death.
. . . He wished her to think of death and it might be to prepare her mind
and more especially her soul (if she had a soul) against this likely contingence.

"Death?" she said. "How can I die? God, God, oh, God! I do not want
to die." At the first moment she was afraid of death like any other wicked
woman. She closed her eyes and leaned back against the masonry of her cell,
remaining a long, long time silent, but her lips moved. Mr. Zelley sat beside
her. His head was in his hands. When next she spoke she had conquered fear of
death. She spoke bravely in a clear, strong voice. Then she told Mr. Zelley
more concerning the fiend whom Hell had sent to love her. She said that he
had promised her that, when she should come to die, he would stand at her
bed's head. After death he would be with her and she with him forever and
ever. She said boldly that she did not fear to die. But she flung herself to her
knees and laid her tousled head in Mr. Zelley's lap and then confessed that
she had a most hideous horror of gallows and halter. As he could he comforted her. Tears streamed from his eyes, though hers were always dry. He
knelt and seemed to pray to God.

John Ackes at his chink saw him pray and heard his prayer. He said it
was an unseemly prayer—not like those one hears in church—not like the
majestic and awful utterances of Mr. Increase Mather. Zelley talked to God
as you might talk to a friend. So many thought that it was not to the true
God that he prayed, but to some demon whom he privately worshipped. When
his own day came to hang, this thing was remembered against him.

The witch-woman crouched upon her straw bed the while he prayed.
She had put her hat on her head again and was wrapped in her scarlet riding-
coat. She stared out of round cat's eyes at the man who prayed for her.

5

Abortive attempts to save a soul *and more infernal manifestations of the*
Demon Lover.

Now was her physical body in sore plight, for she was bound in irons
heavier than a strong man might bear. The jailors feared her, and, although
an eye was forever at the chink, they did as little for her as might be. The
Court permitted only these to go to her: her jailors; the two ministers of God,
labouring in Salem; and Mr. Increase Mather whose mind was at that time big
with a demonology.[10] He wished to study and examine her. It was three weeks
before Mr. Zelley got a permit from Boston to visit her. He guessed by the
cold, tardy manner in which his request was answered that he himself had
fallen into ill-repute. This was true. His people thought him a warlock and
feared and hated him.

When twenty years later, in the days of the great witch-hunting and hang-

---

[10] See Increase Mather, *An Essay for the Recording of Illustrious Providences . . . Espe-*
cially in New England, London, 1684.

ing in Salem, Mr. Zelley himself came to be tried, John Ackes was commanded
to tell the Court (if he could remember) of what it was the witch and the
warlock had talked through those long hours they had sat side by side upon
the witch's straw bed. He testified (swearing to his truth upon the Bible)
that they talked but little. Zelley's head was forever in his hands. He did not
see the witch-woman's face—nor her eyes. He did not see how constantly she
gaped at empty corners; how she smiled and nodded into space; how sometimes she would close her eyes and raise her mouth for the empty air to kiss.
All this she did behind Mr. Zelley's back. They asked John Ackes if Mr.
Zelley made no attempt to save the woman's soul. No, he only sat. Sometimes he talked a little to Doll and sometimes he talked to one whom he
designated as "god." But he did not really pray at all—not as Mr. Mather
prayed—him you could hear through stone walls and up and down the street.
The crowd would gather outside the jail when Mr. Mather prayed. He was
a most fearful and righteous suppliant before the Throne of God. After his
prayers the wonder was no lightning came to destroy the young witch where
she sat—grimacing and leering at spectres. When one considered Mr. Mather,
one could not say that Zelley prayed at all.

However, it was true that Zelley would sometimes seem to beg Doll
Bilby to turn to God before it was too late. She would always explain to
him that she wanted no other God than Lucifer and no Heaven, for where
her parents were and her foster father and her dear husband—there with
them was her Paradise, not in Heaven with the cold angels singing psalms
forever to an angry and awful God; not in Heaven where doubtless Hannah
Bilby would be found and all her cruel neighbours—no, no, a thousand times
no. Hell was her true home—her Paradise.

Sometimes he would read to her from a stout big book, and John Ackes
swore he thought it was a Bible, although it was possible that the book was
a book of magic—perhaps this was even probable. Still the stories he read
to her from this book sounded to him like Bible stories. What would he
read to her? He read to her of Mary of Magdala, how she laid her head
upon our Saviour's feet and wiped them with her hair. He read to her the
holy promises of John. It was evident, said John Ackes, that Zelley was not
for a long time conscious of the fiend which lurked forever in the witch's
cell.

Towards the end no one but Mr. Zelley dared go to her dungeon. They
were all afraid. It was remembered and marked against him that, where other
and more godly men felt fear, he felt no fear. At last even Mr. Zelley knew
that he and the witch were never alone. There was another and more awful
presence about.

Now he would look up quickly from his reading and catch her eyes as
they sought those of some one or something close behind his own shoulder.
When their eyes met, she would smile so softly and happily he knew that
the invisible presence must be that of the one she loved. Mr. Zelley confessed that this consciousness of a third and unseen party in the cell sadly
upset and confused him. He sweated, he could not read. One afternoon she
gave him such close attention he decided that the fiend had left, so he closed

his book and asked her abruptly if her demon lover had come back again. She was surprised that he asked this question. "Of course he is back," she said. "Now he will not leave me until the end." It was not he, she said, whom the Thumb twins saw at the trial, and Doll again wickedly said that perhaps that creature had been an angel. "My fiend never came near me as I stood all day on trial. Now he has sworn to stay with me. If I go to Gallows Hill, he will go with me. If I die here first, he will hold my hands."

Zelley asked her if she could really see this demon. For instance, was he at that very moment in the room? Oh, yes. He sat yonder by the cupboard. His head, she said, rested upon his bosom. "Last night I had a fearful fit of terror. I thought I could not face the gallows. He held me in his arms and sang to me until sunrise. Now he sleeps."

"Is he now in seaman's clothes and has he the likeness of proper man?" (Mr. Zelley whispered. He feared to wake the demon.)

"No. He has returned in shape of true fiend. For he is horned, naked, scaly, black. His feet are cloven. He has vast leathery bat-pinions. His tail is long and spiked."

"How, then, can you know that this is your own fiend and not another one?"

"By his eyes and by his loving voice. These things have not changed."

"How is it he returned to you? In what manner did he make himself manifest?"

"You recall that day after the trial when you came to me and let me know beyond a doubt that I must die? All the next day I felt him in the cell with me. Then little by little he took visible form. At first he was a vapour that seemed to rise between the flags of the dungeon floor, and then I could see the shadow of his great and most awful form—a transparent shadow through which one could look, even as one looks through smoke. But daily he gained more and more in body and he now is as hard and sturdy as mortal man. At first seeing horns, tail, and so fearsome a scaly black body, I cried out in my disappointment and despair. I, in my simplicity, had imagined he would always be to me as he had been—shaped, dressed, and coloured like comely, mortal man. He seemed monstrous to me—more likely to inspire fear than love. At last I could see his eyes and they were unchanged. And his voice (for, having gained complete actuality, he could speak) was the same. So I knew him as my own husband, and now I love him more in his present infernal majesty than I did in seaman's form. This shape is fairer to me." (Thus twenty years later Mr. Zelley testified in court as to his conversation with Doll Bilby.)

On being pressed, Mr. Zelley confessed still further. He said he asked her why it was that no one—not even the jailors—dared go to her cell. Did they fear the spectral presence? She was amazed that he had heard no gossip. Surely the village must by now be buzzing with the tricks her demon had performed. Had he not heard what had befallen her peeping jailors? They used (to her unutterable torment and vexation) to watch her through a chink in the masonry. But the demon punished them by blowing into their eyes. This had given them the pink-eye. Surely he must have noticed that her jailors suffered from pink-eye? Now that she mentioned it he said he believed he had noticed it. And she was to tell him further. Why did the great Mr. Mather come no more? She clapped her hands, laughing and purring. Her demon had hated Mr. Mather so bitterly, and had so resented his long, loud prayers, that he had several times been on the point of strangling him. In his utter foolishness the man had dared to read the story of Tobit to her—how Sara was beloved of the fiend Asmodeus and how this fiend strangled her many husbands upon their marriage beds, but how at the last this fine fiend Asmodeus had been driven to farthest Egypt by the stench of a burning fish's liver. This story the wicked witch claimed to be utterly false —it made no jot of difference to her that it was found in Holy Writ. She said it was a black lie that did much to minimize that dignity of Prince Asmodeus—who was a close friend to her own lover. She put up her hand and whispered to Mr. Zelley that, although her fiend had never told her his own true name, she had reason to suspect that he himself was none other than this same Asmodeus, for he was touchy beyond all reason for the dignity of the Prince and he had told her at some length how dull, tedious, and complaining a woman Sara had been, and how gladly her lover had surrendered her in the end to the young Jew. The burning fish's liver had never driven him forth—he went as it pleased himself. The stench had almost expelled the bride from her bridal chamber, but it had had no effect upon the stalwart demon Prince.

Mr. Mather had insisted on reading this story thrice over to her, and on the last reading he had also endeavoured to burn the large liver of a codfish. Then her husband rushed at the fire. His tail stood up rigid in rage; he shook his horns like an angry bull; he rustled his vast pinions, and, as he snuffed out the fire that made the stench with his two horny hands, Mr. Mather looked up and of a sudden saw him there and was close to dying of terror. Doll begged the fiend again to assume invisibility and not to strangle the distinguished Divine. So Mr. Mather went away and never came again. But surely, surely Mr. Zelley had heard this thing spoken of? And how her demon had served the two Salem clergymen—the tricks he had put on them —surely these things were common gossip? No, of these things he had heard never a word. No one gossiped with him—now.

It was then at that moment he first came to know he was under suspicion. Doll knew this too. She told him how she had never heard that the Thumb twins were bewitched until the very day Captain Buzzey rode up and accused her of their bewitchment. She said she pitied Mr. Zelley and he said his life grew strange. Every one in all the world was far removed, and even God had turned His face away from him. He said (foolishly) that all his life he had felt that if he believed in witches, demons, etc., he could not believe in God; for that God Whom he worshipped would not tolerate such evil things. Yet now had he seen the proof that such things were true—and, if true, where, then, was that great and good God whom he had long worshipped? "My Doll," he said, "you have taken away my reason and my God —now I have nothing. I have not even one man I may call 'friend.'"

She comforted him, not by words, but by putting her small hands (now thin as a bird's claws) upon his bent head. She kissed his forehead. He got up and went away. He did not stay as he should have stayed with his flock in Cowan Corners. He slept at the Black Moon, for such was the bewitchment that Doll had set upon him he must see her again and that early upon the next day.

6

The Labours of a Witch and the Prayers of the Godly.

The year was nine days old and no more. Then was Doll Bilby taken in labour and brought prematurely to bed.

The Salem midwife—ancient Nan Hackett—would have none of her, and it seemed that, whatever it was she must bear, she should bear alone. Nor did she ask for mortal aid. She was content with that phantom which stood night and day (as many saw) at her bed's head. Mr. Zelley remembered that Goody Goochey, when first she came to Cowan Corners, had served the beginning as well as the end of life—that is, she had been a midwife as well as a layer-out of the dead. He went to the woman and begged her, in pity's name and partly commanded her in the name of the General Court, to get herself to Salem jail and there give such service as might be.

She was afraid. She did not wish to be midwife to a witch and the first to welcome a black imp into the world. She drank three piggins of ale and took a leather bottle of brandy with her. She set upon her thumbs and fingers those iron rings with which she was accustomed to guard herself against the ghosts of the dead. She thought, after all, is not a live imp of greater danger to a good Christian's soul than the body of a dead church elder? Mr. Zelley went with her to the jail.

The witch at the moment was not in pain. She lay with eyes black as the pits of Hell. Her white mouth was open. She roused herself a little and made Mr. Zelley a brief speech in which she said that she had, as he knew, sought God and spiritual peace, and now, let him look into her face and say that she had failed to find either. It was true, said Mr. Zelley. Her face was fulfilled of heavenly peace. He left her without a word.

Outside he found a conclave of idle men and women who laughed and joked coarsely. One big ruddy wench (who had already borne, to the embarrassment of the community, three fatherless children) was crying out loudly that God knew it was enough for woman to give birth to human child, which is round and sleek as a melon. God help the witch now in labour with an imp, for it would come into the world with spiked tail and horns. Such a thing would be the death of any mortal woman. All were afraid. Some believed a clap of thunder would come down from Heaven and destroy the woman. Others that a fiend would rise up from Hell to succour her. Some said that the witches and warlocks for an hundred miles had gathered together and now, mounting broomsticks, were about to charge down upon Salem. One said, "Have you not heard? Judge Bride has suffered an apoplexy. Judge Lollimour is at death's door." This was not so.

Another said Captain Tom Buzzey's hands (those hands that had held the witch) had withered. They had shrivelled to the size of a child's. This was not so.

All said the witch is in labour. She's with child by the Devil. God will burn her soul in Hell. This was so.

The day wore on. The sun, as sometimes may be in the midst of winter, was so warm the snow melted and water dripped from the eaves of the jail. It was tender as a day in spring. Planks and rugs were laid in the slush, for certain clergymen came to pray and must have dry land to kneel upon. They prayed that God recollect the number of good, pious Christian people there were at Salem and not destroy all, for they feared His wrath might blast the whole village. God made no sign, but the water dripped from the eaves and a sweet spring fragrance rose from the melting snow.

The multitude gaped and feared. Sometimes they smelt sulphur, salt-peter, brimstone, and the stench as of a sloughing serpent. They heard the crying of a phantom voice and the swishing of a thousand brooms. So they waited through the day expecting every moment to see crabbed Goody Goochey hobble out with a black imp upon a blanket to show them.

There was no sound from the cell. Not one cry nor moan from the witch, not one word from Goochey. The jailors would open the door. It stuck. Their keys would not fit it. They could not open the door, and believed devils were holding it fast. They dared not peek in the chink because of their pink-eye.

By sundown most went home.

7
Mr. Zelley opens a Dungeon Door, and what came of it.

The next day dawned cold and grey over an icy sea, and the gulls and terns came in from the harbour crying and lamenting. There was now no tenderness in the air, and the water that had but yesterday melted under the rays of a genial sun froze to glassy ice. A wind sharp as needles came in off the sea and few if any watched the night out on their knees beside the dungeon walls. As soon as it was possible to see six feet ahead, the multitude again began to assemble, but this time they came without laughter or conversation. They were shrouded in hoods, shawls, etc., for warmth, and seemed a spectral band. Now and then one or another of them would raise a pious voice in prayer, lamentation, or thanksgiving, but for the most part they stood bowed and mute. All night there had been no sound from the witch's cell—never a sound. Who was there so bold as to enter in to her and bring back a report, for John Ackes's hand shook so he could not manage the key? Some said Mr. Zelley would go—he had no normal, wholesome fear of witches or demons. Others said, "Where does he lie tonight?" Others, "Go, run and fetch him"; and a boy (it was Widow Hannah's bonded boy Jake Tulley) said the man lay at the Black Moon and that he would run and fetch him. This he did.

Mr. Zelley came in a steeple hat and a greatcoat. He spoke to no one. No one spoke to him. He entered the jail and took the cell key from Ackes, and, after some shaking and effort, he turned the lock and pushed hard on the door, which swung in so suddenly he almost fell on his knees beside that straw bed where he had sat so many wicked hours with the witch-girl. A hundred had crowded down the passage and into the doorway after Mr. Zelley. All stopped at the threshold of the cell. They stood agape, some filled with curiosity, some with fear, others with pious ejaculations and elevated thoughts.

Goody Goochey (who indeed proved to be no woman, but a man) lay in a drunken fit in a corner. His face was purple and his throat twisted and bruised as though he had been half strangled—which he always averred to his dying day was the truth, for he had seen the scaly black demon come at him with great hands outstretched to his throat, and that was the last he could really remember until certain ones tumbled him out into the snow. He was sure, however, that, as he lay thus almost unconscious in a corner, a great concourse of spectrals and infernals had filled the cell. They had danced, sung, and made much of the witch, praising her, encouraging her, etc. Because the man was known to be an impostor (he had for many years made all think him a woman) and because of his swinish, drunken ways, many did not believe what he said.

All could see that Bilby's Doll was dead. She lay with her round eyes open to the ceiling, and her expression was one of peace and content. Whatever she might have borne was dead within her.

8

Without HELL *where is* HEAVEN? *And without a Devil where is* GOD? *Also the last of Doll Bilby and an end to these instructions.*

There are court records, affidavits, etc.; there are diaries, letters, and such; there is the memory of old gaffers and goodies to prove that once Doll Bilby flourished. But of physical, inanimate objects nothing that was associated with her evil life and awful end now exists. The house she lived in mysteriously rotted and fell into the cellar hole. The grave they dug her is now lost under a ploughed field (a sterile field that yields little). Where the dungeon was now is a brick house, a fine big house of red bricks had out from England. No one will live there. Yet any gamin, for a copper penny, and any courting couple, for wanton pleasure, will show you the very spot in the white birch thicket where Doll met her demon lover night after night under the moonlight, in that world of witchery which none today will ever see. For in those days there were sights and wonders that will not come again. In those days God was nearer to man than He is today, and where God is there also must be His Evil Opponent—the Prince of Lies, for show me Paradise, and there, around a corner, I will show you Hell.

Finis coronat opus

Topics for Writing and Research

The following headings are intended for classes that will use the witch-craft materials for several weeks, combining preparation for the longer research paper with practice in several traditional rhetorical techniques. The headings, of course, are not mutually exclusive—the writer of an extended definition must use comparison and contrast—but they do represent expository problems that deserve class discussion. Experience suggests that a total of three short papers should precede the long paper.

For suggestions on footnote form, see Preface pages vii-viii.

I. *Short Papers* (600-1000 words)

A. "Objective" Narration

Write a 300-word, "objective" account of an examination, refraining from explicit or implicit judgment of the proceedings and from explanations and descriptions based on what you might infer from other documents. Then write a 500-word account of the same examination, giving as full and fair a description as you can and employing not only your judgment but all the available information (your observation of discrepancies in the witness's testimony or inadequacies in the court reporter's transcription; your knowledge of how the bewitched girls behaved when suddenly "afflicted"; your recognition of increasing tension, of climax). In this second version you are not invited either to "slant" or to preach, but only to present your most accurate version of the whole truth, circumstantial and emotional. The examination of Sarah Good (pp. 4-5), or of Bridget Bishop (pp. 21-23), or of Deliverance Hobbs (pp. 66-69) is recommended.

B. Definition

Write an essay that includes an extended definition of one of the following terms:
1. spectral evidence
2. witchcraft (See Cotton Mather's sermon, pp. 96-106.)
3. original sin
4. bewitchment (See, for example, pp. xiii, 6, 83.)

C. Comparison and Contrast

1. Compare the behavior of any two defendants at their respective examinations.

2. Compare the objections that Increase Mather and Thomas Brattle made to the Salem trials.

3. Compare two or more depositions.

4. Compare Cotton Mather's letter to John Richards and *The Return of Several Ministers*.

5. Compare Doll Bilby in the forest (pp. 181-85) and Goodman Brown in the forest.

D. Process

1. Describe the procedure against a witch, from arrest to execution.

2. Describe the methods of examination used in 1692.

3. How does Esther Forbes build up the "case" against Captain Bilby's wife?

E. Classification and Analysis

1. What kinds of evidence were used in a particular trial? What kinds in the trials generally?

2. What kinds of argument (or, if you prefer, fallacy) were used against a particular defendant? Against the defendants generally?

II. *Long Papers* (2000-2500 words)

*1. A critical, comparative essay on the technical "point of view" in *A Mirror for Witches* and "Young Goodman Brown."

2. The portrayal of innocence and guilt in Doll Bilby and Goodman Brown.

3. A narrative of one defendant's experience from accusation to execution (Sarah Good, Bridget Bishop, Susanna Martin, John Proctor, George Burroughs).

4. What part did spectral evidence play in the convictions?

*5. The value of spectral evidence.

Either of the latter two subjects would require a careful definition of spectral evidence. Topic 5 would require an evaluation of spectral evidence in a seventeenth-century witchcraft trial. (Was it sensible to admit spectral evidence in court? Was spectral evidence reliable as corroborative evidence? What are its dangers?)

6. The Minister and the Skeptic: Increase Mather and Thomas Brattle.

*7. A comparative essay on three historical accounts of the same trial (for example, George Burroughs': Cotton Mather, in *The Wonders of the Invisible World* [reprinted on pp. 112-16]; Charles W. Upham, *Salem Witchcraft* [see Bibliography]; Marion L. Starkey, *The Devil in Massachusetts* [see Bibliography]).

8. A comparison of the actions, attitudes, and (thus) the character of two of the condemned witches.

* The instructor might well require students to ask his approval before choosing this topic.

9. A study of irrelevant evidence in the Salem trials.

10. The role and importance of the confessed witch in the Salem trials.

11. The court reporter: his value as an historical source.

*12. What is a witch hunt? A critical analysis of the value of comparing the Salem trials with congressional investigations in the years from 1948 to 1954.

13. Arthur Miller's use of the Salem trials in *The Crucible* (see Bibliography).

14. Arthur Miller's portrayal of John Proctor: a study in the transformation of historical evidence.

15. The portrayal of the supernatural in *A Mirror for Witches*, "Young Goodman Brown," *The Crucible*, and Lyon Phelps's *The Gospel Witch* (see Bibliography).

16. Compare Esther Forbes's Cowan Corners with Salem Village.

Selected Bibliography

I. *Sources*

Calef, Robert, *More Wonders of the Invisible World*, reprinted in *The Witchcraft Delusion in New England*, ed. Samuel G. Drake, Vols. II, III, Roxbury, Mass., 1866.

Mather, Cotton, *Diary, 1681-1708, Collections of the Massachusetts Historical Society*, Seventh Series, Vol. VIII.

————, *Magnalia Christi Americana*, 2 vols., Hartford, 1820.

————, *Late Memorable Providences, Relating to Witchcrafts and Possessions*, London, 1691.

————, *The Wonders of the Invisible World*, London, 1862.

Mather, Increase, *Cases of Conscience Concerning Evil Spirits Personating Men*. See Mather, Cotton, *The Wonders of the Invisible World*.

The Mather Papers, Collections of the Massachusetts Historical Society, Fourth Series, Vol. VIII.

Narratives of the Witchcraft Cases, 1648-1706, ed. George L. Burr, New York, 1914.

Records of Salem Witchcraft, Copied from the Original Documents, ed. William E. Woodward, 2 vols., Roxbury, Mass., 1864.

Sewall, Samuel, *Diary, 1674-1700, Collections of the Massachusetts Historical Society*, Fifth Series, Vol. V.

Willard, Samuel, *Some Miscellany Observations on our Present Debates Respecting Witchcrafts . . .* , Philadelphia, 1692.

II. *Authorities*

A. Witchcraft

Boas, Ralph P., and Louise Boas, *Cotton Mather*, New York, 1928.

Kittredge, George L., *Witchcraft in Old and New England*, Cambridge, Mass., 1929, New York, 1958.

Miller, Perry, *The New England Mind: From Colony to Province*, Cambridge, Mass., 1953.

Murdock, Kenneth B., *Increase Mather: The Foremost American Puritan*, Cambridge, Mass., 1925.

Robbins, Rossell Hope, *The Encyclopedia of Witchcraft and Demonology*, New York, 1959.

Starkey, Marion L., *The Devil in Massachusetts*, New York, 1949.

Taylor, E. W., "Some Medical Aspects of Witchcraft," in *Problems of Personality*, New York, 1925, pp. 165-88.

237

Upham, Charles W., *Salem Witchcraft; with an Account of Salem Village* . . . , 2 vols., Boston, 1867.

Wendell, Barrett, *Cotton Mather, the Puritan Priest*, Cambridge, Mass., 1926.

————, *Were the Salem Witches Guiltless?* Salem, 1892.

B. Historical Background

Channing, Edward, *A History of the United States,* Vol. II, New York, 1936.

Morison, Samuel Eliot, *Harvard College in the Seventeenth Century,* 2 vols., Cambridge, Mass., 1936.

————, *The Intellectual Life of Colonial New England,* New York, 1956 (orig. publ. as *The Puritan Pronaos: Studies in the Intellectual Life of New England in the Seventeenth Century,* New York and London, 1936).

The Puritans, ed. Perry Miller and Thomas H. Johnson, New York, 1938.

Sibley, J. L., *Biographical Sketches of Graduates of Harvard University,* 3 vols., Cambridge, 1873-1875.

Walker, Williston, *The Creeds and Platforms of Congregationalism,* New York, 1893.

III. *Historical Fiction and Drama*

Barker, Shirley, *Peace, My Daughter,* New York, 1949.

Forbes, Esther, *A Mirror for Witches,* Boston, 1928.

Hawthorne, Nathaniel, "Young Goodman Brown," in *Mosses from an Old Manse,* Boston, 1857.

Levin, David, "Salem Witchcraft in Recent Fiction and Drama," *New England Quarterly,* XXVIII (December 1955), pp. 537-46.

Miller, Arthur, *The Crucible,* Bantam Books, New York, 1959.

Phelps, Lyon, *The Gospel Witch,* Cambridge, Mass., 1955.